# PERENNIALS

# PERENNIALS

*Darrel Apps*, Editor

Principal Photography by

*Andrew Lawson*

HEARST BOOKS

New York

**Library of Congress Cataloging-in-Publication Data**

Darrel Apps
    Perennials / compiled from the Good Housekeeping illustrated encyclopedia
    of gardening: completely rev. by Darrel Apps; photography by Andrew Lawson.
    —1st U.S. ed.
        p.   cm. — (Hearst garden guides)
    Includes index.
    ISBN 0-688-10042-2
    1. Perennials.  2. Perennials — United States.
    I. Apps, Darrel.  II.  Series.
    SB434.P4732  1993
    635.9'32—dc20                                     92-23042

Printed in Singapore
First U.S. Edition
1 2 3 4 5 6 7 8 9 10

Produced by Smallwood & Stewart, Inc.
New York City

Editor: Charles A. de Kay
Horticultural Consultant: Ruth Lively
Designer: Michelle Wiener
Managing Editor: Robin Haywood

HEARST
GARDEN
GUIDES

# CONTENTS

chapter

# 3

# ENCYCLOPEDIA OF PERENNIALS   33

# 1

# INTRODUCTION

Since the early 1980s there has been what some call a "perennial renaissance" in America. Because of this renewed interest, thousands of different perennial plants have been introduced or reintroduced to the marketplace. This proliferation creates something of a dilemma for the editor of books such as this: which plants to include and which to exclude?

Obviously, this volume of the *Hearst Garden Guides* cannot present a complete listing of all perennials; however, the third chapter does offer a compendium of some of the most important home landscape and garden plants presently being used in the U.S. It includes the most commonly available perennials, as well as many interesting and unusual varieties that are well worth the effort to find. Each entry also provides key facts and opinions—an information capsule that will enable gardeners to apply everyday gardening techniques successfully—for each perennial discussed.

Care has been taken to present a broad spectrum of perennials, and special attention has been devoted to describing important varieties. Some older varieties were left out because they have been superseded by better forms, and others were omitted because they are no longer carried by the majority of retailers.

With some perennials there are literally hundreds of varieties from which to choose. For example, the American Hemerocallis Society has registered more than 35,000 different types of daylilies. In such cases, of course, it was possible to discuss only a few of the major award winners.

Because perennial interest is at an all-time high, the introductions of new plants will probably continue. One way to keep abreast of what is happening in this exciting field is to read *Perennial Plants*, published by the professional Perennial Plant Association for its 1,400 members.

Taxonomists—scientists who classify plants—have been just as busy as plant breeders; they continue to reexamine plant names and make changes. Current botanical names are used in this book, except in cases where a plant is still universally known by an old name. *Chrysanthemum × rubellum*, for instance, has a new first name, *Dendranthema*, which is not yet well-known. As few gardeners would know to search for the new name, the plant is discussed under the listing for *Chrysanthemum* and cross-referenced under *Dendranthema*.

The standard hardiness map published by the U.S. Department of Agriculture (USDA), which divides the country into plant climate zones, has also been subject to change. In January 1990, the USDA issued a new map (see pages 178–179) that more accurately reflects average minimum winter temperatures. Although the zonal boundaries have shifted, the temperature ranges assigned to each zone are unchanged. Many plants have yet to be tested within these new zones.

Hardiness ratings are intended to be guidelines, and not hard-and-fast criteria denoting whether a plant will live or die in a particular climate. They are based solely on the average minimum winter temperatures of a location. In reality, though, there are many other factors that affect plant hardiness: average high temperatures in summer, extremes of both heat and cold, rainfall, humidity and soil moisture.

When considering zone hardiness ranges and seasons of bloom, it is important to remember that microclimates and unusual weather patterns influence the success or failure of any given plant. Experienced gardeners know that there is no "normal" perennial flowering year. Perhaps it is this unpredictability that makes the "gardening journey" so enticing!

**PLANT CLASSIFICATION**

Understanding the basics of botanic nomenclature (the system of naming plants used by scientists) is essential to identifying and learning about plants. Over the ages, people have classified plants in various ways. The ancient Roman writer Pliny the Elder (A.D. 23-79), who used size and form as his criteria, set up three major groupings: trees, shrubs and herbs. In the Middle Ages, plants were classified according to whether they were medicinal, edible or poisonous. Later the great eighteenth-century Swedish botanist Carolus Linnaeus (1707–1778) used the number of stamens (pollen-producing structures) in the flowers as his basis for classification.

Such systems are considered arbitrary today, and even though most gardeners continue to classify plants much as Pliny did, modern taxonomists have moved to a so-called natural system of classification in which plants are grouped according to their generic and evolutionary relation-

ships. Under this system, related species of plants make up a genus. Related genera (plural of genus) make up a family. Related families make up an order. Related orders make up a class. Related classes make up a subdivision (or subphylum). Related subdivisions make up a division (or phylum) and related divisions make up the plant kingdom.

The following classification of *Aquilegia canadensis* (wild columbine) and *Belamcanda chinensis* (blackberry lily) illustrate this method.

| COLUMBINE | BLACKBERRY LILY |
|---|---|
| Kingdom *Plantae* | Kingdom *Plantae* |
| Division *Tracheophyta* | Division *Tracheophyta* |
| Subdivision *Pteropsida* | Subdivision *Pteropsida* |
| Class *Angiospermae* | Class *Angiospermae* |
| Subclass *Dicotyledonae* | Subclass *Monocotyledonae* |
| Order *Ranunculales* | Order *Liliales* |
| Family *Ranunculaceae* | Family *Iridaceae* |
| Genus *Aguilegia* | Genus *Belamcanda* |
| Species *canadensis* | Species *chinensis* |

Note that, in both examples, the names on the same line (except at the genus and species levels) have the same endings. This helps to identify the classification level. Generally, division names end in "-phyta"; subdivision names in "–opsida"; class names in "-ae"; order names in "-ales"; and family names in "-aceae."

**Nomenclature**

Most familiar garden plants have one or more common names and a scientific name. Because the common names are in English, they are easier for the average person to remember and pronounce, and that is probably why most gardeners prefer them. Unfortunately, common names lead to much confusion. For one thing, many plants have several common names. For example, *Lychnis coronaria* is called mullein pink, rose campion or dusty miller. Frequently, two or more totally different plants have the same common name: dusty miller is a name given not only to *Lychnis coronaria*, but also to *Artemisia stelleriana*, *Centaurea cineraria*, *Centaurea gymnocarpa*, *Centaurea ragusina*, *Chrysanthemum ptarmiciflorum*, *Senecio cineraria* and *Senecio vira-vira*. Occasionally, closely related plants have such different common names that their relationship is obscured: sweet Williams, pinks and carnations, for example, are all closely related members of the genus *Dianthus*.

Since common names are so imprecise, they cannot be the basis for plant classification. To identify a plant accurately, botanists adapted the binomial system devised 200 years ago by Linnaeus. This system identifies each plant by two names, the genus followed by the species, both usually derived from Latin or from Greek rendered into Latin. Thus, the scientific name of the wild columbine is *Aquilegia canadensis* (which may be abbreviated *A. canadensis* once the generic name has been spelled out in reasonably close context). If a species of plant includes varieties or cultivars, that name is added directly after the specific (or species) name.

The selections starting below and continuing on the next page explain the various elements that make up a plant name.

## Genus

The first part of the scientific name stands for the genus, or the group of closely related plants to which the specified plant belongs. The generic name is italicized or underlined when written, and the first letter is always capitalized.

A plant family may comprise any number of genera, and a genus any number of species. For example, the family *Papaveraceae* contains some twenty-five genera, including the genus *Papaver*.

This genus includes many perennial species, most notably the striking and showy Oriental poppy (*Papaver orientale*), which is featured in this volume; but the genus also embraces many annual species, such as the corn or Flanders poppy (*Papaver rhoeas*) and the opium poppy (*Papaver somniferum*).

## Species

The second part of the scientific name connotes the species, the specific plant within a genus. Each species will be different from the others in the genus, but all will have one or more characteristics in common. For instance, all members of the genus *Papaver* have milky sap and one flower per stem in shades of red, yellow, orange, lavender or white. A genus may contain anywhere from one to more than a thousand species (the word is both singular and plural). In turn, a species may (but does not always) have a number of varieties.

Species can reproduce themselves from seed. Occasionally two different species may interbreed, one pollinating the other by means of wind or insects, resulting in a natural hybrid. Intentional interbreeding or hybridization occurs all the time in the laboratories and gardens of seed developers and plant breeders.

To the gardener, species are of the utmost importance because they are specific types of plants. If a person wants to plant a penstemon, for instance, and simply orders *Penstemon*, any one of a dozen types might be sent. To get a particular *Penstemon*, a distinct species must be ordered—a *Penstemon barbatus* for the bearded penstemon, for example, or *P. digitalis* if the foxglove penstemon is preferred. To be absolutely precise, the varietal or cultivar name must be added, provided the species contains varieties, as do both *P. barbatus* and *P. digitalis*.

As a rule, most specific names are descriptive of some feature of the plant—for instance, *grandi-*

*flora* (large-flowered), *odorata* (fragrant) and *lutea* (yellow) are common species names. Some specific names, however, are derived from names of geographical regions (for example, *japonica*) or individuals (for example, *sieboldiana*).

The specific name is always italicized or underlined and lower-cased. The word "species" can be abbreviated when referring to many or all of the species in a genus—for example, *Penstemon* spp.

*Variety*

The lowest, or final, natural classification of plants is the variety. Not all species have natural varieties, but most species have several. These varieties occur in nature, although they often go unnoticed until brought to public attention by plant breeders who wish to popularize the plants.

Each variety within a species retains the basic character of that species but has one or more distinctive characteristics of its own. For example, the leaves of *Arabis albida* (wall rock cress) are gray, but there is a natural variety that has yellow-white borders on the leaves. The variety name, usually derived from Latin, appears in lower-cased italics preceded by "var." in unitalicized letters—for example, *Arabis albida* var. *variegata*. (It is also correct to omit the "var." when referring to a natural variety.)

*Cultivar*

A cultivar (from *culti*vated *var*iety) is a new plant produced under controlled conditions by plant breeders. It is selected in cultivation, propagated (usually as a clone or exact genetic duplicate of the original) and named.

A cultivar continues to exist in cultivation only because there is a market for it. For example, at some point someone discovered that in a planting of *Lychnis coronaria*, one individual had white flowers instead of the bright crimson or magenta blossoms characteristic of the species. It was prop-

agated vegetatively—by division, probably—and named *L. coronaria* 'Alba' in honor of its white flowers.

Cultivar names are in English or another modern language (usually the national language of the country in which the plant was first propagated). They are noted by the abbreviation cv. or by single quotation marks (*Lychnis coronaria* cv. Alba or *Lychnis coronaria* 'Alba') and never appear in italics. A cultivar name can consist of more than one word, each beginning with a capital letter.

*Hybrid*

A plant resulting from the crossing of two specific plants is a hybrid. Hybrids are noted with a multiplication sign. The symbol precedes the genus when the genus itself is a hybrid. It is written between the generic and specific names if the species is a hybrid. Cultivars can be (but are not always) selected from hybrids.

Hybridization is unusual in nature, but it can occur; most hybrids are developed as the result of human actions, either accidental or intentional. A famous example of an accidental hybridization is × *Cupressocyparis leylandii* (Leyland cypress). It resulted when *Cupressus macrocarpa* (Monterey cypress) from California and *Chamaecyparis lawsoniana* (Lawson false cypress) from Oregon were planted next to each other in a garden in England. The pollen from one fertilized the seed of the other, a seedling grew and it became a hybrid genus. One of the seedlings of Leyland cypress was found to be bluer than the others. It was propagated (in this case by cuttings, since it roots easily), named, and so became × *Cupressocyparis leylandii* 'Naylor's Blue'.

Intentional crosses are more common, such as the hybrid *Delphinium* × *elatum*, which was created by a complex series of crosses between *D. elatum* and *D. exaltatum* and *D. formosum*.

# PARTS OF A FLOWER

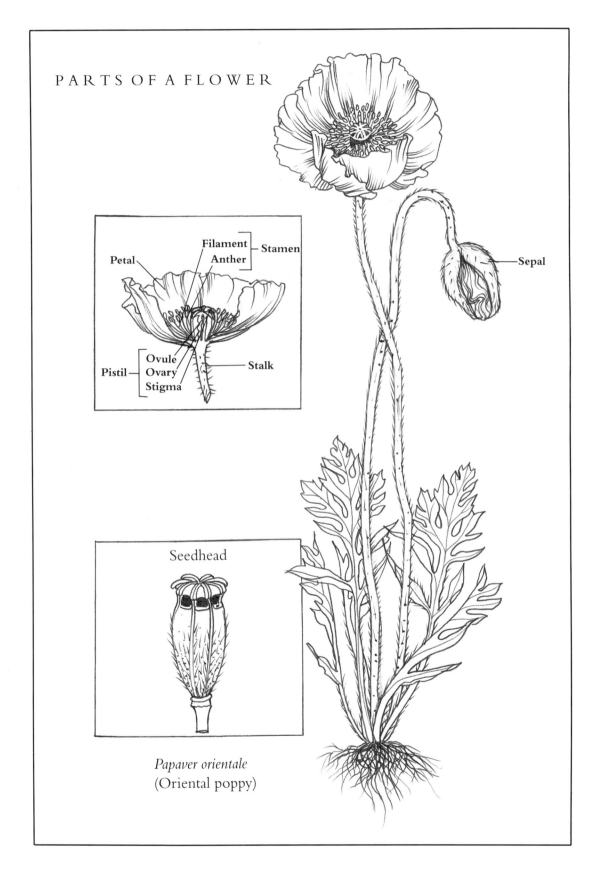

Petal
Filament
Anther
Stamen
Pistil
Ovule
Ovary
Stigma
Stalk
Sepal

Seedhead

*Papaver orientale*
(Oriental poppy)

## FLOWER FORMS

The word "flower" is the popular term for the combination of structures that comprise the reproductive organs of complex plants. Without flowers, these highly evolved plants could not produce seed with which to reproduce their kind.

The variety of colors, shapes and sizes of flowers is almost bewildering. In color, only a true black is missing. As to shape and form, while the majority of flowers are symmetrical, many, such as mountain bluet (*Centaurea montana*), are highly asymmetrical. In size, flowers range from the microscopic to diameters of almost a foot. Some flowers are borne singly on the plant stems, others in clusters (see "Inflorescence" on page 16).

The point at which the flower is connected to the stem is the receptacle. Next are the sepals, which collectively make up the calyx. These are the outermost, petal-like structures, usually green, which enclose and protect the flower bud before it opens.

Inside the sepals are the petals, which collectively form the corolla. (The petals and sepals together make up the perianth. In cases where the sepals and petals cannot be distinguished from one another, as for example in lilies, they are known as tepals.) Some flowers have only a few petals; others have hundreds. Usually the petals are separate, but they are often united into a single tube or cup.

The reproductive organs of the flower are surrounded by the petals. The male organs are the stamens, collectively called the androecium, which produce pollen. The female organs are the seed-bearing carpels, collectively known as the pistil or gynoecium, which collect pollen and protect the ovule.

Each stamen consists of a filament (usually a short, slender stalk) bearing at the apex a single, enlarged anther.

## SOLITARY FLOWER FORMS

Simple Flower

Tube Flower

Composite Flower

# INFLORESCENCES

**Umbel**
*Cluster whose flower stalks grow from the same point.*

**Spadix**
*Thick flower spike with fleshy, cylindrical center characteristic of plants in the Arum Family and some others.*

**Raceme**
*Elongated cluster whose flowers have short stalks.*

**Cyme**
*Branching cluster of flowers that bloom from center toward edges; flower-tipped axis.*

**Spike**
*Elongated cluster whose flowers are stalkless.*

**Corymb**
*Flat-topped cluster of flowers that bloom from edges to center; formed by flower stalks growing from different points on axis.*

**Solitary**
*Flower that grows alone on a stalk; not part of a cluster.*

**Panicle**
*Open cluster of flowers that bloom from bottom toward top; flowerless tip.*

Pistils may have three parts: the swollen ovary in which seeds are formed, above this the slender style, and at the end of the style the stigma—often rough or sticky—on which the pollen falls or is deposited to produce fertilization. The pollen germinates on the stigma, grows down the style and fertilizes the ovary, producing seed.

Flowers are often categorized as perfect or imperfect. Perfect flowers have both stamens and pistils and are thus capable of self-fertilization if pollen ripens and the stigma becomes receptive to it at the same time. Imperfect flowers may have either stamens (these are called staminate flowers) or pistils (pistillate flowers). When the staminate (male) and pistillate (female) flowers are borne on separate plants, the plants are said to be dioecious. Monoecious plants, on the other hand, have both staminate and pistillate flowers.

**Inflorescence**

Most plants produce just one flower head—a single flower at the end of the flower stalk—and are called solitary flowers. The most common shapes that solitary flowers take are shown in the illustration "Solitary Flower Forms" on page 14.

Many flowers, however, are borne in clusters; the shape of the flower head, which is determined by where the flower cluster is branched, varies with the type of plant. The flowers of *Acanthus mollis* (common bear's breech), for instance, forms a flower spike; *Arisaema triphyllum* (Jack-in-the-pulpit) blooms as a spadix and the ever popular *Dianthus barbatus* (sweet William) flowers as flat-topped cymes. *Aconitum napellus* (monkshood) and *Digitalis grandiflora* (yellow foxglove) form spike-like clusters, in which the flowers appear on short stalks, called racemes. The most important flower-cluster arrangements are shown in the "Inflorescence" illustration on the preceding page.

chapter

*2*

# PERENNIALS: FLOWERS FOR SEVERAL SEASONS

Perennial plants grow back year after year, as compared to annuals, which bloom and die in a single season, and biennials, which complete their life cycles in two seasons. Trees, shrubs and woody vines are perennial; but when gardeners say "perennial" they refer to flowering plants, usually those that die to the ground each year, that brighten beds and borders from spring until fall. Perennials that have fleshy, green stems are called herbaceous perennials to distinguish them from those that have woody, persistent stems. Examples of herbaceous perennials include *Anemone* × *hybrida* (Japanese anemone), *Platycodon grandiflorus* (balloon flower), and many species of *Aster* (Michaelmas daisy) and *Paeonia* (garden peony). Examples of woody-stemmed perennials include species of *Artemisia* (wormwood), *Lavandula* (lavender) and *Nepeta* (catmint). Such woody perennials are sometimes called subshrubs, and though their branch tips may die back in winter, they retain their basic shape throughout the year. Both kinds of perennials are covered in this book.

Not all herbaceous perennials stay green until frost; some, such as *Papaver orientale* (Oriental poppy) and *Mertensia virginica* (Virginia bluebells),

die back soon after flowering. Other non-woody perennials may be evergreen, at least in certain climates; *Helleborus* (hellebores), *Chrysanthemum* × *superbum* (Shasta daisy), certain *Hemerocallis* species (daylily) and *Limonium* (statice) often maintain at least a rosette of green foliage through most of the winter. The influence of climate is significant. In Mobile a given daylily cultivar may be evergreen; in Little Rock it will hold its foliage until mid-winter, then brown off; in St. Louis it is quite deciduous; and the same daylily will not survive the winter in Des Moines. Many species of *Dianthus* (pink and carnation) are evergreen throughout their range.

Often gardeners fail to realize that many garden plants that they treat as annuals may be quite persistent—truly perennial—in a milder climate. *Begonia*, *Pelargonium* (houseplant or bedding geranium), *Justicia* (shrimp plant) and several other "annual" bedding plants are perennial, perhaps even semi-woody, in their tropical native habitats. *Antirrhinum* (snapdragon) and *Petunia* frequently grow back for two or more years in the Pacific Northwest. (Tender perennials are treated in the volume *Annuals*.) Gardeners should consider how perennials behave where they grow naturally, in addition to how they behave in the garden. A gardener who attempts to reproduce, within reason, the conditions of a plant's native habitat is more likely to be successful than one who treats all plants the same.

Perennials are the backbone of most gardens. In a rock garden, almost every plant is a perennial. In the border, many, often most, plants are perennial. Some English garden lovers would think it heresy to plant anything but perennials in a border. American gardeners are more flexible, and borders here are often fortified with flowering masses of annuals and biennials throughout the summer.

Most of the flowers in the wild garden are perennial. *Lilium* (lily), *Narcissus* (daffodil), *Hyacinthus* (hyacinth), *Tulipa* (tulip), *Crocus* (crocus) and similar dependable bulbs, corms and tubers are, of course, perennials. So are the more tender sorts, such as *Dahlia, Gladiolus, Acidanthera, Canna* and *Crocosmia*, although many of these will not overwinter in northern zones. Gardeners, however, generally consider all of these bulbous plants as "bulbs," and thus all of these lovely flowers are featured in a separate volume of the same name.

It is hard to think of a private garden without perennial flowers; beds of nothing but annuals conjure up thoughts of Victorian park plantings or masses of petunias at a shopping center. Perennials mean home gardening.

A careful selection of perennials provides flowers in the garden month after month. Very early in the spring the low-growing perennials begin to bloom. *Helleborus* often blooms in the snow; in the rock garden, *Arabis*, the earliest species of *Dianthus* (moss pink) and some *Primula* species (primrose) come out in March or early April. In most climates the greatest showing of perennials appears during May, June and July. Autumn is climaxed by displays of *Chrysanthemum, Aster, Artemisia* and *Anemone × hybrida*.

## STRUCTURE OF PERENNIAL PLANTS

When considering the development and physical characteristics of perennials, a helpful place to begin is with the roots. Perennial plants have strong root systems, with the roots continuing to grow outward year after year. At the soil line some perennial plants develop a mass of stem-root tissue—more or less well-defined—called a crown. *Delphinium* crowns, for example, are somewhat woody, producing thick, very tender shoots above and rather weak but long roots below. The crowns of *Phlox paniculata* (garden phlox) and hardy *Aster* become extremely woody with age; so woody, in fact, that eventually movement of water and minerals from roots to shoots is retarded and bloom becomes poor. The crowns of *Primula* and *Myosotis* (forget-me-not) remain soft. Other perennials do not have well-organized crowns but thickened, fairly woody main roots. The roots of the garden species of *Paeonia*, *Dicentra spectabilis* (common bleeding-heart) and *Baptisia* (false indigo) are intertwined, tangled and thick, becoming woody with age; these produce strong buds (eyes) near the soil surface that grow into flowering shoots. Smaller, fibrous roots extend outward from the thickened roots, and these absorb water and nutrients.

Perennial roots go deep into the soil. Before planting, study the natural habitat of the perennials you plan to grow. Select a site with growing conditions that most closely approximate those where the plant grows naturally, and prepare the soil accordingly. When a perennial is planted in the wrong site (even though the soil is deeply worked), the plant will do poorly.

The stems of border perennials usually arise straight up from the crown or from the roots. Sturdy, well-spaced stems produce masses of large, long-lasting flowers. So on older clumps, clip out all weak stems at the base when the leafy shoots are half-developed; it usually pays to remove half of the remaining stems on perennial clumps older than three years.

For strong bloom and healthy plants, lift and divide border perennials every three to five years. (For the different methods of dividing plants, see the section called "Division" on page 30.) Some perennials resent disturbance, however; *Paeonia, Hosta,* and *Dictamnus albus* (gas plant) make little or no bloom for two to three years after being lifted. The stems of woodland and aquatic perennials are usually not thinned.

Perennials bloom in many ways. *Delphinium, Lupinus* (lupine) and *Kniphofia* (red-hot-poker) produce flowers on a strong vertical stem. While most of the perennials with flowers in spikes bloom from the bottom upward, a few—notably *Liatris* (Kansas gay feather, blazing-star)—bloom from the top downward. Other perennials, such as *Phlox paniculata,* bloom with flowers in close-set panicles or clusters. Still others, such as *Heuchera* (coralbells), bear flowers in loose clusters, or in very open sprays, as does *Aquilegia* (columbine). A few perennials bloom on unbranched stems, or with branching limited to second-crop flowers that originate low on the stem of the primary flower, as is the case with Shasta daisies. For more on flower clusters, see "Inflorescence" on page 16.

Seed formation saps the strength of the plant, putting a stop to the current flowering, or reducing the number or size (or both) of next year's flowers. To prevent seed formation, remove flower heads of perennials as soon as blooms fade. All perennials benefit from this "deadheading." The only times not to do it are if the seedheads are required for dried arrangements or for decoration in the garden, or if you want the the plant to self-sow.

## DESIGNING WITH PERENNIALS

A landscape design can include a variety of habitats to meet the various needs of perennials. A perennial border likes full sun and requires a well-drained site. So choose an open location that is sunny for as much of the day as possible, and preferably one that is not in a low-lying area. If no such site exists on the property, opt for one that gets sun all morning and part of the afternoon. Two or three closely planted shade trees, positioned to form a northern boundary and underplanted with low-growing, understory trees, such as dogwood, redbud or black haw, will provide a wind break, sheltering the garden from cold weather. Gardeners lucky enough to have a low place where the ground is soggy throughout the year can make a bog garden, with or without a pond, for aquatic perennials. A rock garden is wonderful; quite a few rock-garden perennials will thrive in a properly laid-up dry wall, and the maintenance is very light.

## The Perennial Border

Because today's gardens are often quite small, most perennials are used in entrance gardens, near the outdoor patio or amongst the shrubbery. With the resurgent interest in perennials, however, many gardeners are planting borders again. Ideally, a border is a flower bed designed to be approached from one end, so that the expanse of the bed seems to stretch away from the viewer. The bed appears to advantage when set against a natural background; trimmed or informal hedges, garden walls and solid fences all make good backgrounds for a perennial border. It is wise to leave a space of 3 to 5 ft. from the background to promote good air circulation and thus reduce the chance of disease, but this is not always possible.

Double digging is recommended for the perennial bed—that is, digging in such a fashion that the soil is turned to a depth of 15 to 24 in., with ample well-decayed manure, humus-yielding products such as peat and compost, and various

*(continued on page 24)*

# DAYLILIES

Few plants are as popular as daylilies (*Hemerocallis* spp.) in American perennial gardens. This appreciation seems to grow with each passing year. The phenomenon is a particularly American one; even our English cousins, who can take credit for the first interspecies hybrid—George Yeld hybridized daylilies in the early 1880s—have not found daylilies to be all that colorful or useful. But this ambivalence toward these beautiful plants may soon change.

Until recently most daylilies were diurnal (day-openers), dependent on warm summer nights to open properly. When temperatures fell below 65°F, they opened slowly, if at all, the next morning. The cooler the preceding night the less likely it was that they would open the following morning. Only an occasional problem during the summer in most of the United States, this "cold night phenomenon," greatly hindered their practicality in other parts of the globe, including England, where on many summer nights the temperature drops into the 50s. Aware of this problem, American hybridizers have created a new "race" of daylilies that open nocturnally and are less effected by the cold. In fact, one of the most successful daylilies worldwide is 'Stella de Oro' whose flowers open conveniently the night before. Hybridizers are now breeding and introducing cultivars that are fully open by 6:00 A.M. even on cold mornings. These new plants may prove irresistible to English gardeners.

For the most part, modern daylilies are exactly that: cultivars produced in the last decade or so. At the turn of the century, there were only two major daylilies in America, *Hemerocallis lilio-asphodelus* and *H. fulva* 'Europa'. In 1934 A. B. Stout from the New York Botanical Garden published a book, *Daylilies*, based on his work with several new species and species hybrids. Later, following the World War II, the American Hemerocallis Society was founded. Today the society boasts over 7,500 members, more than 200 of whom breed daylilies as a hobby or business.

The success of these amateurs and professionals alike in changing a genus is almost unbelievable. The flower color now varies from off-white through all shades of yellow, orange, pink, lavender and salmon to reds, maroon and true purple hues. Some flowers are eyed or watermarked, some are bicolor, and often the throat is chartreuse, lemon or another shade. A few of the newer cultivars have "bubbled" or "wire edges" of different colors than the petals. Ruffling has been perfected to the point that there are many different forms. Doubles in a wide range of colors and shapes are popular with collectors. Cultivars that bloom from 6 in. up to 5 ft. in height are now available. There are cultivars ranging in bloom season from May to September. Many newer sorts bloom early and continue to bloom all season.

The official registrar for new daylily cultivars, the American Hemerocallis Society reports that there are now over 34,500 cultivars with nearly 1,000 new cultivars registered each year. The awards program of the American Hemerocallis Society is useful in helping gardeners select the best performers.

The highest honor is the Stout Silver Medal, which is awarded to one plant each year by a panel of judges. Recent winners are: 'Betty Woods', double gold; 'Fairy Tale Pink', melon-pink; 'Brocaded Gown', yellow; 'Martha Adams', pink; and 'Becky Lynn', pink.

The Lenington All-American Award recognizes overall performance and is voted on by the American Hemerocallis Society Board. Winners in recent years have included: 'Condilla', a double gold; 'Joan Senior', near-white; 'Russian Rhapsody', wine-colored with a deeper eye; 'Lullaby Baby', light pink; and 'Golden Prize', a deep gold.

The Donn Fischer Memorial Cup recognizes the top performing miniatures (flowers under 3 in.). The judges vote on their selections, which in recent years have included: 'Siloam Grace Stamile', bright red; 'Texas Sunshine', gold; 'Siloam Bertie Ferris', pink with a red eye; 'Yellow Lollipop', reblooming gold; and 'Siloam Tee Tiny', a deep pink with a purple eye.

The Annie T. Giles Award is also given by the society for small flowered daylilies (3 to $4^1/2$ in.); recent award winners include: 'Enchanter's Spell', beige with a violet eye; 'Janice Brown', peach-pink with a rose eye; 'Sugar Cookie', cream; 'Siloam Jim Cooper', red with ruby eyezone; and 'Pandora's Box', near white with burgundy eyezone.

A non-profit corporation called the All-America Daylily Selection Council (AADSC) was recently formed to evaluate daylily cultivars. Its central mission is to help gardeners select daylilies that consistently perform well. The council sponsors a three-tiered series of horticultural testing. Plants are evaluated for foliage, beauty of bloom, bud count, length of bloom, spent blossoms, sun resistance and plant increase. If a cultivar scores high here, it is sent on to cooperator gardens in each of the hardiness zones and more data is gathered over a period of two years. The group plans to name the first All-America Winners shortly.

Most daylilies are propagated by simple division. This method is somewhat slow because many only increase by one or two plants each year. In the mid-1970s micropropagation methods were tried and became somewhat successful. These "test-tube babies" have helped to make newer cultivars available at modest prices. Hybridizers also produce seeds to create new daylilies. Most of these are inferior or similar to their parents. On the average, only about one or two of every thousand seedlings is worthy of introduction. Seedlings bloom in the first year in the southern states and in about two to three years in northern areas.

The local clubs and regions of the American Hemerocallis Society are a good source of information about the newest sorts, and those that perform best locally. While most daylilies are quite hardy, there is considerable variation in modern cultivars. In the colder zones (Zones 3 and 4), dormant daylilies are usually most successful. In Zones 9 and 10, evergreen cultivars are often the best choice. However, in the intermediate zones (Zones 5 to 8), both dormant and evergreen cultivars usually succeed.

No serious pests or diseases bother daylilies, though local infestations of aphids, nematodes, slugs, spider mites and thrips may cause trouble; and soft rot has also been known to be a problem in newly set plants in the southern states. For more information on daylilies, see pages 101–105 in the encyclopedia.

# PEONIES

For centuries the peony (*Paeonia* spp.) has been the "grande dame" of flowers. Native to Eurasia and western North America, peonies are renowned for their uniquely graceful shapes, which have probably graced more priceless porcelain bowls than any other flower save the rose. Hardy perennials of both herbaceous and shrubby tree forms (the latter are covered in *The Hearst Garden Guides* volume *Trees & Shrubs*), peonies continue to be one of the most popular flowers.

Grown in temperate regions for their showy single or double blossoms in shades of rose, pink, white and yellow, peonies bloom in late May and early June. The herbaceous types feature unique, long-lasting blooms, which are excellent for cutting. The decorative foliage, consisting of erect compound leaves on string stems, endures well until the first frosts. The herbaceous cultivars are bushy, ranging from $1^{1}/2$ ft. to $3^{1}/2$ ft. in height.

Five wild species, all native to China, account for most of the hybrids available today: *Paeonia lactiflora, P. officinalis, P. peregrina, P. tenuifolia* and *P. wittmanniana*. The Chinese perfected the peony a thousand years ago, almost to the degree we know it today. The American Peony Society provides continued impetus for cultivar improvement. Each year more new peonies are being hybridized and registered. So much is going on, in fact, that even those in the thick of the matter seem uncertain as to who is breeding what.

Most of the showy garden hybrids were derived from *P. officinalis*. Five different types of flowers are now recognized by the American Peony Society:

**Single**—five or more petals arranged around a center of pollen-bearing stamens and carpels.

**Japanese**—five or more petals and a center of stamens bearing abortive anthers nearly or completely devoid of pollen, which appear in many different forms and are commonly called staminodes.

**Anemone**—five or more petals and a center of stamens fully transformed into small, narrow petals called petaloids.

**Semidouble**—five or more guard petals and a center of broad petals, with many pollen-bearing stamens intermixed. These stamens may be rings among the petals, or there may be a center of all stamens; they are always a prominent feature. The carpels may be normal or transformed, either whole or in part.

**Double**—five or more guard petals, with a center of stamens and carpels, more or less fully transformed into petals, which make up the main body of the flower.

Peony crosses that were never thought possible before are now being made. The original discovery occurred in Japan with a new race of golden peonies. The *P. lutea* hybrid 'Alice Harding' was crossed with the white *P. lactiflora* 'Kakoden.' This cross was then repeated in the U.S. on a much wider scale.

The catalogs of peony specialists offer a bewildering array of peony cultivars, all of which promise to be glorious. To see which cultivars win in shows and which ones breeders are talking about, one guide to read is the bulletin of the American Peony Society. Also much in the limelight among growers in the know are the "estate" and "rock garden" peonies bred by Roy Klehm of Charles Klehm & Sons Nursery of South Barrington, Illinois.

From the gardener's point of view, the most exciting news is that by careful selection from today's cultivars, six weeks of continuous bloom (four toward the southern ranges) are possible. There are also more colors than ever before. The development of these fabulous new hybrids is hindered only by the fact that peonies are slow to propagate. By present methods it can take fifteen to twenty years for a new cultivar to become widely available. One answer may be tissue culture, which has totally changed the orchid business. But whereas other plants are easy to propagate by the tissue-culture method, peonies remain somewhat elusive. Scientists predict, however, that a breakthrough is imminent.

Peonies are heavy feeders and should be grown in full sun where they will have full growing space, well-drained soil and little or no competition from large shade-tree roots. The choice of planting site and preparation of the soil is particularly important with peonies, because they will last for several decades once established. The plants should be set out in September or October, as dormant roots. The site should be well-prepared, dug deeply and enriched with rotted manure, peat moss and compost. If the site is sandy, adding compost and peat—to increase the water-retention capacity—is especially important.

The most essential part of peony planting, outside of correct site preparation, is the proper planting depth. The buds of the root clump should be no deeper than 2 in. below the soil surface. Too-deep planting is a common reason for lack of bloom. Once planted, the peonies will last well with little care. An application of a fertilizer high in phosphorus, such as 5-10-5 or 4-12-4, is recommended in spring. The leafy stems should be cut to ground level after the first frosts brown off the foliage.

Mulching of peony plants is not recommended, as this can encourage disease. About the only major disease to which peonies are susceptible is botrytis, a fungus that causes brown shoots as the plants are developing in spring. Insect pests are a rarity. Ants crawl over the flower buds because they are attracted to the sticky sap, but they are harmless to the plants.

To encourage large flower buds, many growers like to disbud their peonies, that is, remove all the small buds from the side of the flower stem when they are the size of peas and allow only the central terminal bud to develop into one large flower. Propagate by root division in fall when plants are dormant.

chemical fertilizers (particularly root-producing phosphates) turned deeply into the bed.

If trees or large shrubs grow close to the border, dig a trench between the bed and the woody plants each spring. This cuts roots that would invade the border and compete with the flowering plants.

Perennial borders are usually laid out with low-growing, almost prostrate plants at the front, higher plants planted in drifts behind them, and very tall plants—*Macleaya cordata* (plume poppy), *Thalictrum* (meadow rue), *Artemisia*, *Digitalis* (foxglove), tall *Delphinium* cultivars and the like—clumped at the back of the border. There must, however, be some undulation in height within the border, or the design will appear rather sterile.

Dozens of designs for perennial beds and borders have been published, with lists of flowers for each area of the planting. While this sort of diagram has some value as an illustration of design principles, too often it is taken literally. The best perennials for a Midwestern border would not necessarily be suited for New England, the Deep South or the Southwest.

A perennial border may be very long and narrow or relatively short and broad. But the concept of a border calls for an elongated rectangle. Perennial borders that are fairly long—20 to 30 ft., with a width of 5 to 8 ft.—are adequate; even longer is better. While, for proportion, a 100-yd.-long border might be 20 ft. wide (and require a battalion of gardeners to maintain!), generally a perennial border is less than 12 ft. in depth.

With few exceptions it is best to plant perennials in groups of at least three, even in the smallest garden. One or two plants of a kind simply do not make enough of a show, save for very statuesque perennials like *Crambe cordifolia* (sea kale) or a mature *Baptisia australis* (false indigo). The size of the "patches" of plants varies with the size of the border and with the scale of the various

plants; 3 to 4 sq. ft. is the minimum for many plants.

The best borders feature long, narrow strips of "front-row," low-growing plants in front of more rectangular clumps of moderate-sized flowers. These clumps of intermediate and background perennials change in size according to the boldness of their foliage and flowers. Three or four clumps (growing together) of soup-bowl-size *Papaver orientale* (Oriental poppy) flowers, for example, easily balance a 1-ft.-across patch of misty *Gypsophila paniculata* (baby's-breath).

When compiling a list of plants for the perennial border, refer to the USDA Zone Hardiness Map on pages 178–179 and select plants that are hardy in your area. To ensure a continuous show of color, mark those that bloom in April–May, May–June, June–July, July–August and August–September, and add or drop plants as necessary. Next, subdivide each of these lists of plants by height to help determine their position within the border. Finally, list the color of each plant.

With this information in mind, draw up a border design plan, filling in plant names where appropriate. Stick to those plants that bloom longest and are best suited to the soil and weather conditions of the site. Blend colors to suit personal tastes. A perennial border can be a collection of faded pastels or a mix of bright flowers with just enough white, pale yellow and cool colors to keep the strong colors from clashing.

Given that the selected plants are hardy, the exact composition of a perennial border is largely a matter of personal choice. Although most borders endeavor to provide color and interest for as long as possible, a border can be designed to be at its peak for just a month. In a garden where spring bulbs put on a long and showy display and dahlias and chrysanthemums are featured in fall, a perennial border need only peak in midsummer. In another scheme, color rather than timing may be the overriding factor in plant selection, and perhaps only pink or blue plants will find a place in the design.

While true perennials make up the main planting, showy biennials and hardy bulbs in the perennial border generally add more color and foliage texture.

## The Island Bed

Allan Bloom, the famous English gardener, has done much to promote the concept of island beds. In this scheme, perennial plants become the focal point rather than just one of the components of an overall landscape scene. An island bed differs from a border in that it is not adjacent to a structure, such as a stone wall. An island bed, to be seen equally well from all vantage points, is generally surrounded by grass, or another neutral, flat surface.

This design idea is a great favorite of large estate gardens, municipalities, parks and public display gardens. In such large landscapes, island beds are useful for breaking up great expanses, and they help to create diversity and intimacy. But they can be equally successful in a home garden.

The success of island beds comes from the juxtaposition of large masses of contrasting foliage and flower color. It is best to select plants that need less staking and less maintenance. Unlike borders, the island bed is viewed from all sides, so careful attention must be given to the height of plants throughout the island. Most designers try to avoid the monotony associated with the bedding-out concept, in which entire beds are filled with rows of annuals that are generally of one height.

Textural variations can be introduced by adding clumps of fine-leaved vertical grasses among the flowering perennials. A few of these gardens have become rather pedestrian because the palette of plants is restricted to just a few

species of grasses and long-blooming perennials. Obviously, the choice of plants is limited only by gardening knowledge and experience. As the "perennial renaissance" continues, island beds offer a promising new era for gardeners.

## Perennials for Foliage

When choosing perennials, do not overlook those whose foliage is as important or more important than their flowers. Bold or finely divided leaves in various shades of green, bronze and silver are a great addition to any garden. For instance, borders can be done entirely with white- and silver-leaved plants of various sizes and shapes.

Among the foliage plants with bold leaves are *Rodgersia*, *Bergenia*, *Rheum* (ornamental rhubarb) and some *Hosta*. Upright plants with large, showy leaves include some species of *Ligularia* and *Macleaya cordata* (plume poppy).

Silver-leaved plants are not too uncommon; most gardeners grow *Stachys byzantina* (lamb's-ears) and *Veronica incana* (woolly speedwell). *Artemisia*, particularly the spreading 'Silver Mound' and tall 'Silver King', are grown in old-fashioned gardens, and they are finding a place in very contemporary settings, too. *Anaphalis margaritacea* from the roadside and *A. triplinervis* from the Himalayas (both are called pearly everlasting because of their use in dried arrangements) wear woolly white leaves and small, pearly flowers. Among the rock-garden perennials are a number with silvery white foliage. Some of these make ideal edging plants for the border, as their leaves contrast nicely with the dark green turf and most of them bloom well.

Foliage of many colors can be used to advantage to accent or complete a color scheme, but blue foliage is probably the quietest and most restful color for a border. It is a good contrast for gaily

(continued on page 28)

# HOSTAS

Long considered indispensable shade plants, hostas (*Hosta* spp.) were thought to be too common only few years back, but now they are in the limelight and have again become fashionable. These Chinese and Japanese natives came into fashion in America in the late 1960s with the founding of the American Hosta Society, which now claims 2,000 members. With every passing year, hostas have grown in popularity, becoming important staples of the perennial garden, and increasingly sought after by gardeners with expansive grounds and small plots alike.

There are twenty to thirty species, depending on whether the taxonomist consulted is a "lumper" or a "splitter." But interest during the last fifteen years has been so great as to encourage the selection of many new cultivars—there are now more than a thousand. The development of these new plants has been so rapid that even the experts are unsure as to the lineage of many of the new cultivars; some are suspected to be hybrids, while others are thought to be mutations of the species.

Still grown primarily for their large, dense, decorative clumps of luxuriant leaves, these plants have generated such enthusiasm that breeders have selected a marvelous array of foliage colors—from green to blue and from chartreuse to gold with assorted subtle variegations—as well as flower forms, fragrance, texture and adaptability. They vary in height from 12-in.-tall-types, such as *Hosta tardiflora* (late-flowering hosta) and *H. lancifolia* (lance-leaf hosta), to significantly larger clumps, like *H. sieboldiana* (Siebold hosta), which grows to be 3 ft. tall and 5 ft. wide. If given some sun, most hostas produce distinctive spikes of aromatic, funnel-shaped flowers of white and lavender, which ascend from the foliage from midsummer to fall. The flowers are long-lasting when cut, adding an unusual touch to bouquets.

Hostas, or plantain lilies as they are sometimes called, are among the most versatile and useful plants in the garden. Delightful as edgings for the shrub border or along a path, they also provide color to the rock garden and texture to the perennial border or wild garden. Native to the Far East, they add a touch of the exotic to any waterside or damp, shady corner.

Essentially shade- and moisture-loving plants, they are best known for their capacity to fill in difficult areas. Shady areas can be trying for gardeners, but plant a combination of a few different varieties of hosta side by side and these areas become lush, verdant sites. Useful in pots, planters and other containers, they can provide a sense of greenery alongside steps or even on a city terrace. Borders of perennials, which come in and out of bloom during the growing season, find handsome, long-lasting companions in hostas.

Hostas make excellent partners in a number of combinations—blue-leaved hostas, such as the well-known *H. sieboldiana* 'Elegans', *H. ventricosa* (blue hosta) or *H. lancifolia* 'Kabistan', provide a neutral backdrop to the hot colors of candelabra primroses alongside a riverbed; the large leaves (18 in. long and 12 in. wide) of *H. sieboldiana* act as a counterpoint to frilly and soft-textured companion plants, such as astilbe or ferns; the undulating lines of *H. undulata* (wavy hosta ) set off the straight lines of iris foliage.

Exciting new cultivars are being introduced every year, expanding the range of foliage color (to include chartreuse and gold, for instance) and the range of sizes from very short and wide to quite large. Popular new forms include: 'Francee', 24 in. tall and 30 in. wide, has leaves bordered by regular, narrow, white margins; 'Gold Standard', a medium-sized variety (24 in. tall and 30 in. wide), has leaves that unfurl to chartreuse-green with an irregular deep-green margin; 'Golden Tiara', a small plant for edging (2 in. tall and 16 in. wide) has medium green blades with a chartreuse-yellow margin and purple flowers in midsummer; 'Great Expectations', a medium-sized plant (20 in. tall and 30 in. wide), has leaves with blue-green edges and cream-yellow centers; the pest-resistant and somewhat sun-tolerant 'Invincible' (10 in. tall and 12 in. wide) has bright, thick, glossy green leaves and fragrant blue flowers that appear in late summer; 'Krossa Regal' is a large plant (36 in. tall and wide) that holds its silvery blue leaf blades at distinct angles; 'Sum and Substance', which can take quite a bit of sun if the soil is moist, makes upright mounds (30 in. high and 24 in. wide) of chartreuse to gold foliage; and 'Sun Power', 30 in. tall and 36 in. wide, has gold foliage that lasts all season long.

Hostas thrive in rich, humus-enriched soil in moist locations with partial shade. They need ample space and at least three to five years of undisturbed growth in a single location to develop into truly handsome specimens.

(When considering buying plants, note that the sizes listed in most catalogs tend to be their full size at maturity.)

While hostas are known for thriving in the shade, there are exceptions—'Sun Power', for instance, grows best in full sun—and no matter which variety, a hosta's shape and color will depend on the amount of sun to which it is exposed. Gold-leaved plants will generally be green in deep shade, while blue-leaved varieties will become green in the sun. Hostas rarely flower in full shade, where their leaves will generally be larger but fewer in number.

Hostas are fairly free of pests, with the exception of slugs and snails, which are capable of stripping a plant's leaves overnight. Commercial slug and snail baits are available, although homemade slug traps (little containers filled with beer) are less toxic to children and neighborhood pets. All varieties of hosta can be injured by late frosts in early spring; avoid planting in known frost pockets. Propagate by crown division or by seeds.

For further information, see the specific entries in the encyclopedia (pages 107–110). Because of the tremendous number of selections and the complexity of the subject, the types discussed there are limited to a select group of highly recommended species and cultivars. For further reading, pick up one of the new books devoted solely to the subject, or contact the American Hosta Society, which publishes four newsletters and a bulletin annually for its members. It also provides a plant identification service and a seed exchange.

colored flowers, and if planted in the shade it makes the shadowy places softer and mistier. There are numerous variations in blue coloring. Some plants have foliage of a striking steel blue; some have leaves of varying shades of blue-green; others have whitish, grayish, frosty or silvery blue leaves; some have opalescent blue. The stronger the shade, the more care should be exercised in its use.

*Dianthus* is a perennial favorite for its grassy bluish foliage as well as for its delightfully perfumed flowers. It is frequently used as an edging, and the lower kinds can be used as a ground cover in a sunny spot. There are hundreds of species, with much variation in height and growth habit— from tiny, low mounds to some that grow about 1 ft. high. The foliage of all species, in both texture and color, is indispensable in the garden.

One of the best and most useful of the plants with blue-gray leaves is *Hosta sieboldiana* (Siebold hosta). This stately border plant is handsome and survives well in shady places. In fact, hot, dry conditions seem to produce better color in the foliage. The plant makes a large, compact mound of beautiful, large blue-gray leaves and produces short spires of lavender bells. It is more useful for its leaves than for its flowers, but it has a fine effect wherever planted and is an excellent accent.

Some *Thalictrum* (meadow rue) species have foliage of a lovely, soft, bluish tone. *T. delavayi* (Yunnan meadow rue) is perhaps the best of these, with elegant, finely cut foliage of blue-gray and open, airy panicles of lilac flowers. It grows 4 to 6 ft. tall and blooms in July. It is beautiful in the border, with flowers good for cutting.

## CARE AND PROPAGATION

Well in advance, schedule the seasonal chores required to keep the perennial bed or border in good shape. Plantings that are tended only in time left over from the rest of life's duties often reflect that lack of care in their appearance.

In early spring, when danger of frost is past, gradually remove the mulch (whatever material was applied to protect plants over winter); a daily partial removal of mulch spread over ten days is better than lifting all of it at once. As the ground is cleared, apply a light dressing of an all-purpose balanced fertilizer. Generally, 3 lbs. of a 5-10-5 fertilizer dressed over 100 sq. ft. of bed will suffice. After the fertilizer is spread, cultivate shallowly with a three- or four-pronged cultivator. Working around each clump, remove moldy, decayed and discolored leaves. If slime trails indicate the presence of slugs and snails, apply a slug and snail bait. Keep the bed in clean cultivation— that is, keep the soil loose and free of weeds— throughout the summer, or, when all the plants are up and new growth has hardened off, apply a summer mulch of old sawdust, coarse compost or chopped straw. Perennial beds look best when cultivated weekly.

### Staking for Better Perennials

When taller-growing plants reach 6 to 8 in. in height, thin the crowded and weak shoots. Set stakes at this stage, so foliage will cover them by blooming time. There are several alternative methods of staking. Some gardeners tie each plant to a support stake with a wire loop at the top through which the plant will grow. Others put three bamboo stakes in a triangular pattern around the plant and ring them with string, creating a pen. Still others push brush into the perennial clump. This last method came into use in English gardens during the labor shortage of World War II and proved so successful that it has continued to be a common practice. Brush staking is a one-time job, while the use of clean stakes requires weekly visits to add more ties.

During fall and winter assemble twiggy brush, called pea stakes (the method was first used to stake peas). Upper branches of brushy trees, such as elm, beech, birch, hazelnut and hornbeam, work very well. Each piece should be a finger-sized main stick with plenty of twiggy branches growing from it, broom fashion.

To stake a clump of Michaelmas daisies, for instance, ring the clump closely when the shoots are 15 in. high with half a dozen or more of the brushy sticks, butts pushed firmly into the soil. The brush should make a loose, continuous ring around and among the daisy shoots. The daisy stems will grow upward through the twigs; their soft branches, well furnished with leaves, will grow outward through the brush and mask it. Brush twigs that show can be clipped away in a few weeks. A well-brushed clump of perennials is seldom knocked crooked by even the strongest wind.

### Insects and Diseases

As new growth develops, watch for insect pests and diseases. It pays to learn what insects and diseases can be expected. Experienced gardeners know that mildew fungal disease is liable to attack garden phlox, for instance, and that green plant beetles will strip the foliage from evening primroses. With most insect pests, wait until they appear, then estimate how severe the damage will be. If it seems that great harm is likely, consider spraying with an insecticide specifically approved to control the insect that is doing the damage. Light infestations can be contained by destroying the insects by hand, or occasionally by spraying them off with a strong stream of water. Predator insects may help, too. Encourage the various "beneficial insects" by not using insecticides.

Since some fungal diseases cannot be cured, they must be prevented. (In some cases, spreading can be inhibited.) So with diseases such as mildew on phlox, the gardener must get there first. Knowing this, spray disease-susceptible species frequently with a recommended fungicide. Most large garden centers have knowledgeable staff members who can help in selecting approved pesticides.

Certain other species are subject to crown rot. *Delphinium, Lupinus, Chrysanthemum × superbum*, some *Campanula* species and some other perennials can all suffer from crown rot. Plants with this disease look fine until the soil warms up. Then, very quickly, new shoots wither and die, and a film of fungus appears at the base of the plant. Drench the crowns of susceptible plants with specific chemicals approved for crown rot early in the spring and once or twice again later.

### Watering and Fertilizing

Never let perennials suffer for want of water. Usually, spring and early summer rains provide enough (sometimes too much) water. During the dry season, soak the beds and borders once each week. Watering with soaker hoses or with an underground watering system is recommended in order to keep the foliage dry and thus avoid diseases.

The pre-blossom routine in the perennial garden is fertilization, continuous cultivation of the surface, staking, and disease and insect control. As plants come into flower, feed again. In cool climates spread a light fertilizer application over the bed. Many gardeners prefer to fertilize each clump individually, adjusting the time of application and the amount to the blooming time and the size of the plant. Midsummer care is limited largely to snipping off dead flowers and guarding against drought, insect pests and diseases.

As a clump goes out of flower, cut back the flower stalks so the plant looks neat, but preserve as much foliage as possible. The leaves are vital to the health of the plant, as they make the food that is to be stored in the roots for growth the following year. In the fall, when frost blackens the foliage, cut back the plants immediately and carry the debris to the compost pile or have it hauled away. Removing the foliage minimizes the risk of diseases and insect eggs overwintering in the garden. Cultivate the bed one last time; all plants will probably not die back at the same time, so these cleanup jobs will have to be done two or three times a month through October and November. Do not fertilize in the fall. Do not mulch early. But do carry on with clean cultivation as was done in the summer.

## Division

Most vigorous, multi stemmed, clump-forming perennials should be divided every three years, such as *Dianthus*, while others must be divided every year. Not only is this one of the simplest and perhaps the most reliable method of propagating plants, but many perennials, such as *Artemisia stellariana* (beach wormwood) and *Stachys byzantina* (lamb's- ears), suffer when they become too woody (as it becomes increasingly difficult for them to absorb and metabolize nutrients). Note, however, that not all perennials should be divided. Slow-growing plants, such as *Dictamnus* (gas plant) and *Paeonia* (peony), are best left alone.

The best time to divide a plant is during its period of dormancy, so divide spring- and summer-blooming plants in the fall, after the plant has died back, but before the onslaught of lethal frosts. Divide fall-blooming perennials in the spring— before they show signs of new growth. Do not divide plants that have foliage taller than 2 in.

Water loss during the procedure is one of the worst dangers to divided plants, so water the day before if the ground is dry and avoid dividing on bright, sunny days. It is worth waiting for cool weather, or at least the evening. If the plant is very overgrown, cut it back to the ground before dividing.

Lift the clump from the ground with a spade and separate the young offshoots from the larger woody center. There are three basic techniques for dividing perennials. The type of crown and root system of a particular plant determines which technique to use. Perennials that form a mat of thin roots, like *Chrysanthemum*, *Achillea* and *Phlox*, can be pulled apart by hand. Perennials with woody crowns, such as *Aquilegia*, *Geranium* and *Artemisia*, should be cut apart with sharp shears or a knife. Perennials with thick, dense crowns and nearly impenetrable root masses, such as *Hemerocallis*, should be pried apart using two gardening forks inserted in the clump, back to back. See the illustration, opposite, for a quick guide to these techniques.

Discard the central, woody stem and replant the young growth immediately. The shoots should be planted to the same depth as they were when attached to the parent. Water thoroughly, and mulch fall divisions to protect developing roots from frost heaving.

## Winter Protection

A mulch is a layer of any material that covers the surface of the soil around growing plants. One of the most effective labor- and time-saving measures a gardener can take, mulch helps keeps the soil cool and moist, reducing the amount of watering that will be necessary, and helps to keep down weeds. Mulching in the fall protects plants from frost heaving. In cold climates, unmulched soil freezes and thaws repeatedly. As this happens, the ground alternately shrinks and swells and can actually heave a perennial out of the ground, where its roots will dry out or freeze. Either occurence will kill the plant.

Popular mulches include both organic and inorganic (including synthetic) materials. Organic materials have the advantage of breaking down to add humus to the soil. Most perennials can be mulched with straw, prairie hay, salt-marsh hay or shredded wood products. Avoid materials that

## DIVIDING PERENNIALS

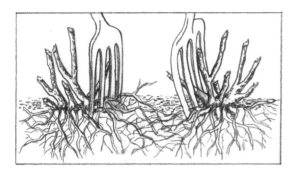

Large, hard, woody crowns can be pried apart with two digging forks positioned back to back. Make sure there are growing stems on each part that you plan to replant.

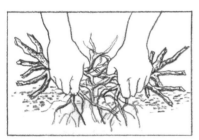

Many small clumps of stems can be pulled apart with your hands.

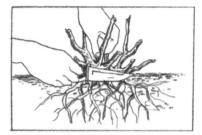

With a clean knife or a pair of clippers, cut midsize clumps apart.

compact, such as sawdust, unshredded leaves or grass clippings.

Some gardeners, on the other hand, prefer to use inorganic materials as they would rather see stones or brick shavings than decaying clippings. Black plastic, while not particularly attractive, can be covered with a second more pleasing mulch, and has the added attraction of holding heat from the day's sunshine until evening.

When the ground has frost in it, begin protecting sensitive species by covering the crowns with an appropriate material. In gardens where slugs or snails are a problem, scatter a few pellets of bait near each plant and cover them with hand-sized pieces of broken flowerpot.

Moisture-sensitive perennials, such as delphiniums, should be mounded. Years ago, sifted cinders from the coal furnace were used to accomplish this. Today, coarse grit is used: granite chips, screened sharp river pebbles or crushed brick.

This material should be scraped away and carried off in the spring. Over winter, the mound sheds excess moisture, deflecting it from the crown beneath, and the weight helps prevent frost heaving.

After the Christmas holidays in northern climates, when the ground is frozen hard, it helps to pile evergreen boughs over the entire border to keep the winter sun from thawing the soil on mild days.

### SOURCES OF PERENNIALS

Perennials have been greatly improved over the last decade. Most of the improved forms of many species can only be propagated asexually, and a whole new propagation industry has sprung up to supply the demand. These producers are called plug growers, a name taken from the cell plugs that make up the insides of plastic flats. Some specialize in only one genus, while others cover the entire range of perennials. These plants are then

gardener who wants one of the best purple-leaved heucheras will probably select an asexually propagated plant such as *H. micrantha* 'Montrose Ruby', although it is also possible to grow purple-leafed forms from seeds.

Despite the improved cultivars, there are still a large number of perennials that are seed-grown. Most perennials are as easy to start as annuals; sow seeds in the cold frame in midsummer, overwinter the young plants in the frame and bed them in the spring. Or start seeds in early spring, indoors under lights or in a home greenhouse. Set out the young plants in the vegetable garden in rows when danger of frost is past. There they are cultivated and cared for just like so many vegetable plants, for an entire summer. In the fall they go into the perennial border, the mixed garden or wherever else they happen to be needed.

Perennial plants are available from local specialists and from various mail-order nurseries. When plants are shipped, they suffer. Typically, they are packed semi-dormant and slightly damp. If the package is delayed (especially in a warm place), the plants begin to grow, and then decay. The quickest delivery service is usually the best. When the plants arrive, open the package immediately. Set the plants in a windless, bright place, out of direct sunlight. Those that appear to be dry should be soaked in a shallow pan of water. Hold the plants until late afternoon, then plant them, giving each a thorough watering. After transplanting, protect plants from direct sunlight for three or four days with two wood shingles stuck in at an angle over the plants.

Some perennials, such as Oriental poppies, are shipped dormant during the summer. Others are shipped semi-dormant after flowering; bearded irises are an example of this type.

Many perennials grow well from cuttings. Shoots of delphiniums, chrysanthemums and coralbells, for example, root easily in perlite or other rooting mediums. Root cuttings of others, such as Oriental poppy, bleeding-heart and globe thistle, are equally successful. Try a few cuttings each year. Friends with unusual plants are generally very willing to furnish the material for propagating.

chapter

# 3

# ENCYCLOPEDIA
# OF PERENNIALS

The following encyclopedia lists the perennials best suited for the garden, including the most commonly available species and cultivars, as well as a substantial selection of lesser known varieties that are well worth the effort to grow. Comprehensive in scope, it encapsulates all the information necessary to make informed choices when selecting and cultivating perennials.

In this chapter, perennials are listed by genus under their botanical names (with a pronunciation key). Species of each genus appear for every entry, together with varieties and cultivars. For instance, the various kinds of sunflowers are all listed under their genus, *Helianthus*. If you know only the common name of a plant, you can use the Common Name Index to find its correct botanical name. Look up "sunflower" in the index, for example, and it points to the genus *Helianthus*.

**Plant Ratings**

The encyclopedia singles out the most outstanding plants for the garden. Virtually indispensable genera, such as *Hemerocallis* (daylilies), *Hosta* (hostas) and *Paeonia* (peonies), are noted with two stars (★★). Unusually outstanding species or varieties, such as *Pulmonaria saccharata* (Bethlehem sage), are indicated by a single star (★).

**The Encyclopedia Entries**

General horticultural information, such as the type of soil and amount of light that plants require, their susceptibility to disease, overall hardiness, planting times and appropriate methods of propagation, appears with each genus. General gardening information, such as the valued ornamental aspects of the plants—flowers, form and foliage to name a few—is also outlined.

Each species entry contains a detailed botanical description of the plant, which includes average mature height; flower shape, size, color and blooming period; and leaf structure, color, size and texture. Also included are suggestions as to where plants might best be used in the garden or indoors to highlight each species' aesthetic strong points, as well as descriptions of recent and time-tested subspecies, nursery-introduced series, varieties, hybrids and clones.

Geographical information, such as the plant's place of origin (a key to the conditions under which it thrives in nature) and the most northern hardiness zone, alerts gardeners to the ability of each species to grow well in a given region. Wherever possible, a zone range has been supplied for the most complete hardiness information. The U.S. Department of Agriculture Plant Hardiness Zone Map is reproduced on pages 178-179.

# UNDERSTANDING
# THE ENCYCLOPEDIA ENTRIES

Two stars indicating genus indispensable to the home garden. ——— **★★ Hemerocallis** (hem-er-oh-*kal*-lis). ——— Genus. A plant group that includes many related species.

Common name of this genus. Cross-reference entry appears listed in the Index of Common Names. ——— DAYLILY.

Lily Family (*Liliaceae*). ———

Pronunciation key. Accent on italicized syllable.

Botanical name of the plant family.

Each entry gives you a ——— detailed description of the perennial, including average height; flower shape, size, color and blooming period; and leaf structure and size. In-depth cultivation information, including zone ranges where known, light and soil requirements and propagation techniques are covered. Design suggestions and reliable strains, varieties, cultivars, hybrids and clones complete the information.

Mostly hardy, mostly herbaceous perennials, native from central Europe to China and Japan. While these do best in a deeply dug, well-fertilized, sunny bed or border, they tolerate a wide range of conditions—poor or dry soil, boggy soil, high shade or northern exposure. Species daylilies are experiencing something of a renaissance, but it is the continued introduction and improvement of the newer cultivars that has made this genus so popular.

The plant produces a fountain of roughly 1-in.-wide, strap-shaped foliage. Flowers are borne one, two or a few at a time on a tall, naked scape over a three- to six-week period.

Stands for *Helleborus orientalis,* a species belonging to the *Helleborus* genus. ——— **★ H. orientalis** (or-ee-en-*tay*-lis).

LENTEN ROSE.

Single star indicates species of outstanding merit. ———

Quite similar to *H. niger* in appearance and culture, except that the flowers range from white, pink, maroon or purple fading to green, and several appear together on a branched, leafless stem. Blooms from March to May. Propagation is by seeds or by division in spring or fall. Zone 4. ———

Entry listed alphabetically under the plant's common name in the Common Name Index. All entries are listed under both their common and botanical names so they can be located by either.

Zone map on pages 178-179.

BUTTERFLY WEED. ———
See *Asclepias tuberosa.*

## Acanthus (ak-*kan*-thus).

Bear's-breech.

Acanthus Family *(Acanthaceae).*

A perennial of southern Europe. The elegant, elongated leaves are irregularly scalloped along the edges, and the lobes of most species end in spines. These leaves are familiar in sculptured form on the capital of the Corinthian column. The stately plant is striking in the border and makes a dramatic accent among shrubbery in landscape plantings. Full sun, rich, well-drained soil and not too much water give best results. Propagate by seeds, by crown division or by root sections in spring.

### A. mollis (*mol*-lis).

Common Bear's-breech.

A large plant, to 3 ft. and more. The leaves are up to 2 ft. long and 6 to 9 in. across. Flowers are white or purple with spiny bracts at the base of the blossoms, which grow in bold spikes 2 to 4 ft. high and bloom in July and August. The cultivar 'Latifolius' grows to 4 ft. or more and is much less spiny (and much more hardy) than the species. It does not flower as freely as the species but has exceptionally beautiful, wide, glossy foliage. The purple flowers are displayed on loose spikes. Propagate by root cuttings. Zone 6.

### A. spinosus (spin-*oh*-sus).

Spiny Bear's-breech.

It differs from *A. mollis* in that it has spiny leaf margins and is more free flowering, and the 12-in.-wide leaves are more deeply divided. The flowers have three to four veins on the purplish bracts rather than the five to seven on common bear's-breech. This species is somewhat more tolerant of spring frosts and can be grown in colder zones. The variety *spinosissimus* (spin-oh-*siss*-ee-mus) has more finely cut foliage and appears

*Acanthus mollis*
Common Bear's-breech

more silvery in clump form. The flower stalks have long spines. Zone 6 (Zone 5 with protection).

## Achillea (ak-i-*lee*-uh).

Yarrow.

Composite Family *(Compositae).*

One or more species native to almost every continent. These familiar, long-lived perennials have clusters of small, single or double flowers in white, pink or yellow shades. The taller species are useful in the border and cutting garden, the shorter species in rock gardens or as a substitute for grass in sandy, dry areas, especially in sections of California. Yarrows grow in any well-drained, well-dug garden soil, but ample moisture and full sun will give best results. Divide every two to three years to avoid a weedy habit of growth. Propagate by seeds, sown early for bloom the first year, or by crown division. Only the most impor-

## Achillea

tant species and cultivars are listed below; rock-garden enthusiasts cultivate several more. The flat-headed fern-leaf yarrow, *A. filipendulina*, and woolly yarrow, *A. tomentosa*, are fine for winter bouquets. Cut the long stems as the heads reach full flower; tie in bunches and hang upside down in a sunless, airy place to dry.   The color holds well.

★ **A.** × 'Coronation Gold'.
CORONATION GOLD YARROW.
A cultivar that resulted from a cross of *A. filipendulina* and *A. clypeolata*. It is perhaps the most popular yarrow in American gardens today. The finely dissected foliage is gray-green and aromatic. The 3- to 4-in. gold flower heads are held on 3-ft. self-supporting stems. This is considered one of the most reliable plants for mass planting by landscape contractors. It prefers well-drained soils that are not overly fertile. It can be propagated by terminal cuttings or by crown division. Zones 3 to 9.

**A. millefolium** (mil-ef-*foh*-lee-um).
COMMON YARROW.
MILFOIL.
A wild flower commonly seen along roadsides and in fields. The usual color is white, but there is a rosy-pink cultivar, 'Rosea'. There are several named cultivars of the pink variety. The flower clusters, $1^1/2$ to 2 in. across, are made up of tiny florets, $1/4$ in. across. The foliage is fragrant when touched. Among the recent cultivars are the Galaxy hybrids from Germany. These hybrids are made by crossing *A. taygeta* and *A. millefolium*. The flower heads of these are larger than those of *A. millefolium*, but the foliage is similiar. 'Appleblossom' is a 3-ft. cultivar that starts out deep pink and fades to a soft appleblossom-pink. It is a free-standing clone. 'Salmon Beauty' is also 3 ft. tall and comes in various shades, depending

*Achillea* × 'Coronation Gold'
CORONATION GOLD YARROW

*Achillea millefolium* 'Summer Pastels'
COMMON YARROW

on the age of the flowers. In fertile soils it needs staking. More than a dozen cultivars are now available in this series. 'Summer Pastels' is a 1990 All-America Selection winner and represents hybrid forms that can be started from seed. When sown early enough they bloom the first year. Colors include apricot, salmon, scarlet, lilac, cream, orange, white and gold. Culture as above. Zones 3 to 9.

**A. ptarmica** (*tar*-mi-kuh).
SNEEZEWORT.
Single-flowered parent of two double-flowered hybrids, 'The Pearl' and 'Boule de Neige'. These cultivars are grown for their double white flowers, which are $^1/_2$ in. across, chrysanthemum-like in form, held in loose, attractive clusters. The plants are $1^1/_2$ to $2^1/_2$ ft. high and are useful in the perennial border for their summer bloom and in the cutting garden. They spread rapidly and have to be transplanted frequently. Zones 3 to 9.

**Aconitum** (ak-oh-*nye*-tum).
ACONITE.
MONKSHOOD.
Buttercup Family *(Ranunculaceae)*.
Handsome perennials, chiefly of Europe and Asia, with dark green, deeply divided leaves and showy, helmet-shaped flowers in purple, blue, yellow or white spikes. They are important as the source of several pharmaceuticals derived from the thick, heavy roots. All parts of the plant are dangerously toxic in all the species. When grown from seed, they flower in two to three years. Monkshood are cool-climate plants and prefer a rich, moist soil and partial shade. By planting a range of different species, one can have monkshood in bloom from late June into late fall. Do not disturb the plants unless they become overcrowded to where flowering suffers. Important plants for the perennial border, they thrive at the edge of the bog garden.

**A. × bicolor** (*bye*-kul-or).
BICOLOR MONKSHOOD.
A cross between *A. napellus* and *A. variegatum*, this hybrid grows to 3 to 4 ft. tall. The leaves are deeply divided with five to seven segments. The margins of the segments are toothed. It flowers in summer with colors ranging from blue and white through navy blue to violet-blue, depending on the dominant parent. The flower spikes are made up of small 1-in. flowers in the shape of a hood. Plant in full sun to partial shade in cool, moist, deep, highly fertile soil. Zones 3 to 7.

**A. californicum.** See *A. columbianum*.

**A. carmichaelii** (kar-mye-*keel*-ee-eye).
AZURE MONKSHOOD.
(Syn. *A. fischeri*.) The latest of the monkshoods to bloom. Some cultivars are only 2 to 3 ft. tall. 'Barker's Variety' and 'Kelmscott Variety' grow to 6 ft., with blue or white flowers in September and October. The plants are valuable at a time when good border perennials are hard to come by, and the tall cultivars are especially beautiful as backgrounds for chrysanthemums. *Wilsonii* (wil-*soh*-nee-eye) a tall, showy variety that is generally handsomer than the species. Plants may need staking. Zones 3 to 7.

**A. columbianum** (kol-lum-bee-*ay*-num).
(Syn. *A. californicum*.) A blue or white species similar to *A. carmichaelii*, about 3 ft. tall. Zones 4 to 5.

**A. fischeri.** See *A. carmichaelii*.

**A. napellus** (nap-*pell*-us).
COMMON MONKSHOOD.
This European species, blooming in July and August, has beautiful, dark blue blossoms on strong stems, 3 to 4 ft. high, sometimes taller.

## Aconitum

*Aconitum napellus* 'Carneum'
COMMON MONKSHOOD

The finely cut leaves add to the plant's beauty. Increasing slowly, it persists for years without extra care. There is a white variety, handsome but not as hardy as the type. 'Carneum' is a pale pink cultivar best used in areas of the country with cool nights. In the South its blossoms fade to a washed-out white. *A. napellus* is the species commonly grown as the source of the drug aconite, and it should be remembered that its roots are very poisonous. Zone 4.

### Actaea (ak-*tee*-uh).

BANEBERRY.

COHOSH.

Buttercup Family *(Ranunculaceae)*.

Native to the Northern Temperate Zone. These long-lived, sturdy perennials are grown for their deeply cut leaves and showy clusters of small white flowers, followed by shiny red or white berries (which are poisonous) in late summer.

*Actaea alba*
WHITE BANEBERRY

*Adonis vernalis*
SPRING ADONIS

They are easily grown in a moist, humus-rich soil and partial shade. The plants are useful in the shady border, the rock garden or the wild garden. Propagate by seeds sown early in spring or by root division.

**A. alba** (*al*-buh).
WHITE BANEBERRY.
(Syn. *A. pachypoda*). A native plant found in the woodlands of eastern North America. It grows to 3 ft. Conspicuous white or pinkish berries, each with a dark blue eye, follow the fluffy white flower clusters that bloom in May. There is a red-fruited form of this species. Zones 3 to 7.

**A. pachypoda.** See *A. alba*.

**A. rubra** (*rue*-bruh).
RED BANEBERRY.
A native plant similar to *A. alba*, but it flowers about a week earlier. The $^1/_4$-in. red berries are borne on greenish pedicels that turn an attractive red color when the seeds mature. Zones 3 to 7.

# Adenophora (ad-e-*noff*-o-ruh).
LADYBELLS.
Bellflower Family *(Campanulaceae)*.
Perennials native to mountain regions of the Far East and very similar to *Campanula*. They prefer rich, well-drained loam and full, or nearly full, sun. Once established, they should not be disturbed. Propagate by seeds, cuttings or division.

**A. bulleyana** (bull-ee-*ay*-nuh).
From western China. A tall species, it is often seen in European gardens. It features light blue, funnel-form flowers, $^1/_2$ in. long. Zones 3 to 8.

**A. confusa** (kon-*fuse*-uh).
COMMON LADYBELLS.
FARRER'S LADYBELLS.
Grows to 2 to $2^1/_2$ ft. tall with racemes of nodding, 1-in., dark blue bell-shaped flowers. Flowering starts in late spring and lasts for about three to four weeks. Plant in full sun to partial shade in deep, well-drained soil. Fleshy roots make the plant difficult to divide or move. Propagate by seeds. Zones 2 to 8.

**A. liliifolia** (lil-ee-eye-*foh*-lee-uh).
LILYLEAF LADYBELLS.
The stem leaves are wedge-shaped and 3 in. long. It bears fragrant, light blue flowers.

# Adonis (ad-*doh*-nis).
PHEASANT'S-EYE.
Buttercup Family *(Ranunculaceae)*.
Hardy annuals and herbaceous perennials from Europe and Asia, with feathery foliage and pretty yellow or red flowers, usually daisylike in form. The plants are easily grown in almost any rich garden soil, in full sun or partial shade. Propagate by seeds or by root division.

**A. amurensis** (am-moor-*ren*-sis).
AMUR ADONIS.
Perennial, from Asia, with large, bright yellow-cupped flowers, 2 in. across, blooming in late winter and early spring. This species grows 1 to $1^1/_2$ ft. high, with fernlike, finely cut foliage. It needs rich soil to grow well and is fine in the spring border with early bulbs and for cutting. There is a sulfur-yellow double-flowered cultivar, 'Fukuju Kai'. Zones 3 to 7.

**A. vernalis** (ver-*nay*-lis).
SPRING ADONIS.
This perennial species from southern Europe grows to 1 ft. or higher, with large, bright yellow

flowers, $2^1/2$ in. across. It blooms from April to June, with dense whorls of finely cut leaves, and is useful in the rock garden or the spring border. A white variety and a double form are available. Zone 3.

## Aegopodium (ee-goh-*poh*-dee-um).

GOUTWEED.

Carrot Family *(Umbelliferae)*.

A small genus of sturdy perennials from Europe and Asia. The species described below grows about 1 ft. high and spreads by slender, creeping rootstocks. Foliage is bold and divided. The plants are useful for edging perennial or shrubbery borders. They like partial shade and ordinary garden soil, well turned to a spade's depth. Propagate by seeds or division.

**A. podagraria** (pod-ah-*gray*-ree-uh).

BISHOP'S WEED.

The green-and-white-leaved cultivar 'Variegatum' is usually grown. This plant is found almost throughout the U.S. Its lively foliage sets off other familiar and equally sturdy garden perennials. The flowers are small, greenish-white and inconspicuous, growing in 3- to 4-in. flat clusters. It grows in both sun and shade, and makes an excellent plant for the base of large rocks as a transition to lawn, for edging the herb garden and as a ground cover on shady slopes, as well as in the perennial border. As a ground cover, it needs thinning every two to three years; otherwise it will spread away, trying to escape its own tangled stems. The green-and-white foliage is effective when cut for arrangements. Zone 3.

## Aethionema (ee-thee-oh-*nee*-muh).

STONE CRESS.

Mustard Family *(Cruciferae)*.

Masses of candytuft-like rose, magenta or lilac flowers smother these low, shrubby perennials from the Mediterranean region. Usually grown in the rock garden or rock wall, they are also useful in the spring border when adequate drainage can be provided. They require full sun, a dry location and a sandy, coarse soil with lime added. Prune back after flowering. Propagate by seeds sown in early spring or by cuttings in summer.

**A. coridifolium** (kor-id-i-*foh*-lee-um).

LEBANON STONE CRESS.

(Syn. *Iberis jucunda*.) This is a low-growing, shrubby, compact plant, 6 to 10 in. high, with small, creamy-white to rose-lilac flowers in thick, short clusters in June. It is best in the rock garden or a dry wall. Zone 5.

**A. grandiflorum** (gran-di-*floh*-rum).

PERSIAN STONE CRESS.

(Syn. *A. pulchellum*.) Similar to the above but with bluish foliage. Small pink or rose flowers, $1/4$ in. across in upright heads, cover the entire plant. It is a choice plant in the border, rock garden or dry wall. The cultivar 'Warley Rose' is dense, with rose flowers and blue leaves; 'Warley Ruber' has dark rose flowers. Zone 6.

**A. pulchellum.**  See *A. grandiflorum*.

## Ajuga (aj-*yew*-guh).

BUGLEWEED.

Mint Family *(Labiatae)*.

Low-growing, modest, European perennials, extremely useful for ground covers or edgings in shady places. Ajugas grow into a heavy mat of foliage and are very hardy. These need rich soil for best results but will grow under almost any conditions, in sun (in the North only) or shade. Propagate by seeds or by division of roots or rooted runners. Zone 3.

**A. pyramidalis** (peer-ruh-mid-*ah*-lis).

UPRIGHT BUGLEWEED.

This slowly spreading species of ajuga bears 4- to 6-in. pyramidal spikes of blue in late spring. The foliage is dark green and almost evergreen. Each clump sends out stolons late in the season, and the plant makes an excellent ground cover. It likes sun or shade and moist, average soil. 'Crispa' (syn. 'Metallica Crispa') has crinkly bronze-red foliage and deep blue flowers. Zone 3.

**A. reptans** (*rep*-tanz).

BUGLEWEED.

CARPET BUGLEWEED.

Often seen naturalized in fields and along road-sides in the eastern U.S., this trailing species has bluish-purple flowers and a matlike carpet of

*Aethionema grandiflorum* 'Warley Rose'
PERSIAN STONE CRESS

*Aegopodium podagraria* 'Variegatum'
BISHOP'S WEED

*Ajuga reptans* 'Atropurpurea'
BUGLEWEED

# Ajuga

foliage. Varieties and cultivars can be selected based on the color of their flowers and foliage. 'Alba' is a white-flowered form. 'Pink Beauty' has pink-flowered spikes, while the tall 'Gatlin's Giant' has blue flowers and burgundy foliage. 'Atropurpurea' is one of the best cultivars, with bronze-purple leaves and blue-violet flowers. 'Burgundy Glow' is a popular plant, with foliage in shades of white, pink, rose and green; its flowers are blue. A recent cultivar is 'Jungle Beauty Improved', selected by Beth Chatto, a prominent English gardener, and introduced through the U.S. National Arboretum. It is a vigorous-growing, thick-leaved plant with individual leaves often measuring up to 6 in. across, and blue flowers. The dark leaves of the purple and bronze cultivars make a heavy mat, giving a strong color accent when used as an edging or in the rock garden. The stems root freely to form new plants. Hardiness varies with the cultivar selected; the species is hardy in Zones 3 to 9.

## Alchemilla (al-kem-*mill*-uh).

Rose Family *(Rosaceae)*.
European perennials and annuals of strong, almost weedy growth, whose principal attraction is their silvery foliage. The species listed are useful in borders and rock gardens. Small, yellow-green flowers in loose heads are negligible. Plants prefer partial shade and ordinary, well-drained garden soil. Propagate by seeds or by root division.

★ **A. mollis** (*mol*-lis).
LADY'S MANTLE.
A mounded plant up to 18 in. high and 24 in. wide. The leaves are 4 to 5 in. long, orbicular, with palmately veined lobes. Densely pubescent, the leaves are best described as velvety. The small chartreuse flowers are borne in clusters held above the foliage. Flowering occurs from June through August, and flowers are long-lasting

when cut. This plant is excellent at the front of the border or along a walk, softening the edges. It prefers partial shade with moist soil but can take full sun if given extra water. Remove old, spent flowers before they go to seed, as it spreads readily by seed and can be invasive. Zones 4 to 7.

**A. vulgaris** (vul-*gay*-ris).
LADY'S MANTLE.
The large leaves, 3 to 4 in. wide in velvety-gray clusters, make this perennial an effective accent plant in the border. Although the flower stalk grows to 1 ft., the plant can be placed toward the front of the border, since the heavy leaf clusters make it a low accent. The flowers are smaller than those of *A. mollis* and the foliage less pubescent. This species appears in the earliest herbals and is much used in old-fashioned gardens and in herb gardens. Zones 4 to 7.

## Alyssum. A genus now classified under *Aurinia*.

## Amsonia (am-*soh*-nee-uh).

Dogbane Family *(Apocynaceae)*.
Easily grown perennials with small, funnel-shaped flowers, native to North America. The species below is useful in the flower border and as a filler in shrub borders, as it thrives in full sun or half shade. Plants prefer ordinary garden soil, well turned to a spade's depth. Propagate by seeds, by root division in spring, or by stem cuttings in spring or summer.

**A. tabernaemontana**
(tab-bur-nee-mon-*tay*-nuh).
WILLOW AMSONIA.
Grows $2^{1}/_{2}$ to 3 ft. high, in partial shade or full sun. The light blue flowers, $^{1}/_{2}$ to $^{3}/_{4}$ in. long in dense terminal clusters, make a fine display in May and June. The foliage is attractive all sum-

*Alchemilla mollis*
LADY'S MANTLE

*Amsonia tabernaemontana*
WILLOW AMSONIA

mer long and turns yellow to scarlet in the fall. Zones 3 to 9.

## Anaphalis (uh-*naff*-uh-lis).
PEARLY EVERLASTING.
Composite Family *(Compositae)*.
Gray-white, fuzzy-leaved perennials, native to Europe, Asia and North America. They are valued for dried arrangements and are also good in the hot, dry border of the sunny wild garden. They like any soil and full sun. Propagate by seeds or by root division.

### A. margaritacea (mar-gar-it-*tay*-see-uh).
CAD-WEED.
PEARLY EVERLASTING.
RABBIT-TOBACCO.
Found in all Northern Temperate regions, this species has tiny white flowers, $1/4$ in. across, closely packed in small heads and blooming from mid-spring to early summer. It grows 2 to 3 ft. high. People living in Kentucky and the Ozarks used to smoke the dried leaves for asthma. Zones 3 to 8.

### A. triplinervis (tri-plee-*ner*-vis).
PEARLY EVERLASTING.
The silvery-gray leaves of this plant are covered with white hairs and form a distinct textural accent when set against plants with dark green leaves. The leaves are very dense. Dense white flower heads, called corymbs, appear in July and continue until frost. Each grayish-white flower has a yellow center. When cut and dried the flowers will last all winter. The plants grow to 1 to $1^{1}/2$ ft. tall. They prefer full sun in average, well-drained soil, but, unlike other members of the genus, will tolerate damp soils. 'Summer Snow' is a cultivar with clear white flowers and silver-gray foliage. Zones 3 to 8.

# Anaphalis

*Anaphallis margaritacea*
PEARLY EVERLASTING

*Anemone × hybrida* 'Honorine Jobert'
JAPANESE ANEMONE

*Anchusa azurea* 'Loddon Royalist'
ITALIAN BUGLOSS

*Anemone × hybrida* 'Queen Charlotte'
JAPANESE ANEMONE

## Anchusa (an-*kew*-suh).

ALKANET.

BUGLOSS.

Borage Family *(Boraginaceae)*.

Annuals, biennials and perennials mostly from Europe, some of which are found escaped from cultivation and naturalized in eastern North America. Plants are coarse, usually with hairy leaves and stems, and produce showy clusters of shallow funnel-shaped flowers, typically a fine, clear blue. These sturdy plants are most effective when planted in large groups. They are easily grown in ordinary garden soil and full sun. Propagate by seeds or by root division.

**A. azurea** (a-*zoo*-ree-uh).

ITALIAN ALKANET.

ITALIAN BUGLOSS.

(Syn. *A. italica*.) A tall perennial, 3 to 5 ft. high. The cultivar 'Dropmore' has brilliant blue flowers in large clusters and reaches a height of 4 ft. 'Loddon Royalist' is only about 3 ft. in height and has gentian-blue flowers. 'Royal Blue' is similar to 'Loddon Royalist' but is deep blue in color. The blooming season begins in June and may be extended into early fall if faded sprays are cut. Zone 3.

**A. italica.** See *A. azurea*.

**A. myosotidiflora.** See *Brunnera macrophylla*.

## Anemone (an-*nem*-oh-nee).

WINDFLOWER.

Buttercup Family *(Ranunculaceae)*.

A large genus of perennials, many of them rhizomatous or tuberous-rooted; some are among our loveliest and most delicate native spring woods flowers, while others, native to Europe or Asia, bloom in summer and fall. Enormously var-ied in size, form and flowering characteristics, they are valuable in borders, rock gardens, wild gardens and cutting gardens. All like rich, well-drained soil, plenty of moisture and partial shade. All portions of these plants are usually quite poisonous. Propagate by seeds sown when ripe in the fall or by offsets.

★ **A. × hybrida** (hye-*brid*-uh).

JAPANESE ANEMONE.

Hybrid forms originally made by crossing *A. hupehensis* var. *japonica* and *A. vitifolia*. The foliage grows to 18 in. high in a clump. Each leaf is made up of three leaflets, each of which is lobed and serrate with a point at the end. The flowers appear on branching stems up to 5 ft. above the foliage mound. Blooming starts in late August and continues into the fall. The flowers come in single and double forms. The single forms have a center of yellow stamens. There are white and pink cultivars available.

While these anemones are sometimes slow to establish, if the plants are located properly the wait is rewarded with large clumps of beautiful flowers. They prefer morning sun over late afternoon sun. Also, give them rich, moist, well-drained soil with lots of organic matter and do not let them dry out in full sun. Mulch and good drainage are needed in the winter. Once established, they send their roots deep and it is hard to transplant them, so site them carefully.

'Honorine Jobert' is considered a white sport of the usual pink hybrid. It has been in cultivation for more than 130 years. Plants grow to 5 ft. tall and display their pure white $2^{1}/_{2}$-in. flowers with gold anthers in September and October. 'Lady Gilmore' has 4-in.-wide semidouble flowers. 'Margarete' has semidouble deep pink flowers on short 2- to 3-ft.-tall plants. 'Max Vogel' has 4- to 5-in. single pink flowers on 4-ft. plants. 'Pamina' is a more recent cultivar

## Anemone

from Germany growing 30 in. tall and covered with double rose-purple flowers in late summer and fall. 'Prince Henry' has deep rose, semidouble flowers on 3-ft. plants. 'Queen Charlotte' has beautiful pink semidouble flowers that are 3 in. across. 'September Charm' (an allied cultivar, probably belonging to *A. hupehensis*) produces 3-in. pink flowers on 3-ft. plants. 'Whirlwind' has 3-in. semidouble white blossoms on 4- to 5-ft.-tall plants. Zone 6 (some hardy in Zone 5).

**A. tomentosa** (toe-men-*toe*-suh).
GRAPE-LEAVED ANEMONE.
(Syn *A. vitifolia* 'Robustissima'.) An extremely winter-hardy anemone from Tibet. Many of the *A.* × *hybrida* cultivars are limited to Zones 5 and 6; *A. tomentosa* is hardy to Zone 4. It is an extremely vigorous species, producing a multitude of 2- to $2^1/_2$-in. pink flowers two to three weeks ahead of *A.* × *hybrida* cultivars. Its leaves are large, divided and veined; they have silver-gray undersides. Zone 4.

**A. vitifolia** 'Robustissima'. See *A. tomentosa*.

# Aquilegia (ak-wil-*lee*-jee-uh).
COLUMBINE.
Buttercup Family *(Ranunculaceae)*.
Native to the Northern Temperate Zone. They are sturdy, long-lived perennials that, once established, will persist and multiply. Graceful blooms, often with prominent spurs in many colors, nod above blue-green, divided foliage. Among the indispensable standbys of the flower garden, the species are variously effective in the rock garden, the perennial border, with bulbs and in the wild garden. They are useful as a cut flower as well. Plants like full sun or partial shade and reasonably light soil; good drainage is essential. Although leaf miners may make white tracks on leaves, spraying is seldom worthwhile, but early applica-

tion of a systemic insecticide prevents damage. Beware of self-sown seedlings which are produced freely and are often of inferior quality. Propagate by seeds or by root division in spring.

**A. caerulea** (see-*rue*-lee-uh).
COLORADO COLUMBINE.
ROCKY MOUNTAIN COLUMBINE.
A lovely native plant with large blue flowers, $2^1/_2$ to 3 in. across, that bear slim spurs and bloom in May and June. It grows $^1/_2$ to $2^1/_2$ ft. tall. This species sometimes fails to live more than two or three seasons, but it usually self-sows when established, and so seems as permanent as some of the more durable species. It should be planted in good-sized groups in the border or the rock garden. There are varieties with white, yellow or pink blossoms. Zone 4.

**A. canadensis** (kan-a-*den*-sis).
WILD COLUMBINE.
Native to eastern North America, this very attractive wild flower bears red and yellow blooms in April and May. The plant, 1 to 2 ft. high, makes compact growth and is effective in the rock garden in clumps or in the wild garden in masses. It grows easily from seed and does best with some leafmold in the soil. 'Corbett' is a recent introduction selected near Corbett, Maryland. Its flowers are a pale yellow. Zone 3.

**A. chrysantha** (kris-*an*-thuh).
GOLDEN-SPURRED COLUMBINE.
A tall, handsome plant, 3 to 4 ft. high, from the southwestern U.S. and Mexico. It produces large, fragrant, yellow flowers, 3 in. across, with spurs 2 in. long. Many fine, long-spurred hybrids have been developed from this very hardy species. It grows in full sun. Zone 3.

**A. flabellata** (flab-el-*lay*-tuh).

FAN COLUMBINE.

Lavender blossoms are produced in late April on this species from Japan, on stems 1 to 1¹/₂ ft. high. There is a dwarf variety, *nana* (*nay*-nuh), which is much smaller. Both the species and the variety have white forms. Zone 3.

**A.** × **hybrida** (hye-*brid*-uh).

COLUMBINE.

Years of breeding the various species have produced distinct cultivars for modern gardens. The long-spurred types, from crosses of *A. canadensis, A. chrysantha, A. caerulea* and *A. formosa,* are the most popular. 'McKana Hybrids' won the All-America Selection bronze medal in 1955 and are still much in demand. This selection is represented by various pastel shades in rather large 3- to 4-in. flowers on 2- to 3-ft. plants. 'Biedermeier' is a dwarf 9- to 12-in. plant for edging and bedding out. It comes in various shades, but blue and white bicolor blossoms are most prevalent in the mix. 'Nora Barlow' is a unique double-flowered form whose sepals are reddish-pink with cream edges. 'Spring Song' is a 2¹/₂- to 3-ft. plant with flowers in soft pastel shades and spurs nearly 3 in. long. Zone 3.

## Arabis (*ar*-a-bis).

ROCK CRESS.

Mustard Family *(Cruciferae).*

A large genus of plants native to temperate North America and Eurasia. They are easily grown and suitable for the perennial border, the rock garden or niches in a dry rock wall. The species described below makes a fine show in spring, when the entire gray-green mat of small leaves is dotted with fragrant little white blossoms. Some cultivars also make fair ground covers for rocky slopes. Plants prefer full sun and almost any gritty, well-drained soil. They

*Aquilegia* × *hybrida* 'Biedermeier Mixed'
COLUMBINE

*Arabis albida* var. *variegata*
WALL ROCK CRESS

## Arabis

are easy to propagate by seeds or by division in spring.

**A. albida** (*al*-bid-uh).
WALL ROCK CRESS.
(Syn. *A. caucasica*.) A Mediterranean plant with gray, tomentose foliage that forms mats over rocks and in the crevices of walls. Numerous white flowers appear over the gray foliage in early spring. Plants benefit from hard pruning after flowering to discourage legginess. *Arabis* is sometimes treated like pansies in the South and replanted each fall. A double form, *A. albida* var. *flore-plena* (*floh-re-plee*-nuh), has persistent flowers because of its sterility. 'Rosabella' has rose-colored flowers, while 'Snow Cap' has large white flowers. The variety *variegata* (var-ee-*gay*-tuh) has yellow-white stripes on the leaves. Zone 4.

**A. caucasica.** See *A. albida*.

*Arisaema triphyllum*
JACK-IN-THE-PULPIT

**Argyranthemum.** See *Chrysanthemum*.

## Arisaema (ar-ri-*see*-muh).
JACK-IN-THE-PULPIT.
Arum Family *(Araceae)*.
Tuberous-rooted plants, native mostly to the Old World, with single flower stems and single fleshy stalks bearing one or two divided leaves. The small, inconspicuous flowers are borne in a dense cluster that surrounds the stalk just below a long, fleshy prolongation of the stem known as a spadix. The conspicuous part of the plant, often referred to as the "flower," is actually the spathe, a sort of large bract that curls around the real flower and is usually colored with varying stripes and streaks of green, white, brown and purple. All parts of the plant contain an acrid element that is not poisonous but is extremely irritating to the mouth and throat when chewed or swallowed. *Arisaema* are easily grown in loose, humusy soil that is moist but well drained. They are good for naturalizing in the shade of deciduous trees. Propagate by seeds or root division.

**A. sikokianum** (sik-koke-ee-*aye*-num).
SNOW RICE-CAKE PLANT.
A Japanese native with the most exquisite flowering spathe of all the Jack-in-the-pulpits. It blooms in April and May with waxy spathes that are chocolate

*Armeria maritima*
SEA PINK

colored on the outside and green and white on the inside. The spadix itself is pure white. A recent and most attractive introduction to American gardens. Zone 5.

**A. triphyllum** (try-*fye*-lum).
INDIAN TURNIP.
JACK-IN-THE-PULPIT.
A familiar native plant in the eastern U.S. It grows 1 to 2 ft. high, with two leaves, each divided into three segments that are 3 to 6 in. long. The spathe is held upright between the leaves and is usually green on the outside and purplish-bronze on the inside, with the upper point bent over, forming the "pulpit" around the "Jack," or spadix, in the center. The May blooms are followed by a fruit cluster like a huge blackberry, turning red as it ripens to a bright scarlet in fall. Suitable for shady, moist places in the wild garden. Zone 5.

**Armeria** (ar-*mee*-ree-uh).
THRIFT.
Plumbago Family *(Plumbaginaceae)*.
Long-known, these sturdy low perennials, mostly from northern Europe, form small, neat tufts of evergreen foliage and bear small, attractive, globe-shaped flowers. They need full sun and a light, gritty, well-drained soil. Especially useful and effective as edgings and in rock gardens, they also make pleasing additions to wall gardens or to spring and summer borders. In addition, they are pretty in pots in the cool greenhouse. Plants are easy to propagate by seeds or by division.

**A. maritima** (mar-*rit*-im-uh).
SEA PINK.
The most familiar species, this is a small plant rarely more than 12 in. high. Narrow, evergreen leaves form tight rosettes. The small, rose-colored flowers in dense, cloverlike heads, $^1/_2$ to 1 in.

across, are borne on slim, wiry stems and bloom profusely from mid-May to mid-June. Plants are easily grown and suitable for cut flowers. As its common name implies, this species flourishes on the seacoast. There are many hybrids, cultivars and varieties available, including the variety *laucheana* (law-kee-*ay*-nuh), with pale pink flowers from mid-April to June; 'Alba', an especially fine white-flowered form; and 'Ruby Glow', with ruby-colored blossoms. *A.* × 'Bloodstone' is a 9-in. hybrid of *A. maritima* and *A. plantaginea* with extremely bright flowers. Zone 3 but intolerant of hot, humid summer weather.

**Artemisia** (ar-tem-*miz*-ee-uh).
WORMWOOD.
Composite Family *(Compositae)*.
A large and interesting genus of perennials, some with important flavoring and other herbal uses, and widespread throughout the world. Almost all have inconspicuous flowers and gray or whitish foliage. Many are extremely drought-resistant. The sagebrushes of the Western plains and mountain areas are among the species of *Artemisia*. All are easily grown in ordinary garden soil well turned to a spade's depth. Full sun and very good drainage are necessary. Plants are easy to propagate by division.

**A. abrotanum** (ab-*roh*-tay-num).
SOUTHERNWOOD.
Green-foliaged, graceful perennial plant, 2 to 4 ft. high, with very slender, threadlike leaves and tiny, pale yellow, buttonlike flowers in a drooping cluster. The foliage has a pleasant fragrance. These plants are often grown in herb gardens. Cut back severely in spring, otherwise they grow too leggy. Zone 5.

## Artemisia

**A. absinthium** (ab-*sin*-thee-um).

WORMWOOD.

Evergreen plants growing 2 to 3 ft. tall, with silky-gray, much-divided leaves. 'Lambrook Silver' is an excellent 2$^{1}$/2-ft. form. 'Huntington' (syn. 'Huntington Garden') is a recent selection from California. It grows 4 ft. tall and nearly as wide. 'Powis Castle' is thought to be a hybrid of *A. arborescens* and *A. absinthium*. It has beautiful filigree-gray foliage and grows to 3 ft. Zone 4; 'Powis Castle' is less hardy, Zone 6.

★ **A. ludoviciana** var. **albula**

(loo-doe-vis-ee-*aye*-nuh *al*-bew-luh).

SILVER-KING ARTEMISIA.

Native to the southwestern U.S., this perennial species is popular in flower borders for its sturdy growth, to 3 to 4 ft., and its striking, silvery-white leaves. The tiny florets are grayish white and produced in late October. The plants are useful at the back of borders and for cutting, and they may be used in flower arrangements fresh or dried, lending an airy lightness. To dry, cut when the flower buds have formed, tie in loose bunches and hang in a shady, airy place. In the garden the plants are beautiful at night when the leaves reflect the moonlight. Silver-king is the common name for this botanical variety, but it is also sometimes listed as 'Silver King', implying cultivar designation. Zone 4.

**A. schmidtiana** (shmit-ee-*ay*-nuh).

SILVER-MOUND ARTEMISIA.

A silky-haired artemisia, 2 ft. tall, sturdy, long-lived and useful in the perennial border. The cultivar 'Nana' is shorter, about 1 ft. high, and grows in solid mounds, 2 ft. across. Usually sold as 'Silver Mound' artemisia. Zone 3.

**A. stelleriana** (stel-la-ree-*ay*-nuh).

BEACH WORMWOOD.

Familiar on every seashore of the eastern U.S., where its thick, evergreen, felty, deeply lobed leaves scramble about in the sandy beaches above the tide. Plants are low-growing, 1 to 1$^{1}$/2 ft. high. They are good in seashore gardens and in other gardens where the soil is sandy and the drainage good. Zone 4.

## Aruncus (ar-*runk*-us).

GOATSBEARD.

Rose Family *(Rosaceae)*.

The most important cultivated species is a striking perennial, native to the rich woods of North America, Europe and Asia. Plants produce graceful, feathery foliage and showy masses of small white flowers in June. They are easily grown in ordinary garden soil, well turned to a spade's depth, with plenty of moisture. They will self-sow when established. Propagate by seeds or by division.

**A. dioicus** (dye-oh-*eye*-kus).

(Syn. *Spiraea aruncus*.)  A handsome, native wild flower, 5 to 6 ft. tall, with tiny white flowers in spikes. This is a dioecious species, with both male and female plants. Female plants have attractive seed heads after flowering and may be more desirable.  Leaves are dark green and compound. The plants are very striking in large clumps in moist places, in partial shade, at a brookside or at the back of perennial borders that can be watered abundantly. The cultivar 'Kneiffii' has more delicately cut foliage and makes an extraordinarily graceful addition to the woodland garden in summer. It is difficult to establish but is well worth the trial and error required. Zone 3.

*Artemisia ludoviciana* var. *albula*
SILVER-KING ARTEMISIA

*Artemisia stelleriana*
BEACH WORMWOOD

## Asclepias (as-*klee*-pee-as).

MILKWEED.

Milkweed Family (Asclepiadaceae).

Tall, showy wild flowers, native mostly to the U.S. Vigorous, sometimes weedy plants, they are beautiful in masses in a native setting. Some are valuable for the perennial border or the pond margin. The elongated, pointed seedpods, with their silky-haired seeds, follow pretty clusters of small flowers. Milkweeds are difficult to transplant but are easily grown from seed or from root cuttings.

**A. tuberosa** (too-ber-*roh*-suh).

BUTTERFLY WEED.

ORANGE MILKWEED.

This handsomest of the milkweeds needs full sun and well-drained soil. Often grown in perennial borders, it is 2 to 3 ft. high. The small, orange-red florets, in showy clusters in June and July, are notably attractive to butterflies, which adds to

*Aruncus dioicus*
GOATSBEARD

their garden value. Occasionally, a yellow, pale orange or scarlet seedling appears. The plants are able to compete with grasses in meadow gardens and are very useful in midsummer when many flowering perennials are least effective. A fine cut flower. Zones 3 to 9.

## Asphodeline (as-fod-el-*lye*-nee).

JACOB'S ROD.

Lily Family *(Liliaceae)*.

Sturdy perennials from the Mediterranean region. Only one species is common in the U.S., a handsome plant easily grown in ordinary garden soil, well turned to a spade's depth, in full sun or partial shade. Propagate by seeds or by root division, early or late in the planting season. Plants should be dug up, divided and replanted every two years.

### A. lutea (*lew*-tee-uh).

ASPHODEL.

JACOB'S ROD.

The asphodel of classical mythology, this fragrant perennial, 3 to 4 ft. high, has bright yellow flowers, 1 in. long, in thick clusters as much as 1 ft. across. It makes a fine show in the perennial border in June and July and is excellent for cutting. Zone 6.

## Aster (*as*-ter).

MICHAELMAS DAISY.

Daisy Family *(Compositae)*.

Native to North and South America, Europe, Asia and Africa. Perennial asters are familiar and cherished summer and fall wild flowers found over a large part of the North American continent. They grow in wet and dry places and at many altitudes. Leaves are simple and alternate, from 2 to 6 in. long. Asters range in height from 6 in. to 6 ft., with flower heads that are $1/4$ to 4 in. across in white and shades of purple, blue, pink and red. Their flowering period ranges from July to late fall, depending on the variety and the location.

The small, daisylike blooms in loose heads are pretty both at close range and in massed drifts. Asters are especially useful in wild gardens, where they can spread and flower until frost. Some native varieties have been selected and improved in cultivation. These are effective in strong clumps at either the back or the front of the perennial border, depending on size. A number of non-native species are useful in the garden.

Native asters may be raised from seed. Plant them in spring for blooms the following year. Garden cultivars seldom come true from seed; it is therefore best to propagate them by division or by cuttings. Root divisions are easily made. Plants increase rapidly and need good garden soil, well dug, with added humus. Divide every second or third year, as shoots are thin in late spring when crowded. Full sun brings the best results, but asters will also flower well in dappled shade. The native, fall-flowering asters are hardy and have a long flowering period. Some summer-flowering kinds are less hardy. Other than dividing the plants, ordinary garden care will suffice. Asters are usually free of insect pests and diseases, although some late cultivars occasionally show mildew on the leaves. But look out for rabbits, which have a fondness for aster foliage.

### A. amellus (a-*mel*-us).

Native to Europe and Asia Minor, a short, 1-ft.-tall plant with rough leaves and stems. Usually the selections within this species are quite refined compared to the wild forms. 'King George' is an especially fine cultivar with purple flowers on 2- to 3-ft.-tall plants. Zones 5 to 8.

### ★ A. × frikartii (frik-*art*-ee-eye).

A Swiss hybrid made by crossing *A. amellus* with *A. thomsonii*. A useful garden aster, it grows to 2 ft. Fragrant purple flowers with golden centers bloom from July to October. Two cultivars are common in American gardens. 'Mönch' grows to 3 ft. and has flat, attractive, lavender-blue daisy flowers. 'Wonder of Staffa' is much like 'Mönch', but the flowers are not as flat and are less blue. It is also more likely to need staking. Zone 5.

**A. lateriflorus** (lat-ter-i-*floor*-us).
CALICO ASTER.
Stems of this plant are 4 to 5 ft. tall, branching along their entire length. These branches end in one-sided flower clusters, which open in fall. The typical composite flower heads are $1/2$ in. wide, with the ray flowers white or violet and the disk flowers purplish. Grow in full sun in almost any soil type. 'Horizontalis' has tiny coppery-purple foliage and lilac flowers with rosy stamens. It looks like a woody shrub by the time it flowers in late September. It is a very fine garden plant because of its form and clean foliage all season long. Zone 3.

**A. novae-angliae** (*noh*-vee-*ang*-li-ee).
NEW ENGLAND ASTER.
Tall, growing 3 to 5 ft. high, with leaves 3 to 4 in. long. One of the finest native asters, it has showy, dark purple flowers in late summer. The many beautiful and long-established cultivars are much more suitable for garden use than are the species. They include 'Alma Potschke', bright rose, 3 to 4 ft.; 'Autumn Snow' (syn. 'Herbstschnee'), white, 3 ft.; 'Barr's Pink', rose-pink, 4 ft.; 'Fanny's Aster', violet-blue, 3 ft., which blooms in November and takes hard frosts; 'Harrington's Pink', soft pink, 4 to 6 ft.; 'Mt. Everest', clean white, 3 ft.; 'Purple Dome', deep purple, 18 in.; 'September Ruby', ruby-red, 4-ft.; and 'Treasure', violet-blue, 4 ft. Zones 3 to 4.

**A. novi-belgii** (*noh*-vye-bell-*gee*-eye).
NEW YORK ASTER.
Best known in its named cultivars but grows 2 to 3 ft. high in the wild. Bluish-violet flowers

*Asphodeline lutea*
JACOB'S ROD

*Aster amellus* 'King George'

## Aster

are produced in large, handsome heads. As with other species, many garden cultivars have been derived from this one: 'Ernest Ballard', reddish-pink, 3 ft.; 'Eventide', semidouble, violet-blue, 3 to 4 ft.; 'Patricia Ballard', semi-double, rose-pink, 18 in.; 'Prof. Anton Kippenburg', semidouble, lavender-blue, 15 to 18 in.; and 'Snowsprite', semidouble, white, 15 in.  Zone 5.

**A. tataricus** (ta-*tar*-ri-kus).
TATARIAN DAISY.
Native to Siberia. One of the tallest asters, this plant grows 6 to 8 ft. high, with basal leaves up to 2 ft. long and 6 in. wide. In spite of its height, it seldom needs staking. Each stem ends in a corymb of violet-purple flower heads, typi-cally composite-type. Flowers open in late fall. Grow in full sun in any soil type. Zone 4.

**Astilbe** (as-*till*-bee).
FALSE GOATSBEARD.
Saxifrage Family *(Saxifragaceae).*
Astilbes are handsome plants for the perennial border, where they are all but indispensible. They have soft muted colors that blend well among other summer perennials (and shrubs), almost without equal. Also popular as forcing plants in commercial greenhouses, where they are grown for indoor use, they are good in any small, warm greenhouse. Tiny, white or vari-ously pinkish flowers in graceful panicles, 2 to 4 in. long, rise above the compound, dark green leaves of good substance in June and July.  Some are quite fragrant. Astilbes are often incorrectly called spireas. Rich, moist soil and some shade give the best results. Propagate by seeds (species) or by division, the latter being preferable.

*Aster novae-angliae* 'Autumn Snow'
NEW ENGLAND ASTER

*Astilbe × rosea* 'Bonn'

**A. × arendsii** (ar-*end*-see-eye).

Much hybridized, this species is known chiefly in many improved cultivars, all 2 to 3 ft. tall. Colors range from white to dark rose to purple. These hybrids resulted chiefly from the crossing and recrossing of several species. Almost all named cultivars belong in this group. Examples include the white 'Bridal Veil', 'Deutschland', 'Irrlicht', 'Snowdrift' and 'White Gloria'; the pink and salmon 'Bressingham Beauty', 'Cattleya', 'Erica', 'Europe', 'Finale', 'Ostrich Plume' and 'Rheinland'; and the red 'Fanal', 'Federsee' and 'Garnet'. Zones 4 to 9.

**A. chinensis** (chin-*nen*-sis).

CHINESE FALSE GOATSBEARD.

A graceful plant, $1^1/2$ to 2 ft. tall. It grows best in partial shade. Pale pink flowers are produced in July and August. It is not as particular about soil and moisture as are some of the other species. The dwarf variety *pumila* (pew-*mil*-uh) is an especially good rock-garden plant, flowering in late summer. The variety *davidii* (day-*vid*-ee-eye) is a very tall species from China, growing 4 to 6 ft., with panicles (clusters) 1 to $1^1/2$ ft. long of rose-pink flowers. It is a striking plant for the wild garden or the back of a generously proportioned perennial border. It tolerates light shade and blooms for four weeks. Zones 3 to 8.

**A. × rosea** (roh-*zee*-uh).

A pink-flowered hybrid of *A. chinensis* and *A. japonica*. It has a compact habit, $1^1/2$ to $2^1/2$ ft. high, and is very handsome in the perennial border. Foliage is deeply cut and feathery. 'Bonn', 'Peach Blossom' and 'Queen Alexandra' are cultivars resulting from these crosses. Zones 4 to 8.

**A. simplicifolia** (sim-pli-si-*foh*-lee-uh).

STAR ASTILBE.

The leaves of this species, unlike those of most other astilbes, are simple, not compound. They are about 3 in. long, with deep lobes and a deep, glossy green color. This foliage forms a compact mound. The flowers appear in summer and attain a height of about 1 to $1^1/2$ ft. The star-shaped white or pink flowers are borne in narrow panicles. Put this plant in a partially shaded spot with lots of organic matter and plenty of moisture. Cultivars include 'Bronze Elegance', 'William Buchanon', 'Inshriach Pink' and 'Sprite'. Zones 4 to 8.

**A. taquetii** (ta-*get*-ee-eye).

FALL ASTILBE.

Native to eastern China, this species is usually represented by a tall upright clone, 'Superba'. It grows to 4 ft., extending the flowering season into late summer. This makes an excellent cut flower. 'Purple Lance' (syn. 'Purpurlanze') is a newer German cultivar in a darker hue. Zones 4 to 8.

# Astrantia (as-*tran*-tee-uh).

MASTERWORT.

Carrot Family *(Umbelliferae)*.

Hardy, herbaceous European perennials for the shady garden, or better, near the stream, in deep, woodsy soil. These have basal leaves vaguely like those of wild geraniums and almost daisylike umbels of small flowers on sparsely branched, naked scapes. Propagate by fresh seed sown immediately (in a cold frame) or by division in spring.

**A. major** (*may*-jor).

To 2 ft., it produces pink and white flowers in spring. 'Involucrata' (syn. 'Shaggy') and 'Sunningdale Variegated' are cultivars frequently found in this species. Zones 4 to 7.

# Astrantia

*Astrantia major*

*Aurinia saxatilis*
BASKET-OF-GOLD

*Aubrieta deltoidea*
PURPLE ROCK CRESS

*Baptisia australis*

**Aubrieta** (oh-bree-*ay*-tuh).

AUBRETIA.

Mustard Family *(Cruciferae)*.

A small genus of perennials from southern Europe to Iran, including very popular and handsome rock-garden plants, described below. It blooms with *Arabis* and *Alyssum* in April and May. Often recommended by English horticultural writers, it is not nearly as hardy in the eastern U.S. as it is in England and often dies out after a season or two. In the Pacific Northwest it is a main feature of spring gardens. Easily propagated by seeds, layers or cuttings, it can be maintained by the persistent gardener and is worth the trouble. Full sun and excellent drainage are essential for success, along with ordinary garden soil with added sand and grit. It will not withstand excessive heat or drought. Garden forms are usually spontaneous or derived hybrids of the various species.

**A. deltoidea** (del-*toy*-dee-uh).

PURPLE ROCK CRESS.

Native to southern Europe and Asia Minor. This showy species grows 3 to 5 in. high in a heavy mat of grayish foliage and produces masses of purplish flowers, ³⁄₄ in. across. There are many fine cultivars in colors from palest pink to darkest purple. Most are started from seed. Zone 6.

**Aurinia** (aw-*rin*-ee-uh).

Mustard Family *(Cruciferae)*.

This genus includes seven species of biennials and perennial herbs native to central and southern Europe and Turkey. Until recently, this genus was included under *Alyssum*.

**A. saxatilis** (saks-ah-*til*-is).

BASKET-OF-GOLD.

An easy rock garden or border perennial, native to Europe. Sprawling, it has rubbery stems that bear three 5-in.-long silver leaves. In early spring the plant is covered with heads of small yellow flowers. Specialists list cultivars such as 'Ball of Gold', 'Compactum', 'Citrinum', 'Flore', 'Sunny Border Apricot' and 'Tom Thumb'. Cut back all of these rather sharply after flowering. The cuttings root, not easily, in damp, coarse sand in diffuse light and should be protected from drying winds. These are best propagated (except the double sort) by sowing seed in early spring. Zone 3.

**Baptisia** (bap-*tiz*-ee-uh).

FALSE INDIGO.

Pea Family *(Leguminosae)*.

Vigorous, shrublike perennials native to the eastern half of the U.S. Leaflets of striking compound leaves are arranged in threes. Foliage is attractive all season long. The plants are particularly good in borders and may also be established easily in the wild garden. They require good drainage, full sun and ordinary garden soil, well turned to a spade's depth. Propagate by seeds or by root division.

★ **B. australis** (os-*tray*-lis).

Handsome sprays of dark blue, lupinelike flowers appear in May and June on stout stems to 3 ft. high. Showy, bright blue-green foliage is produced with an air of casual abundance. Fine in the June border with peonies and irises. The dried seedpods, brown in color, are very decorative in winter arrangements. Zone 5.

**Belamcanda** (bel-am-*kan*-duh).

Iris Family *(Iridaceae)*.

Unpretentious perennials from China and Japan. Only two species are in extensive cultivation, valued for their showy flowers and especially for their glossy black seeds. Full sun or light shade and a rich, well-drained soil are needed. These are easy, foolproof perennials. Propagate by seeds or

# Belamcanda

by root division. Seeds sown indoors in late winter and later transplanted to the outdoor garden after the soil has warmed up will give some bloom the first year.

**B. chinensis** (chin-*nen*-sis).
BLACKBERRY LILY.
This species grows 2 to 4 ft. high, with long, iris-like leaves and bright orange, red-spotted flowers, 1 in. long and 2 in. across, blooming in July and early August. The common name derives from the clusters of black seeds, which are attractive to birds. This plant is often seen in the U.S. along roadsides and in open meadows, where it has naturalized. Zones 5 to 8.

**B. flabellata** (flab-el-*lay*-tuh).
From Japan. The plant and flower are quite like *B. chinensis*, but the flowers are yellow and are not spotted. 'Hello Yellow' is the cultivar usually listed for this species. Zones 5 to 8.

# Bergenia (ber-*jee*-nee-uh).
Saxifrage Family *(Saxifragaceae)*.
(Often listed as *Saxifraga* or *Megasea*.) Asiatic perennials with boldly ornamental foliage in large, low clumps, from which rise thick stems with loose panicles of small pink or white flowers in May. They make excellent rock-garden plants. Sun (partial shade where summers are hot) and well-drained, sandy soil are essential. Propagate by root division or by seed. In recent years English horticulturists have bred some exciting, unusual and free-flowering hybrids. The species listed below is generally available.

**B. cordifolia** (kor-dif-*foh*-lee-uh).
HEART-LEAVED BERGENIA.
The dark pink flowers, in graceful sprays, rise 15 to 18 in. above large, thickly clustered leaves. The variety *alba* (*al*-buh) bears white flowers. A

darker, purple variety is *purpurea* (pur-pur-*ee*-uh), taller than the type. 'Perfecta' is one of the best performers in this group. It has rosy-red flowers. Zones 3 to 8.

**B. purpurascens** (pur-pew-*ras*-enz).
PURPLE-LEAFED BERGENIA.
Native to the Himalayas. Prized most for its purplish winter leaf coloring. In summer the narrow leaves are dark green, but by Thanksgiving they are beet-root colored. The flowers are an irridescent rose color and are borne on graceful reddish stems early in the spring. Plants grow about 1 ft. tall and are about 1 ft. wide. 'Ballawley' is a large plant with 8- to 12-in. leaves. Propagate by seeds or division. Zones 3 to 8.

**Boccania cordata.** See *Macleaya cordata*.

# Boltonia (bolt-*toh*-nee-uh).
FALSE STARWORT.
Composite Family *(Compositae)*.
Sturdy and easily grown perennials, native to the midwestern prairies of the U.S. Small, asterlike flowers of white, lavender or purple bloom profusely in July, August and September, adding an airy, feathery effect to the back of the perennial border. These plants have attractive blue-green foliage and are good for naturalizing and useful for cutting. They like full sun and ordinary garden soil, well turned to a spade's depth. Propagate by seeds or by root division.

**B. asteroides** (as-ter-*roy*-deez).
A tall, well-branched plant, 3 to 5 ft. high, with abundant starlike flowers $3/4$ in. across, much like those of the wild aster. The flowers are white and shades of purple. 'Pink Beauty' is 3 to 4 ft. tall, with masses of soft pink flowers in September. 'Snowbank' is also 3 to 4 ft. tall, with white flowers in September. Zones 4 to 9.

*Bergenia purpurascens* 'Ballawley'

*Brunnera macrophylla*
HEART-LEAF BRUNNERA

**Brunella.** See *Prunella*.

**Brunnera** (brun-*ner*-uh).

Borage Family *(Boraginaceae)*.

There is only one species in cultivation, an attractive perennial of Asia with small blue flowers. In masses, the effect is a shimmering blue. It is effective in the early perennial border, with spring bulbs. Give it sun or partial shade and ordinary garden soil. Propagate by seeds or by division.

**B. macrophylla** (mak-roh-*fill*-uh).

HEART-LEAF BRUNNERA.

(Syn. *Anchusa myosotidiflora*.) This plant grows to 2 ft. high, with tiny, sky-blue, forget-me-not-like flowers in great abundance in April or May. The flower stems rise above large, rough-textured, heart-shaped leaves at the base of the plant. There is a cultivar with leaves with clear white borders, named 'Variegata'. 'Hadspen Cream' has creamy-white leaf borders. Zone 3.

**Callirhoe** (kal-*leer*-oh-ee).

POPPY MALLOW.

Mallow Family *(Malvaceae)*.

A native North American genus of herbaceous annual and perennial plants that thrive in dry, sunny positions and give a long season of bright bloom. Propagate by seeds sown in ordinary soil as soon as the ground has warmed up; also by crown division in spring or fall. Seeds of the perennial kinds should be planted where plants are to remain.

**C. involucrata** (in-vol-yew-*kray*-tuh).

A sprawling perennial, native from Missouri to Wyoming and south to Texas. It grows about 1 ft. high, with rounded, lobed leaves and crimson flowers (various shades exist, some almost white) that remain in bloom for three months. Good for rock gardens if the drainage is adequate, it is also good in the open wild garden. Plants are best raised from seed planted where they are to remain, since the depth of the taproot makes transplanting or dividing mature plants difficult. Zone 4.

## Campanula (kam-*pan*-yew-luh).

BELLFLOWER.

Bellflower Family *(Campanulaceae)*.

A large genus of annuals, biennials and perennials, native mostly to Europe and Asia, and all but indispensable to gardeners everywhere. While the bellflowers are an enormously varied group, differing more in plant size and growth characteristics than in color, the quality of airy and dancing grace is perhaps the most prized of their garden attributes. The flowers of almost all species seem to catch and spill the sunlight, and the leaves of many, particularly the lower-growing species, have a casual but tidy look. To be sure, there is a great difference in every aspect between, say, *C. isophylla* (eye-so-*fill*-uh), on the one hand, and the statuesque and almost pompous *C. pyramidalis* (per-uh-mi-*day*-lis) on the other. But in all there is a family resemblance, which is most pleasing in the clarity of the flower colors. Few flowers can be so well represented in gardens of every kind.

One characteristic, the graceful, bell-shaped flower, occurs in all the species. Bellflowers have many uses but are especially prized in borders and rock gardens, depending on the species. Almost all bellflowers are blue or white, but there are a few pinks in an enormous range of subtle shadings. Well-drained garden soil, full sun or, with some species, filtered shade and adequate moisture are needed. It may be necessary to add lime to the soil. The list below is representative of the many plants of this genus. Propagate by seeds or by division.

### C. carpatica (kar-*pat*-ik-uh).

CARPATHIAN BELLFLOWER.

From eastern Europe, a hardy, very sturdy perennial, 10 to 15 in. high, that is good in borders, in the rock garden and for edgings. Long-lived and persistent where summers are cool, this species often self-sows. The leaves grow in a neat, tufted mound, 6 to 8 in. across. The blossoms, 1½ to 2 in. across, are cup-shaped and lavender-blue or white. The plants bloom from early July until frost, especially when faded flower stems are sheared off. 'Blue Clips' and 'White Clips' are 6- to 9-in. plants with 2½-in. flowers. 'Wedgewood Blue' and 'Wedgewood White' are 6-in. plants with 2½-in. flowers. Zone 3.

### C. cochleariifolia (kok-lee-ah-ree-ih-*foh*-lee-uh).

FAIRY'S-THIMBLE.

SPIRAL BELLFLOWER.

From the European mountains, a low-growing plant forming a dense mat of leaves that is good as a ground cover. The leaves are small and fan-shaped in rosettes, arising from underground stolons. The flowers appear in summer on 3- to 4-in. wiry stems. They are nodding bells in blue or white. Plant where it will receive mid-afternoon sun. Any well-drained soil will do. The cultivar 'Alba' bears clear white flowers. 'Miranda' is a vigorous grower that produces pale icy-blue flowers. Zone 4.

### C. glomerata (glom-er-*ray*-tuh).

CLUSTERED BELLFLOWER.

From Eurasia, a hardy perennial, to 2 ft. high, that is excellent for a strong accent in the mixed border. Flowers are purple, blue or white. The dense, terminal heads of bloom, in which each floret is ¾ in. long, are at their best in June and continue into July. The dwarf variety *acaulis* (ak-*kaw*-lis), 3 to 6 in. high, bears almost stemless blue-violet flowers in July. The variety *dahurica* (dah-*hew*-rik-uh) has dark purple flowers and larger blossoms than the species, in heads up to 3 in. across. 'Joan Elliott' is deep violet-blue. 'Superba Alba' is a white form of the popular cultivar 'Superba'. Zone 3.

# Campanula

*Campanula lactiflora*
MILKY BELLFLOWER

*Campanula persicifolia*
PEACH-LEAVED BELLFLOWER

**C. lactiflora** (lak-ti-*floh*-ruh).
MILKY BELLFLOWER.
From the Caucasus, one of the tallest of the perennial bellflowers, 3 to 5 ft. high, hardy and long-lived. Showy clusters of flowers, white or white with blue edges, appear in July and August on tall branching stems. It grows in sun or shade in rich, well-drained loam. Plant in full sun; do not disturb for three to four years. Propagate by division. 'Pouffe' is a dwarf cultivar only 18 in. high that covers itself with pale blue flowers. 'Pritchard's Variety', 3 ft., ranges from pale to dark blue. Zone 5.

**C. persicifolia** (per-sik-i-*foh*-lee-uh).
PEACH-LEAVED BELLFLOWER.
From Europe, northern Africa and Asia, one of the taller perennial bellflowers, 2 to 3 ft. high. Each strong stem from the terminal raceme is hung with one or more lavender-blue or white

*Campanula portenschlagiana*
DALMATIAN BELLFLOWER

## Campanula

blossoms, each bloom 2 in. across. The slender leaves are mostly in a cluster at the base of the plant. Cultivars and varieties include some doubles and some with very large blossoms. All are handsome in the border in June and early July. They last well when cut. Rich soil, full sun and plenty of moisture are needed. Plants ought to be divided every other year or grown anew from seed to prevent deterioration. 'Grandiflora Alba' has large white flowers and grows to 2 ft. 'Moerheimii' has double white flowers. 'Telham Beauty' has very large, clear blue bells.  Zone 4.

**C. portenschlagiana** (port-en-shlag-ee-*ay*-nuh).
DALMATIAN BELLFLOWER.
From southern Europe, a small perennial, 6 in. high, with purple blossoms, ¾ in. across. It makes especially graceful clumps in a rock wall or a rock garden, where it blooms from late May to July. Sun and a rich, porous, well-drained soil are needed.  Two botanical varieties exist, *alba* (*al*-buh), which is white, and *major* (*may*-jor), a large-flowering type. Zone 3.

**C. poscharskyana** (posh-arsk-ee-*ay*-nuh).
SERBIAN BELLFLOWER.
From Yugoslavia, a loosely spreading perennial with toothed, heart-shaped leaves. Deeply cut, lilac-blue flowers bloom freely in early summer on decumbent 12- to 18-in. stems. Its starry and tumbling effect is well suited to window boxes and hanging baskets. Blooms from June until frost. Zone 3.

**C. rotundifolia** (roh-tun-di-*foh*-lee-uh).
BLUEBELLS-OF-SCOTLAND.
COMMON HAREBELL.
A slender, graceful perennial, 6 to 12 in. high. Its nodding blue flowers, ¾ in. long, on thin, wiry stems, bloom over slim leaves all summer. A

widely variable species, with many forms native to many parts of the world, it is useful and effective in borders, in the rock garden, on rock walls and on slopes. Rich soil, full sun and good drainage are required. The cultivar 'Alba' is white; 'Flore-plena', a double; and 'Olympia', a good performer, bright blue. Zones 2 to 3.

## Catananche (kat-a-*nan*-kee).
CUPID'S DART.
Composite Family *(Compositae)*.
A small genus, native to the Mediterranean region, containing one popular garden perennial valued for its showy flowers. Plants are easily grown in light soil and full sun. Propagate by seeds or by division.

**C. caerulea** (see-*rue*-lee-uh).
CUPID'S DART.
Grows to 2 ft., with handsome heads of blue flowers, 2 in. across. The foliage is clustered at the base of the plant. Useful in the border for its summer-long bloom, it flowers the first year and also makes a fine cut flower, both fresh and dried. Zone 5.

## Centaurea (sen-*taw*-ree-uh).
Composite Family *(Compositae)*.
Annuals and perennials, mostly from Europe and Asia, that are easy to grow and pleasant to have in the garden, in a buttonhole or in a bouquet. Fluffy flower heads in shades of blue, pink, maroon, yellow and white bloom during the summer. Plants vary considerably in size, from 1 to 4 ft. All grow best in full sun. They are useful in borders, edgings and the cutting garden. Propagate by seeds or by root division. These plants will often self-sow in warm regions.

**C. dealbata** (dee-al-*bay*-tuh).
PERSIAN CORNFLOWER KNAPWEED.
This plant grows up to 2¹/₂ ft. tall and 1¹/₂ ft. wide. The basal leaves, coarsely lobed, have long white hairs on the undersides and can be 2 ft. long. The flowers, 2 to 3 in. wide, are pink with a paler or white center and appear in summer, one per stem. It flowers for about four weeks. Plant in ordinary soil, in full sun. The cultivar 'Steenbergii' has pink flowers, larger than the species, with clear white centers. Zone 3.

**C. hypoleuca** (hye-po-*loo*-ka).
KNAPWEED.
Very similar to *C. dealbata* except more compact. The color of the flowers is rose-purple to pink. Plant in full sun, in ordinary soil. The cultivar 'John Coutts' is a superior garden form. Zone 4.

**C. macrocephala** (mak-roh-*sef*-a-luh).
GLOBE CENTAUREA.
Perennial from eastern Europe, with large globelike yellow flowers, 3 to 4 in. across, similar to those of a thistle. The flower bracts are brown and papery, adding detail to the flowering heads. To 4 ft. Zone 3.

**C. montana** (mon-*tay*-nuh).
MOUNTAIN BLUET.
A handsome perennial species, 1 to 2 ft. tall, with large heads of bloom, 2 to 2¹/₂ in. across, above the broad, heavy leafage. Purplish-blue is the usual color, but white, yellow, pink and purple varieties are available. It blooms from May to midsummer, usually with a second bloom period lasting into September. When it finds a spot it likes, it can be a problem by seeding itself profusely around the garden. Fine for cutting and in the border. Propagate by root division. Zone 5.

*Centaurea montana*
MOUNTAIN BLUET

**Centranthus** (sen-*tran*-thus).
VALERIAN.
Valerian Family *(Valerianaceae)*.
A small genus of annuals and perennials native to the Mediterranean region. The most familiar species, *C. ruber*, is an attractive perennial, a favorite in gardens. It needs full sun and ordinary garden soil, well turned to a spade's depth. Propagate by seeds or by root division in spring.

**C. ruber** (*rue*-ber).
JUPITER'S-BEARD.
RED VALERIAN.
VALERIAN.
A bushy plant, 2 to 3 ft. high, with light gray-green leaves, 3 to 4 in. long. Dense clusters of fragrant, funnel-shaped, crimson flowers bloom in

## Centranthus

*Centranthus ruber*
RED VALERIAN

*Ceratostigma plumbaginoides*
LEADWORT

*Cerastium tomentosum*
SNOW-IN-SUMMER

*Chelone lyonii*
PINK TURTLEHEAD

June and July. A white cultivar, 'Albus', and a rose cultivar, 'Roseus', are available. Valuable in the border or the rock garden. Zone 5.

## Cerastium (ser-*ras*-tee-um).

SNOW-IN-SUMMER.

Pink Family *(Caryophyllaceae).*

A large genus, somewhat weedy in northern areas, of low-growing and hardy plants. Any sandy or ordinary garden soil, well turned to a spade's depth, and full sun are the only requirements. Easy to propagate by seeds or by rooted runners.

### C. tomentosum (toe-men-*toe*-sum).

SNOW-IN-SUMMER.

This familiar perennial, native to Europe, grows 3 to 6 in. high, with mats of small gray leaves and dainty white, tubular flowers in June. It makes a graceful picture in the rock garden and as an edging, but it may spread too luxuriantly if not kept within strict bounds. 'Silver Carpet' is more compact than the species. Zone 3.

## Ceratostigma (ser-at-oh-*stig*-muh).

Plumbago Family *(Plumbaginaceae).*

Perennial herbs and shrubs from China and Africa, having alternate leaves with hairy edges, and dark blue flowers in loose heads. The plants are valued in borders and rock gardens, especially for their late-season flowers. They need sun or partial shade and well-drained garden soil. Propagate by seeds or by root division.

### C. plumbaginoides (plum-ba-ji-*noi*-deez).

LEADWORT.

(Syn. *Plumbago larpentiae.*) A handsome perennial, 6 to 12 in. high, with dark, shiny green leaves in a heavy, matlike growth. The foliage turns dark red in fall. The funnel-shaped flowers, 2 in. across, are a fine, dark blue, well set off by the reddish bracts

below each flower. Bloom begins in late July and continues until frost. Useful as a low edging plant for perennial borders, in rock and wall gardens, and as a ground cover. Zone 5.

## Chelone (kee-*loh*-nee).

TURTLEHEAD.

Figwort Family *(Scrophulariaceae).*

Hardy perennials, native to North America, found wild in wet marshes and damp woodlands. The spikes of small, snapdragon-like flowers bloom in July and August. Propagate by seeds or by root division.

### C. glabra (*glay*-bruh).

WHITE TURTLEHEAD.

A sturdy plant, to 2½ ft., with white or occasionally pinkish florets, 1 in. long, in showy spikes. The flowers resemble a turtle's head. It grows well in full sun or partial shade but needs moist, acid soil and plenty of water. Useful in the border or the wild garden. Zone 3.

### ★C. lyonii (lye-*oh*-nee-eye).

PINK TURTLEHEAD.

Probably the best garden species, with showy, rose-purple flower spikes, the florets each 1 in. long. It grows 2½ to 3 ft. high, making large, dense clumps in the perennial border or the wild garden. Partial shade or full sun and any ordinary garden soil, well turned to a spade's depth, are needed. Zone 3.

### C. obliqua (ob-*lye*-kwuh).

ROSE TURTLEHEAD.

To 3 ft. tall, growing in swampy woods from Maryland to Mississippi. Flowers are pink. It makes a good plant for moist gardens. The cultivar 'Bethelii' is more vibrant than the species. Zone 6.

## Chrysanthemum

**Chrysanthemum** (kris-*an*-thee-mum)

Composite Family *(Compositae)*.

Native to the temperate zones of Asia and Europe, a very large genus of annual and perennial herbs, some of which are woody plants.

Recently, botanists have reclassified many plants within this genus to other genera. Tansy-flowered species are now *Tanacetum*; daisy-flowered types are variously assigned to *Argyranthemum*, *Dendranthemum*, *Leucanthemum* and *Nipponanthemum*. While these changes may have significant importance to botanists, they are rather confusing to the everyday gardeners who grow these plants. As these new names remain unfamiliar to most gardeners, all the genus *Chrysanthemum* has been considered intact here.

Of the 160 species of chrysanthemums, some of the most important are:

**C. coccineum** (kok-*sin*-ee-um).

PAINTED DAISY.

PYRETHRUM.

Perennial, from the Caucasus and Persia. The flowers are 3 in. across, daisylike, single, semidouble or fully double, in shades of red and pink and also white. Foliage is fernlike. The cut flowers last exceptionally well. It blooms during June and July and grows in partial shade or full sun. Sow seeds in spring, and divide plants in late summer. A few popular cultivars are 'Atrosanguineum', the darkest red single; 'Brenda', cerise-red with a white eye; 'Eileen May Robinson', single pink; 'Evenglow', a particularly good one with salmon-red flowers; 'Pink Bouquet', double pink flowers; 'Robinson's Variety', double rose flowers; and 'Sensation', double red flowers. Zone 3.

**C. maximum** (mack-*see*-mum).

Often confused with *C.* × *superbum*, but has smaller flower heads, $2^{1}/4$ in. wide as compared to 4 in. on *C.* × *superbum*, as well as spatulate rather than oblanceolate bottom leaves.

**C. nipponicum** (nip-*pon*-ik-um).

NIPPON DAISY.

A shrubby perennial from Japan that reaches from 1 to 3 ft., with white flowers $1^{1}/2$ to 3 in. across, in late fall. Leaves are thick and have attractive glossy surfaces. Zone 5.

**C. pacificum** (pa-*si*-fik-um).

GOLD-AND-SILVER CHRYSANTHEMUM.

Native to Japan. Leaves are lobed at the ends and edged in gold, making them attractive all summer long. Moundlike plants reach 1 ft. tall and 3 ft. across after established. Small tansylike flowers cover the plant in mid-November. Zone 6.

★ **C. × rubellum** (rue-*bell*-um).

HYBRID RED CHRYSANTHEMUM.

There is much confusion as to where this plant belongs botanically. Sometimes it is listed as a cultivar of *C. zawadskii* var. *latilobum* (za-*wad*-skee-eye; lat-i-*loh*-bum), the hardy Siberian daisy, and other times as a hybrid of species. Recently, some authors have listed it under *Dendranthemum rubella* (den-*dran*-thee-mum rue-*bell*-uh). Regardless, the cultivars within this group make excellent garden subjects. Most are free-flowering, compact plants with five lobed leaves. The leaf segments are toothed and somewhat hairy. Cultivars are hardier than most cushion mums and make excellent fall-flowering plants for the border. 'Clara Curtis' is a single pink form with 3-in. flowers that start blooming in July and continue, on and off, until October. It grows 2 to 3 ft. tall. 'Duchess of Edinburgh' has muted red flowers on 2-ft plants in the fall. 'Mary Stoker' has light tangerine flowers on 2- to $2^{1}/2$-ft. plants, and 'Pink Procession' covers itself with soft pink blossoms and is 2 to 3 ft. tall. Both of these bloom in September and October. Zone 4.

**C. × superbum** (sue-*pur*-bum).

SHASTA DAISY.

A hybrid of *C. maximum*, with which it is often confused when listed in the trade because of their similarities. The leaves are dark green, coarsely toothed and up to 1 ft. long at the base of the plant. They are arranged in basal rosettes, which overwinter. The flower stems grow to be up to 3 ft. high, depending on the cultivar, and the plant will spread to 2 ft. across. At the top of each stem is a composite daisy flower, 2 to 3 in. across, with white petals and a yellow center. Some cultivars have double flowers, two or more rows of petals and a paler yellow center. On some, the petals are fringed. They start flowering in June. Some cultivars flower all summer and up to frost if cared for properly.

Plant in full sun or partial shade—the double cultivars tend to prefer partial shade. Give plenty of air circulation and do not overcrowd. The soil should be rich, moist and well drained, with plenty of organic matter. Remove old flower stalks to promote rebloom and good basal-rosette formation for overwintering. These plants need to be divided every two to three years to promote vigor. Some of the best single forms are 'Alaska', with 3-in. flowers on 2- to 3- ft. plants, cold-hardy to Zone 3; 'Everest', with 3- to 4-in. flowers on 3- to 4-ft. plants; 'Little Miss Muffet', 2-in. flowers on 8- to 12-in. plants, which come true from seed; 'Majestic', 3- to 4-in. flowers on 3-ft. plants; 'Polaris', 5- to 7-in. clear white flowers on 3-ft. plants; and 'Snowcap', 3-in. flowers on compact, weather-resistant 18-in. plants. Double-flowered cultivars include 'Aglaya', with fringed petals; 'Cobham Gold', creamy flowers with a raised center; 'Esther Reed', early double; 'Marconi', 4-in. double flowers; 'Mount Shasta', double flowers with a raised center; and 'Wirral Pride', another double flower with a raised center. Zone 4.

*Chrysanthemum* 'Max Riley'

*Chrysanthemum coccineum* 'Brenda'
PAINTED DAISY

# Chrysanthemum

*Chrysanthemum × superbum*
SHASTA DAISY

*Chrysanthemum uliginosum*
GIANT DAISY

**C. uliginosum** (yew-li-ji-*noh*-sum).
GIANT DAISY.
Grows 4 to 7 ft. tall. Flowers are 2 to 3 in. wide, white with green centers and in 2- or 3-flowered clusters in the fall. Foliage is 3 to 4 in. long, coarsely toothed and sharply pointed. Seldom needs staking. Zone 5.

## Chrysogonum (kris-*sog*-oh-num).
Composite Family *(Compositae).*
The only species, native to the eastern U.S., is a low, spreading plant, hairy all over, with bright golden-yellow flowers, blooming in succession from early spring through July. It grows best in rich soil with plenty of humus, an ample supply of moisture and full sun or partial shade. The plant makes a brave show in the border, as well as in the rock garden. Propagate by division (stems root at the nodes as they grow) or by seeds.

**C. virginianum** (vir-jin-ee-*ay*-num).
GOLDEN-STAR.
Perennial, growing to 8 in., with pointed, bright green leaves, 1 to 3 in. long. The charming yellow flowers, starlike because of their pointed petals, are borne singly in the leaf axils. There are two botanical varieties: *virginianum* (vir-jin-ee-*ay*-num), which usually has the most attractive flowers, and *australis* (aw-*stral*-is), which is the most rapid spreader. Zone 5.

**C. zawadskii** var. **latilobum** 'Rubellum'.
See *C.* × *rubellum*.

## Chrysopsis (kris-*op*-sis).
GOLDEN-ASTER.
Composite Family *(Compositae).*
Sturdy perennials, native to dry areas of North America, with alternate leaves and yellow aster-like flowers. The bright yellow, late-summer and

fall bloom and the ability to grow in dry, sandy soils recommend these plants for use in the cultivated garden as well as in the wild garden. They are easily grown in any soil and full sun. Propagate by seeds or by root division.

**C. mariana** (mar-ee-*ay*-nuh).
MARYLAND GOLDEN-ASTER.
A vigorous grower, to 3 ft., with lance-shaped leaves and showy yellow flower heads. Found wild in dry, sandy places. Zone 4.

**C. villosa** (vil-*loh*-suh).
HAIRY GOLDEN-ASTER.
A less showy species, 1 to 5 ft. tall, with oblong leaves and bright yellow blooms. The cultivar 'Golden Sunshine' grows 4 to 5 ft. tall and produces masses of 2-in. flowers in midsummer. Zone 4.

# Cimicifuga (sim-i-sif-*yew*-guh).
BUGBANE.
Buttercup Family *(Ranunculaceae)*.
Handsome, tall perennials, native to moist, shady woodlands of the Northern Temperate Zone. Spires of small, whitish flowers, closely set, bloom in summer or fall. The plants are fine for the back of borders, in the wild garden and for cutting. They are easily grown in sun or shade in moist ground. Propagate by seeds or by root division.

**C. racemosa** (ras-em-*moh*-suh).
BLACK COHOSH.
BLACK SNAKEROOT.
A native North American species, growing to 8 ft., with graceful, feathery spikes of bloom 1 to 1½ ft. long, on tall scapes above large, deeply cut leaves. The flowers are handsome to look at but have a pungent odor that some people find disagreeable. It blooms in July and August. Zone 3.

**C. ramosa** (ra-*moh*-suh).
BRANCHED BUGBANE.
Flowering later than *C. racemosa* and earlier than *C. simplex*, this is a tall plant, often reaching 6 to 7 ft. The cultivar 'Atropurpurea' bears white flowers over dark purple foliage. 'Brunette' has deep bronze foliage and is only 3 to 4 ft. tall. Its flowers are pale pink fading to white and are borne in September. Zone 3.

**C. simplex** (*sim*-plex).
KAMCHATKA BUGBANE.
Native to Russia. This species is a handsome plant, 3 to 5 ft. high, with pretty though rank-smelling spires of white bloom in fall. It lasts well as a cut flower. 'White Pearl' has large flower spikes and is the most frequent cultivar offered in this species. Zone 3.

# Clematis (*klem*-a-tis).
CLEMATIS.
Buttercup Family *(Ranunculaceae)*.
Native to the Northern Temperate Zone, a genus with more than 230 species with both woody and herbaceous types. Many are climbing vines and are included in the volume *Vines, Grasses and Groundcovers*. Foliage ranges from simple, entire leaves to compound leaves with serrations and lobes. Some species bloom on new growth, while others bloom on second-year wood. Flowers are from 1 to 6 in. or more across. A few species are subshrubs and fit the herbaceous perennial limitations of this text.

**C. × eriostemon** (er-i-oh-*stee*-mon).
HYBRID CLEMATIS.
A hybrid species made by crossing the herbaceous *C. integrifolia* (in-teg-ri-*foh*-lee-uh) with the vining woody plant *C. viticella* (vye-ti-*sell*-uh). One of the resulting cultivars is 'Hendersonii', similar to *C. integrifolia* but

## Clematis

superior in many ways. The flowers are larger and deeper blue. Mature plants bloom in May and repeat in July and August. The seed heads have ornamental silky hairs. In rich soils they reach 30 in. in height and need staking. In poorer soils they are only 18 in. tall and are often allowed to sprawl over the ground. Zone 4.

**C. heracleifolia** (he-ra-klee-i-*foh*-lee-uh).
TUBE CLEMATIS.
Native to China and Korea. They are often, but not always, dioecious plants with six to twelve tubular, azure-blue flowers produced in axillary clusters. The four reflected sepals are the showy parts. The leaves are divided into three leaflets, 3 to 6 in. long, with sharp teeth. Flowering occurs in September. The variety *davidiana* (day-vid-i-*ay*-nuh) has wider flowers and is quite fragrant. The cultivar 'Wyevale Blue' has darker blue flowers than the species and blooms a month earlier. They all usually need some staking. Zone 3.

## Convallaria (kon-val-*lay*-ree-uh).
LILY-OF-THE-VALLEY.
Lily Family (*Liliaceae*).
The only species is a hardy perennial native to Europe, Asia and mountainous regions of the U.S. It is widely grown for its delicately scented, nodding, bell-like white flowers and fine, pointed leaves, and it fully deserves its reputation as one of the most adaptable ground covers and charming garden plants. To be most effective, it should be grown in very large masses, and since it needs shade, it is at its best when used as a ground cover under trees whose roots will not give it serious competition. It is also effective with early bulbs (which it may choke out eventually), in the rock garden, as edgings for shrubbery borders and for naturalizing. Rich, moist, but well-drained soil is needed. For abundant flowering, the solid mats should be dug up by the spadeful after several sea-

sons, divided and replanted; otherwise, the plants may crowd themselves out. Propagate by root division in spring.

Lily-of-the-valley pips (roots) can be forced into bloom during the winter, but they must be frozen first. Pips ready to force can be ordered from nurseries, where they have been treated especially for this purpose. If they are brought in from the garden, let them freeze before they are dug. Then plant six to eight pips together in a pot or bowl 6 in. deep, in bulb fiber or sand. Keep them moist and at a temperature of 65 to 68°F, in a dark place. When buds form, bring them out to a sunny window. In about three weeks they will bloom.

**C. majalis** (ma-*jay*-lis).
Grows 6 to 8 in. high, with deliciously fragrant, nodding, cream-white flowers, 1/3 in. across, pendant along thin, wiry stems. The long-lasting,

*Convallaria majalis*

broadly oblong, dark green leaves make a solid ground cover. Blooms appear in May and early June in the North. The cultivar 'Fortin's Giant' is 12 to 15 in. tall and has large flowers. 'Plena' has cream-colored double flowers. 'Rosea' has light pink flowers, and 'Striata' has green leaves with pale white stripes. Zone 2.

## Coreopsis (koh-ree-*op*-sis).

TICKSEED.

Composite Family *(Compositae)*.

A genus of many handsome annuals and perennials from North and South America and Africa, most of them showy and all of them easy to grow. They make a brilliant display in the border from early summer to frost, and survive drought and heat. Leaves are deeply cut and opposite. The white, yellow or occasionally pink flowers are usually single but are sometimes clustered. The plants are excellent for borders, in front of shrubs, in the cutting garden and in the sunny wild garden. They will thrive in full sun and any ordinary garden soil. Propagate the annuals by seeds; the perennials by root division or by seeds, preferably in fall, though this is possible in spring.

### C. auriculata (aw-rik-yew-*lay*-tuh).

MOUSE-EARED COREOPSIS.

This is a dwarf plant, not growing over 1 ft. high. It is stoloniferous, so it spreads, but is not invasive. The leaves are up to 5 in. long and pubescent. The deep gold, daisylike flowers are 1 to 2 in. across and appear in spring. Plant in full sun in well-drained soil. 'Nana' is a 6-in. cultivar that covers itself with deep gold blossoms in April and May. 'Superba' has deep orange flowers, with maroon centers, 2 to 3 in. across. Zone 4.

### C. grandiflora (gran-di-*floh*-ruh).

TICKSEED.

Native to the southern U.S., this perennial species grows to 2 ft., with golden-yellow flowers, 1 to 2 in. across. It blooms from June to frost. 'Early Sunrise' is a compact double yellow form available from seed. It won an All-America Selection Award in 1989. 'Goldfink' has 2-in. single yellow flowers with an orange center and grows to 9 in. 'Mayfield Giant' is an older cultivar with 2- to 4-in. gold flowers on 2- to 3-ft. plants. 'Sunburst' produces semidouble golden-yellow flowers on 2-ft. plants. 'Sunray' blooms for more than ten weeks on 2-ft. plants; its flowers are double and gold in color. Zone 5.

### C. lanceolata (lan-see-oh-*lay*-tuh).

LANCE COREOPSIS.

A dependable and hardy perennial from the eastern U.S., growing 1 to 2 ft. high. Single or double, bright yellow flowers bloom nearly all summer. Plants often self-sow. 'Brown Eyes' is a cultivar representative of this species. The single yellow flowers have a maroon ring near the center. Zone 3.

### C. rosea (*roh*-zee-uh).

ROSE TICKSEED.

A 1- to 2-ft. plant with 1-in. flower heads, native to North America. The ray flowers are pink and the disks yellow. It enjoys moist soils and spreads rapidly by rhizomes. 'Alba' is a white-flowered cultivar, and 'Nana' a dwarf, growing only to 1 ft. Zone 3.

### ★ C. verticillata (ver-ti-sil-*lay*-tuh).

THREAD-LEAVED COREOPSIS.

A showy perennial native to the eastern and central U.S. It grows 2 to 3 ft. high, with deeply divided, narrow leaves. The flowers, 2 in. across, are clear yellow or gold. They have a very long blooming period, starting in July and continuing on until frost. There are three popular cultivars in this species: 'Golden Showers', 18 to 24 in., with 2½-in. gold flowers; 'Moonbeam', 12 to 15 in., with lemon-green flowers; and 'Zagreb', 14 in., with gold flowers. Zone 3.

## Corydalis (kor-*rid*-a-lis).

FUMARIA.

FUME-ROOT.

Fumitory Family *(Fumariaceae).*

A huge but not well enough known genus of hardy, spring- and summer-blooming annuals, biennials and perennials, native to Europe, Asia and North America. They are also known as fume-root because of the strong nitrogenous odor given off by the crushed roots. Graceful plants, they have feathery, finely divided leaves, blue-green in color. Flowers are like those of the bleeding-heart, though smaller, in shades of pink, rose, yellow and blue. The plants are attractive in the open border, the rock garden or the wild garden. Partial shade or sun, a light, porous soil and moderate moisture are needed. Propagate by seeds or by root division.

### C. lutea (*lew*-tee-uh).

YELLOW CORYDALIS.

An adaptable and all but indestructible species from southern Europe that grows about 9 in. high, with bright yellow flowers, ¾ in. long, and attractive rosettes of fernlike, much-divided foliage. It blooms from May to September and grows best in shade. It is a perennial but is usually grown as an annual. Start new plants from freshly collected seed. Zone 5.

### C. ochroleuca (ok-ro-*lew*-ka).

WHITE CORYDALIS.

Somewhat like *C. lutea* but greenish-white in color and 1 ft. tall. The leaves are slightly more gray. The major flowering period is in spring,

with some rebloom in summer. Sow seeds in a cold frame immediately after collecting so that they do not dry out. Seedlings germinate in March the second year after planting. Zone 6.

## Crambe (*kram*-bee).

COLEWORT.

Mustard Family *(Cruciferae).*

A genus with about twenty species of annuals and perennials native from the Canary Islands to western Asia. The leaves are usually large, thick, fleshy and lobed or divided. The surfaces of the leaves are smooth. The main ornamental characteristics of the coleworts are their bold architectural forms and the masses of tiny white four-petalled flowers borne in panicles or racemes. All are foul-odored when smelled closely.

### C. cordifolia (kor-di-*foh*-lee-uh).

COLEWORT.

FLOWERING SEA KALE.

The foliage of this plant can reach 3 ft. tall and spread to 6 ft. Each leaf can be 2 ft. across. Leaves are heart-shaped and a gray-green. The huge panicles of ⁵⁄₁₆-in. white flowers can be up to 5 ft. tall. The plant has the look of giant baby's breath. Plants in bloom are malodorous. Place in full sun in a good garden soil. Propagate from seed. Zone 6.

## Delphinium (del-*fin*-ee-um).

LARKSPUR.

Buttercup Family *(Ranunculaceae).*

A large, handsome and popular genus of annuals, biennials and perennials, widely scattered over the temperate zones of the Northern Hemisphere. The common name derives from the noticeable spur on the florets, which usually occur in showy spikes of bloom. Colors vary from white through every shade of blue and purple and include some pinks, reds and yellows. The plants are easily grown in cool climates that have no extremes of heat or drought.

*Coreopsis verticillata* 'Moonbeam'
THREAD-LEAVED COREOPSIS

*Crambe cordifolia*
COLEWORT

*Corydalis ochroleuca*
WHITE CORYDALIS

*Delphinium* × *elatum* 'King Arthur'
HYBRID BEE DELPHINIUM

## Delphinium

Perennial and biennial species of delphinium are propagated by seeds sown in August (for bloom the second season) or by root division in early spring. Rooted stock may be ordered by mail and planted in early spring. Many of the best hybrids, though technically perennials, are not long-lived and should be treated as biennials. For a complete listing and information on these popular hybrids, see the *Hearst Garden Guides* volume *Annuals*, which incoporates biennials.

For perennial delphiniums make the soil extremely fertile. When starting a border from scratch, dig a 2-in. layer of compost or manure (well rotted, or else a comparable ratio of the dried type) into the bed to a depth of 6 to 8 in. Then spread over it 1 lb. of 10-10-10 fertilizer per 100 sq. ft. (an area 10 ft. x 10 ft.). One nursery recommends adding to this dose yet another 2 in. of manure or compost. Dig the fertilizer, with or without another layer of manure, into the bed, and provide 1 in. of sprinkler watering or wait for a really good rain before planting.

Since the load of food recommended for the delphinium bed works best if it has time to mature a little in the soil, it is a good idea to prepare a delphinium border in the fall for early spring planting. When adding delphiniums to an existing well-fed border, prepare the bed as usual in early spring. When laying out started seedlings or root cuttings, make a hole large enough to accommodate the root ball, add a little bone meal at the bottom, mix well into the soil, cover with another inch of good soil, then set in the delphinium, keeping the crown level with the ground. Planting too deep encourages crown rot. When seedlings have started to grow, dig half a handful of rich organic matter or fertilizer in around each plant.

Through the years, keep the delphinium border well nourished with generous feedings of manure, compost or enriched humus, and fertil-izer. During their growing periods, delphiniums require lots of water. Soak the soil around the roots. Avoid overhead watering to give no encouragement to diseases and to keep from breaking the heavy stalks. (A good rainfall can do that without any help from the gardener.)

Stake all but the shortest species of delphinium because of the brittleness of their soft, hollow stems and the weight of the giant florets. Begin staking when the plants are no more than 12 in. tall. Dark green stakes 4 to 5 ft. tall are inconspicuous enough even when the plants are smaller, and will be needed when they really start to grow. If you prefer, start with shorter stakes. A stake for each stem will be necessary in the largest species. Use soft cord or raffia to tie.

After the delphiniums have flowered the first time, cut off the flower heads before they can set seed, but allow the leaves to stay where they are. They will begin to yellow. At this point, cut off the rest of the stems almost at ground level. Near this time, new shoots will appear at the base, and these will produce a second crop (and in some climates and with some species even a third) in late September or October. To ensure the second crop, feed the plants again when these young shoots first appear.

In cooler areas, particularly where there is a shortage of snow, winter protection is essential to protect the plants from the ravages of premature thawing and heaving. When the ground has frozen, cover the crowns with an inch of sand or other protective mulch. Where winters are especially severe, an additional covering of straw, hay or evergreen branches will guarantee them through the winter.

Porous, well-drained soil is essential to all delphiniums, along with a good supply of ground limestone, potassium and superphosphate. Ample moisture and full sun are important. A location partially shaded some of the day will also suffice.

**D. × belladonna** (bell-uh-*don*-uh).

BELLADONNA DELPHINIUM.

A hybrid resulting from crosses of *D. × elatum* and *D. grandiflorum* (gran-di-*floh*-rum), a 2- to 3-ft.-tall species. Most of the selections in this group are shorter and more branched than the *D. × elatum* species. In *D. × elatum* the central flower stem blooms first and is followed by the side branches. In *D. × belladonna* the central stem and the side shoots bloom at the same time. Examples of the latter are 'Bellamosa', with blue flowers on 4-ft. plants; 'Casa Blanca', with pure white flowers on 3½-ft. plants; 'Cliveden Beauty' with sky-blue flowers growing 3 ft. tall; 'Larmartine', with deep violet flowers on 4-ft. stems; and 'Moreheimii', with white flowers on 3-ft. plants.

**D. cheilanthum** (ki-*lan*-thum).

GARLAND LARKSPUR.

Native to the Caucasus and Asia Minor, it grows to 3 ft. and is the parent of many garden hybrids. It is quite variable but a good perennial in its own right. Good forms can be selected for vegetative propagation out of seedlings that range from white and light blue to dark blue. Zone 3.

**D. × elatum** (ee-*lay*-tum).

HYBRID BEE DELPHINIUM.

Second generation hybrids resulting from crosses of *D. × elatum*, *D. exaltatum* (ex-al-*tay*-tum) and *D. formosum* (for-*moh*-sum). Many nurseries, including those from England, Germany and North America, have been involved in the selection of various plants referred to as "strains" or "series." One of the best known comes from the English nursery firm of Blackmore and Langdon and is called the Blackmore and Langdon strain. In America there is the Pacific Hybrid series (also known as the Round Table series). The Wrexham strain was developed in England and Wales and is sometimes referred to as the Hollyhock strain.

Some of the offspring of *D. × elatum* in the Pacific Hybrid series include 'Astolat', in pink shades; 'Black Knight', which is darkest violet with a black bee; 'Blue Bird', a medium blue with a white bee; 'Galahad', which blooms about ten days earlier than the others in the group and is pure white; 'Guinevere', which has outer petals of light blue, inner petals of lavender and a white bee; 'King Arthur', which has giant, dark royal blue florets with a white bee; and 'Summer Skies', which comes in shades of the lightest blue and has a white bee. A popular series today is the Magic Fountain group. These are short versions of the Pacific Hybrid types, 24 to 36 in. tall. The colors include dark blue, lavender, sky blue and white. Many have contrasting white or black bees. Another group included here is the Connecticut Yankee series. They are similar to the *D. × belladonna* types and are heavily branched. Of interest, too, are the much-admired hybrids being developed by Dr. R. A. H. Legro in Holland. He is perfecting cultivars, through the use of some additional species, with the same high quality as the Pacific Hybrid series, in reds, pinks and salmon. English and American gardeners saw his breathtaking selections in the 1980s, when he spent some time at the Royal Horticultural Society's garden at Wisley, England. Zone 3.

**Dendranthemum.** See *Chrysanthemum*.

**D. rubella.** See *Chrysanthemum × rubellum*.

**Dianthus** (dye-*an*-thus).

Pink Family *(Caryophyllaceae)*.

Primarily Eurasian, extending to South Africa. This genus includes the tall clove-scented florist's carnations, the smaller sweet Williams and the low-growing, fragrant little evergreen forms called border pinks. Pinks and sweet Williams are found in most gardens in the Northern Hemisphere and

# Dianthus

are increasingly loved for their textured clumps of handsome foliage and their lacy blooms.

The border pinks are low-growing, tufted, hardy perennials with narrow, grasslike, opposite leaves that sometimes shade toward a gray-blue, the color of blue spruce. The foliage of many is evergreen and retains shape and color even under snow, a trait that makes them ideal border plants in cooler areas and staples of the rock garden. The flowers are clove scented. Pink and white are the most common colors. If the flowers, which usually bloom in June, are kept picked, many types will produce a second and even a third crop during the season.

Sweet Williams are somewhat less fragrant and usually taller than the border pinks. The flowers are larger and have more brilliant coloring. They range from dark scarlet through reds to pinks and whites, and many cultivars flash circles and stains of contrasting color. Though most are perennials, sweet Williams are best considered as biennials, and so are covered in the *Hearst Garden Guides* volume *Annuals*, which includes all the important biennials.

The carnation is the most imposing of all dianthus and, after the rose, is probably the world's favorite cut flower as well as one of its best greenhouse plants. Some carnations are somewhat hardy when protected through the winter, but most prefer warmer zones and even there may require protection. Parent to the greenhouse carnation is a Eurasian species, *D. caryophyllus* (kar-ee-oh-fil-us), which grows 1 to 3 ft. tall. Its flowers are few to a stem, and colors include pink, rose, purple, red to white, and more rarely, yellow. Greenhouse cultivation of carnations requires a temperature range of from 50°F at night to 60°F during the daytime. To propagate, take cuttings in the midwinter months from shoots growing at the base of the parent plant. Rooted in sand, they will be ready in four to six weeks. In warm climates

such as Zone 8, plant rooted cuttings out-of-doors after all danger of frost is past. Set 6 in. apart in rows 12 in. apart. To obtain extra-large carnation blooms, pinch off all side shoots during the growth period. Plants will generally begin to bloom about seven weeks after planting, and many produce up to eighteen flowers in the following season.

Growing requirements for the smaller dianthus, the pinks and sweet Williams, include light, well-drained soil slightly on the alkaline side. All succeed in full sunshine, though many will also bloom in partial shade. The most common method of propagation for the perennial species is crown division. In areas where winters are severe and less than generous in snowfall, it may be advisable to protect dianthus from premature thawing and heaving with the application of a light mulch or a blanket of pine boughs. The biennial species are generally propagated by seeds.

**D. × allwoodii** (all-*wood*-ee-eye).
ALLWOOD PINK.
Hybrids between *D. plumarius*, the cottage or grass pink, and *D. caryophyllus*, the more imposing carnation. Development of this species is attributed to Montague Allwood, an English nurseryman. Perennial and hardy, the flowers are fringed. Most are double or semidouble, and retain both the charming compact growth habit of the pink and the perennial flowering habit of the carnation if they are kept from setting seed. Mixed seed produces fine plants, which can then be propagated by cuttings throughout midsummer. Cultivars 10 to 18 in. tall include 'Alba', clear white flowers; 'Aqua', white double flowers; 'Baby Treasure', fragrant pink flowers with a scarlet eye; 'Constance', a silver-pink with red flecks on the petals; 'Danielle', a deep salmon that reblooms; 'Doris', a fragrant salmon-pink and one of the most popular; 'Helen', a free-flowering

deep salmon-pink; 'Ian', a long-blooming plant with rich scarlet flowers; and 'Robin', coral-red flowers. Cultivars 3 to 6 in. tall include 'Alpinus', free-flowering single flowers in a mixture of colors from light pink to red, and often bicolored; 'Dainty Maid', single purple flowers with a red eye; 'Elizabeth', pink flowers with a small crimson eye; 'Essex Witch', pink, white and salmon hues, one of the most popular; 'Fay', purple flowers; 'Mars', rounded, double pink flowers; and 'Wink', clear white flowers. Zones 4 to 8.

**D. alpinus** (al-*pye*-nus).
ALPINE PINK.
Native to the Austrian Alps. Leaves are 1 in. long and grass green. Loose clumps coalesce to form large patches. The scentless flowers are up to 1$^1$/2 in. across and cover the foliage for a month or more. Petals are fringed; centers have a central disk. The plants prefer somewhat alkaline soils and cool summers, 85° or less. The cultivar 'Albus' has white petals with small purple spots. Zones 3 to 7.

**D. deltoides** (del-*toy*-deez).
MAIDEN PINK.
A small-flowered perennial with narrow, grasslike leaves in low, heavy mats. Flowers are $^1$/2 in. across, in pink and red, on stems 8 to 10 in. high, in May and June. It often naturalizes and is attractive as an edging plant and in the rock garden. Many hybrid cultivars are offered, including 'Albus', clear white; 'Brilliant', scarlet-red; 'Coccineus', scarlet-red; 'Fanal', scarlet-red; 'Flashing Light', ruby-red; 'Red Maiden', reddish-purple; 'Rosea', shades of pink; 'Samos', crimson-red; 'Vampire', carmine-red; 'Wisley Variety', carmine-red; and 'Zing Rose', deep red, the most frequently offered. Propagate by seeds. Zones 3 to 9.

*Dianthus deltoides*
MAIDEN PINK

*Dianthus gratianopolitanus*
CHEDDAR PINK

## Dianthus

**D. gratianopolitanus**
(grah-tee-ay-noh-pol-it-*tay*-nus).
CHEDDAR PINK.

Sturdy perennial with fragrant, rose-colored, single blossoms on 6-in. stems, above heavy mats of grayish foliage that is practically evergreen. It is useful in rock gardens and rock walls. A few of the modern cultivars are 'Bath's Pink', a soft, fringed pink with 1-in. flowers; 'Flore-plena', with double pink flowers; 'Petite', a 4-in. plant; 'Splendens', with deep red flowers; 'Spotty', a red and white bicolor; and 'Tiny Rubies', a popular double-flowered deep pink.  Propagate by seeds or by terminal cuttings.  Zone 3.

**D. knappii** (*nap*-ee-eye).
HARDY GARDEN PINK.

The leaves are 2 to 3 in. long, $1/4$ in. wide and gray-green. The plants form low mounds of foliage topped by yellow flowers in summer. Flowers form clusters of eight to ten single flowers in each head. Bloom lasts four to six weeks. Plant in full sun in slightly alkaline, well-drained soil. Plants prefer cool summers, otherwise flowers fade. Propagate by seeds. Zone 3.

**D. plumarius** (plew-*may*-ree-us).
COTTAGE PINK.
GRASS PINK.

Hardy perennial, and parent of many hybrids, including the Allwood strain. They differ from *D. gratianopolitanus* by having petals that are more deeply cut and flowers that are in twos rather than solitary. Very fragrant blooms, 1 to 2 in. across and 1 ft. high, rise above grassy mats. Cultivars include 'Agatha', a semidouble, purple-pink with a crimson eye; 'C. T. Musgrave', a single white with a green eye; 'Excelsior', carmine with a darker eye; 'Mrs. Sinkins', an intensely fragrant, double white; and 'White Ladies', a fragrant white.

**Dicentra** (dye-*sen*-truh).
BLEEDING-HEART.
Fumitory Family *(Fumariaceae)*.

Long-lived perennials native to North America and Asia, with fernlike, deeply cut leaves and charming flowers of an unusual heart shape in pendant sprays. The plants are at home in the wild garden or the cultivated border. Partial shade and light, humusy soil are required. Propagate by seeds in late summer, by root division in early spring or by root cuttings in early summer.

**D. cucullaria** (kew-kuh-*lay*-ree-uh).
DUTCHMAN'S-BREECHES.

A native American perennial, low-growing to 6 in., with small, yellow-tipped white flowers in sprays above fernlike foliage in April. The foliage dies down to the ground by midsummer. Useful in the rock, bulb or wild garden. Zone 2.

★**D. eximia** (ex-*im*-ee-uh).
FRINGED BLEEDING-HEART.

One of the most tolerant of variable sun conditions, accepting partial or even full shade, and the species having the longest flowering season—from spring to fall. The flowers are rose-pink. The plants attain 1 to $1^{1}/2$ ft. in height, self-sow readily and are easily transplanted. This is undoubtedly the most useful and adaptable species, though not the most beautiful. A number of named cultivars are available, some with silvery foliage, some with deeper-toned as well as white flowers. Among them are 'Alba', with white flowers and light green foliage; 'Boothman's Variety', a soft pink with blue-green foliage; 'Silver Smith', with white flowers flushed pink; and 'Snowdrift', a pure white.

*Dicentra eximia* 'Alba'
FRINGED BLEEDING-HEART

*Dicentra spectabilis* 'Alba'
COMMON BLEEDING-HEART

**D. spectabilis** (spek-*tab*-i-lis).

COMMON BLEEDING-HEART.

The handsomest species, this is a hardy, long-lived, beautiful perennial from Japan, up to 2 ft. high, with arching sprays of rose-colored, heart-shaped blossoms. Blooms appear from mid-April to late June, then the plant goes dormant in late summer. Indispensable in the spring border and the rock garden. 'Alba' is a white form and 'Pantaloons' a vigorous selection of 'Alba'. Zone 3.

**Dictamnus** (dik-*tam*-nus).

DITTANY.

FRAXINELLA.

GAS PLANT.

Rue Family *(Rutaceae)*.

The only species, from Europe and Asia, is a hardy perennial, long grown in herb and kitchen gardens for its medicinal uses and in perennial borders for its handsome sprays of white or rose-

*Dictamnus albus* 'Purpureus'
GAS PLANT

## Dictamnus

*Digitalis lutea*
STRAW FOXGLOVE

tinted flowers. Its common name, gas plant, derives from the volatile gas of the foliage and flowers, which reportedly flashes in the presence of a lighted match. The plant and seedpods are poisonous, and some people have developed severe dermatitis from this plant. It does not transplant well, so seeds should be sown where plants are wanted. Once established in a favorable location, it will flourish for many years (three generations in one instance). It needs rich soil in partial shade or full sun. It sometimes self-sows.

**D. albus** (*al*-bus).
Grows to 3 ft., with compound, dark green, lemon-scented leaves that need plenty of room to spread. The terminal clusters of white flowers, about 1 in. long, bloom in June and July. The cultivar 'Purpureus' has lovely rose-colored flowers. The foliage tends to dry and turn brown in late summer and may then be cut off.

*Dodecatheon meadia*
COMMON SHOOTING-STAR

*Doronicum caucasicum*
LEOPARD'S-BANE

**Digitalis** (dij-i-*tay*-lis).

FOXGLOVE.

Figwort Family *(Scrophulariaceae).*

More than twenty species from Europe to North Africa, with both biennial and perennial forms. The flowers are borne in tall racemes. The basal leaves occur in rosettes. The plants prefer soils rich in organic matter and a location with partial shade. The name *digitalis* means fingerlike, referring to the flowers, which look like fingers of a glove. A description of the biennial species *D. purpurea* can be found in the *Hearst Garden Guides* volume *Annuals.*

**D. ambigua.** See *D. grandiflora.*

**D. grandiflora** (gran-di-*floh*-ra).

YELLOW FOXGLOVE.

(Syn. *D. ambigua.*) A true perennial from Europe with hairy, toothed, dark green leaves. The flowers are 2 in. long, yellowish on the outside and brown netted on the inside. Propagate from seed. Zone 3.

**D. lutea** (*lew*-tee-uh).

STRAW FOXGLOVE.

Native from southern Europe to North Africa. Creamy-yellow flowers occur on slender racemes in early summer. The 4-in.-wide leaves are a medium green. The plants are truly perennial, persisting for years when sited correctly. The Grecian form is considered superior to the smaller Italian form named *D. lutea* var. *australis* (aw-*stral*-is). Zone 3.

**D. × mertonensis** (mer-toe-*nen*-sis).

STRAWBERRY FOXGLOVE.

A hybrid made by crossing *D. purpurea* (pur-pur-ee-uh) and *D. grandiflora.* The selection made by the John Innes Horticultural Institute in 1925

was a tetraploid that took on the perennial nature of *D. grandiflora.* The leaves are 6 to 8 in. long, and the $2^1/2$-in. rose flowers are bigger than those on either of the parents. Propagate by division of the crown every two years: it can also be started from seed. Zone 3.

**Dodecatheon** (doh-dek-*kayth*-ee-on).

SHOOTING-STAR.

Primrose Family *(Primulaceae).*

Handsome wild flowers, native to North America. They look somewhat like miniature cyclamen and have the same appearance of swift and darting movement. They are not too amenable to garden cultivation, but when woodland conditions, humusy soil and full sun or partial shade can be provided, they are successful and are well worth the trouble of establishing. Effective in the rock garden and the wild garden. Propagate by root division, or by seeds sown as soon as ripe.

**D. meadia** (*mee*-dee-uh).

COMMON SHOOTING-STAR.

This is easily the best of the species seen in cultivation. The long leaves, to 6 in. in heavy basal tufts, form a dark green background for the flowers of dark rose-red, pink (several shades) or white. They have recurved petals, 1 in. long. This interesting and unusual plant reaches a height of 1 to 2 ft. and blooms in May and June. Zone 5.

**Doronicum** (doh-*ron*-i-kum).

LEOPARD'S-BANE.

Composite Family *(Compositae).*

Perennials, native to Europe and Asia, with bright green, heart-shaped, basal leaves and golden-yellow daisy flowers that make a lovely spot of brilliant color in the early spring garden. They are splendid plants to use with spring bulbs.

## Doronicum

Easily grown and long-lived if divided every two or three years, they flourish in full sun or light shade. Propagate by division as soon as flowers cease blooming, or by seeds in the spring.

**D. caucasicum** (kaw-*kas*-i-kum).
CAUCASIAN LEOPARD'S-BANE.
This is the most popular species. It grows $1^1/2$ to 2 ft. high, with golden flowers, 2 in. across, blooming in April and May with tulips. Leaves are kidney-shaped and deeply toothed, and go dormant in summer. It needs a garden loam rich in humus. The cultivar 'Finesse' has semidouble yellow-orange flowers on 18-in. plants; 'Magnificum' has 1- to 2-in. flowers on 2- to $2^1/2$-ft. plants; and 'Spring Beauty' has large double flowers on 12-in. plants. Zone 4.

**Echinacea** (ek-in-*nay*-see-uh).
CONEFLOWER.
Composite Family *(Compositae)*.
(Sometimes listed as *Rudbeckia*.) Tall, sturdy, rather coarse perennials of North America, with large, daisylike flowers with conelike centers. Konrad Moench of Germany named the genus in the late 1700s after the Greek word for hedgehog, *echinos*. The plants grow best in full sun and rich, well-drained soil. Propagate by seeds or by root division at time of planting.

★ **E. purpurea** (pur-pur-*ree*-uh).
PURPLE CONEFLOWER.
PURPLE ECHINACEA.
Growing 3 to 4 ft. high, with purple or pink blooms, 4 to 5 in. across, it makes a bright splash of color in the July and August perennial border. It is long-lasting as a cut flower and also suitable for the wild garden. Popular cultivars in this group are 'Bressingham Hybrids', a seed strain originating from seeds taken off of 'Robert Bloom', with colors ranging from light rose to

red; 'Bright Star', a rose-colored form that performs well in both England and the U.S.; 'Magnus', rose-colored blooms, with petals that do not droop, on 4-ft. plants that come true from seed; 'Robert Bloom', one of the best, with 5- to 8-in. flowers, whose petals do not droop, on 3-ft. plants; 'White Lustre', a warm white with contrasting orange-brown cones; and 'White Star', another white, which comes true from seed. Zones 4 to 5.

**Echinops** (*ek*-i-nops).
GLOBE THISTLE.
Composite Family *(Compositae)*.
Spiny-leaved, prickly-blossomed Old World plants that are a distinctive grayish in tone and fine ornamentals in the border. They bloom from June to August. There is much confusion as to which hybrids and cultivars belong under which species. Most species have bluish flowers. The plants are easily grown, but painful to handle or to weed around, and, like all thistles, will give susceptible persons an unpleasant rash. Most gardeners, however, can handle them safely. Ordinary garden soil, well turned to a spade's depth, and full sun are needed. Propagate by seeds, by root division or by root cuttings.

**E. exaltatus** (ex-al-*tay*-tus).
RUSSIAN GLOBE THISTLE.
From Russia, one of the tallest species, with dark blue flowers. It grows 6 to 7 ft. tall on good garden soils. *E. exaltatus* stems have a white woolly appearance and are unbranched. Zone 3.

**E. humilis** (*hue*-mil-lis).
SIBERIAN GLOBE THISTLE.
From western Asia, this plant is very similar to *E. ritro*. The main difference is the presence of hairs on the upper side of the leaves; it is also less spiny than other species. The flowers form steel-

*Echinacea purpurea*
PURPLE CONEFLOWER

*Echinops ritro*
GLOBE THISTLE

blue balls of tiny florets on 3- to 4-ft. stems. Plant in full sun in well-drained soil. Zone 3.

**E. ritro** (*rye*-troh).
GLOBE THISTLE.
From Europe and western Asia, a perennial to 4 to 5 ft. high, with violet-blue, spherical, thistle-like flowers for six weeks. Leaves are 6 to 8 in. long and have deep, wavy margins. The upper surface is smooth, while the underside is gray-green. Stems branch near the top to display 1- to 2-in. globe-shaped blue flowers. The plants are useful in large groups in borders, in the wild garden or in front of shrubs. The flowers can be dried and used in winter bouquets. 'Taplow Blue' has 2-in. steel-blue flowers and is the cultivar most often offered. 'Veitchii's Blue' is grayer in appearance and has darker steel-blue flowers than the former. Zone 3.

**E. sphaerocephalus** (sfeer-oh-*sef*-a-lus).
GREAT GLOBE THISTLE.
From central Europe and western Asia, a tall, heavily branched perennial, 5 to 8 ft. high. Pale blue, spherical blooms, 2 in. across, make a bold display in the border or the wild garden. The plants are attractive to honeybees. They are especially effective when planted in a border with hollyhocks. Zone 3.

**Epimedium** (ep-i-*mee*-dee-um).
BARRENWORT.
Barberry Family *(Berberidaceae)*.
Choice, low-growing perennials native to temperate Europe and Asia, with both deciduous and evergreen tufted foliage and loose sprays of florets, $1/2$ in. across. Charming, irregular, bicolored flowers—cream and yellow, pink or red, violet or white—appear in spring. Plant in large groups for effectiveness in the border or the wild garden, or as a ground cover under trees. The

plants also make a lovely and graceful addition to the rock garden. The cut flowers last several weeks in water. Plant in partial shade, in moist, peaty loam, well drained yet never completely dried out. Propagate by root division in early spring. Once established, they spread slowly but sturdily.

**E. alpinum** (al-*pye*-num).
Native to Europe. Racemes are displayed above the foliage with twelve to twenty flowers in May. The outer sepals are grayish with red, while the inner sepals are a dark crimson. The petals are yellow. 'Rubrum' is a vigorous cultivar with deeper colors. Leaves are arranged in two groups of three; the leaflets are 2 to 3 in. long. Zone 3.

**E. grandiflorum** (gran-di-*floh*-rum).
BISHOP'S-HAT.
LONG-SPUR EPIMEDIUM.
(Syn. *E. macranthum*.) A dainty plant, 10 to 12 in. high, from Japan. It blooms in May, with outer sepals white, inner ones pale yellow and petals reddish-purple. Spurs are 1/2 in. long, and a dozen or so 1-in. flowers appear on each raceme. 'Rose Queen' has rose-pink flowers and crimson leaves; 'White Queen' is similar to 'Rose Queen' but has white flowers; and 'Violaceum' has dark violet flowers. Zone 5.

**E. macranthum.** See *E. grandiflorum*.

**E. perralderanum** (pe-ral-de-ree-*ah*-num).
Native to Algeria. The red-brown leaflets, in threes, are about 3 in. long. The unbranched inflorescence has twenty to twenty-five yellow flowers. The small brownish spurs are not very noticeable. Zone 5.

**E. pinnatum** (pin-*nay*-tum).
PERSIAN EPIMEDIUM.
Native to northern Iran. Brown-red spurs on yellow flowers in slender sprays (containing twelve to thirty flowers), 1 ft. high, are produced above tufted, red-bronze compound leaves (of five leaflets) in May and June. The foliage arises directly from the roots and turns green as the season progresses; in late autumn, the red-bronze color returns. Beautiful in the spring border, especially in large plantings. The subspecies *colchicum* (*kol*-chi-kum) is shorter than the type, with brighter yellow flowers. Zone 5.

**E. × rubrum** (*rue*-brum).
RED BARRENWORT.
A vigorous hybrid from *E. alpinum* and *E. grandiflorum*. It produces clusters, 1 in. across, of fifteen to twenty flowers. The heart-shaped leaves are tinged with red in spring. One of the most popular garden plants in the genus. Zone 4.

**E. × versicolor** (ver-*sik*-o-lor).
BICOLOR BARRENWORT.
A cross between *E. grandiflorum* and *E. pinnatum* subsp. *colchicum*. When young, the leaves (with nine leaflets) are mottled red. The sepals are rose, the petals yellow and the spur reddish. The cultivar 'Sulphureum' has pale yellow sepals and bright yellow petals. A handsome epimedium that tolerates dry, shady conditions. Zone 5.

**E. × youngianum** (youn-gee-*ah*-num).
YOUNG'S BARRENWORT.
A cross of *E. diphyllum* and *E. grandiflorum*. Leaves arise from the base and are divided into nine leaflets. Flowers are 3/4 in. across and bloom in 3-in. pendulous clusters. 'Niveum' is a very popular garden plant with white flowers, while 'Roseum' has rose or lilac flowers.

*Erigeron speciosus*
OREGON FLEABANE

# Erigeron (ee-*rij*-er-on).

FLEABANE.

Composite Family *(Compositae)*.

A large genus, containing many attractive plants, several of them native to various parts of North America. Some species are weedy in habit and should not be introduced into gardens; they crowd out more desirable but less voracious plants. Plants are easily grown in ordinary well-dug garden soil and full sun. Propagate by seeds or by crown division in spring.

### E. speciosus (spee-see-*oh*-sus).

OREGON FLEABANE.

Native to North America. This is the best species for cultivating in gardens. It resembles a blue aster. It grows to 2 ft., with showy, flat-topped clusters of violet-purple, yellow-centered, daisy-like blooms, 1 1/2 in. across, in June and July. It makes a fine show in the border or the wild gar-

den and is excellent for cutting. Most cultivars listed are hybrids of *E. speciosus, E. speciosus* var. *macranthus* (ma-*kran*-thus), *E. aurantiacus* (aw-ran-tee-*ah*-kus) and *E. glaucus* (*glaw*-kus). 'Azure Beauty' is propagated from seed and shows considerable variation. The species has lavender-blue flowers on 30-in.-tall stems; 'Azure Blue' is similar to the above but has lighter blue flowers; 'Darkest of All' is a popular cultivar with violet-blue flowers; 'Dimity' is a short plant (12 to 15 in.) producing light pink flowers; and 'Forester's Darling' (syn. 'Foester's Leibling') has double pink flowers on 18-in. plants. *E. speciosus* var. *macranthus* is similar to the species but has oval leaves and larger flowers. 'Prosperity', widely available, has a single lavender-blue flower on an 18-in. plant. 'Quakerness' is thought to be a cross of the species and its botanical variety; it has mauve-pink flowers on 18- to 24-in. plants. 'Rose Jewel' has lilac-rose flowers on 30-in. plants, and 'Rose Triumph' bears semidouble rose-pink blossoms on 24-in. plants. Zone 2.

# Eryngium (er-*rin*-jee-um).

SEA HOLLY.

Carrot Family *(Umbelliferae)*.

Native to Europe. Mostly perennial, these plants are handsome and imposing in the border or the rock garden. They have globe-shaped flower heads, usually blue, and are decorative either fresh or dried. The seed heads are also useful for winter arrangements. The plants need full sun and sandy garden soil, well turned to a spade's depth, and plenty of moisture. Propagate by seeds sown in April in a frame of sandy soil, or by cuttings in September or October.

### E. alpinum (al-*pye*-num).

ALPINE SEA HOLLY.

Native to Europe. This species is considered by many to be the handsomest. It grows 2 to 2 1/2 ft.

# Eryngium

*Eryngium alpinum*
ALPINE SEA HOLLY

*Eupatorium purpureum*
JOE PYE WEED

tall, with blue stems and bluish, leathery, spiny leaves. Bright blue blossom heads, 2 in. long, appear in June and July. Occasionally, white-flowered plants are available. Propagate by dividing off plantlets from the mother plant. Zone 4.

**E. amethystinum** (a-me-thist-*eye*-num).
AMETHYST SEA HOLLY.
Native to Europe and one of the most common species grown in the U.S. The basal leaves vary from those of other sea hollies by being pinnately parted. Flower heads are $1/2$ to $3/4$ in. long. The bracts are much longer than the flower heads and are sharply pointed. Propagate by crown division. Zone 4.

**E. planum** (*play*-num).
FLAT-LEAVED SEA HOLLY.
Native to eastern Europe. This species survives better in southern gardens than some of the other species. Flower heads are $1/2$- to $3/4$-in. globes. The basal leaves are heart-shaped, scalloped and not spiny. 'Blue Dwarf' is a 15-in. cultivar. Propagate by crown division. Zone 5.

**E. yuccifolium** (yuk-a-*foh*-lee-um).
RATTLESNAKE-MASTER.
Native to eastern and central U.S. Recent interest in native American plants has brought rattlesnake-master out of the prairie and into home gardens. Leaves are long and strap-shaped, sometimes reaching 3 ft. They are armed with marginal teeth. Several rounded, 1-in., greenish flower heads appear in June. The overall form is rather architectural. Zone 3.

## Eupatorium (yew-pat-*toh*-ree-um).
BONESET.
Composite Family (*Compositae*).
Perennials, mostly tropical and grown under glass. Others, including those described below, are

native to North America and adaptable to outdoor cultivation. These are related and similar in appearance to the annual ageratum, and are sometimes called hardy ageratum. The clusters of blue, purple or white flowers bloom in August and September. All the hardy species need full sun, adequate moisture and ordinary garden soil, well turned to a spade's depth. Propagate by crown division in spring.

### E. coelestinum (see-less-*tye*-num).
MIST FLOWER.

Growing $1^{1}/_{2}$ to 2 ft. tall, it produces compact, flattish clusters of azure-blue flowers, blooming from September to hard frost. It spreads readily and sometimes self-sows. A good combination with fall asters and chrysanthemums in the perennial border, it is also one of the best summer blues and is useful as a cut flower. The cultivar 'Alba' has white flowers. Zone 5.

### E. maculatum (mak-u-*lay*-tum).
This species is very similar to *E. purpureum*, which has purple-specked stems and leaf petioles; a popular cultivar of *E. maculatum*, 'Gateway', has deeper-colored and larger flowers, and can be distinguished based on the number of flowers in the heads. Zone 4.

### E. purpureum (pur-pur-*ee*-um).
JOE PYE WEED.

Native to eastern North America. A familiar wild flower of wet meadows and brooksides, this species grows 5 to 7 ft. tall, with large clusters of fragrant rose pink to purple flowers in August. It is a handsome and imposing plant, though somewhat coarse. Butterflies are attracted to the freshly opened flowers. Sometimes the flowers are used in dried arrangements. 'Atropurpureum' is a cultivar of *E. purpureum* that has deeper-colored flowers and purple stems and petioles. Zone 2.

### E. rugosum (roo-*goh*-sum).
WHITE SNAKEROOT.

Native to eastern North America. It blooms in August and September, producing white showy flowerheads on stems that grow 3 to 4 ft. high. Familiar in wet meadows, it makes a good display in the large border or the wild garden. Some shade is needed. Zone 3.

## Euphorbia (yew-*for*-bee-uh).
SPURGE.

Spurge Family (*Euphorbiaceae*).

A large, widely distributed genus of tremendous variety. There are cactus-like tropical succulents, weeds, popular annuals and perennials, and the striking florist's poinsettia and snow-on-the-mountain. Some of the cactus-like species grow into picturesque specimen plants and may be used for hedges in regions where they are hardy. There are a number of good greenhouse plants. All contain a milky juice, which causes cases of severe dermatitis for some people. Propagate by seeds or by cuttings.

### E. corollata (kor-oh-*lay*-tuh).
FLOWERING SPURGE.

From North America, a hardy perennial, 2 to 3 ft. high. The oblong, linear leaves are 1 to 2 in. long, and filmy clusters of snow-white blooms appear in late summer. It makes a good plant for cutting, for bedding, in the border or in the wild garden. The foliage turns wine-red in fall. Propagate by seeds. Zone 3.

### E. epithymoides (ep-pith-im-*moy*-deez).
CUSHION SPURGE.

(Syn. *E. polychroma*.) Hardy European perennial, about 1 ft. high, that forms attractive, roundish clumps. Showy in the border, it produces bright yellow terminal bracts from April to June. The

## Euphorbia

*Euphorbia epithymoides*
CUSHION SPURGE

*Fragaria frel* 'Pink Panda'
PINK PANDA STRAWBERRY

*Filipendula purpurea*
JAPANESE MEADOWSWEET

oblong leaves are attractive all summer and turn dark red in fall. Propagate by seeds. Zone 4.

**E. polychroma.** See *E. epithymoides*.

## Filipendula (fil-i-*pen*-dew-luh).

MEADOWSWEET.
Rose Family (*Rosaceae*).
(Sometimes incorrectly listed in catalogs as *Spiraea*.) From the Northern Temperate regions, tall perennials with feathery foliage and showy clusters of tiny pink or white flowers. They need full sun or partial shade and ordinary but well-turned garden soil. Propagate by seeds or by crown division in spring or fall.

**F. hexapetala.** See *F. vulgaris*.

**F. palmata** (pahl-*may*-ta).
SIBERIAN MEADOWSWEET.
Native to Siberia. Leaves are made up of one palmately seven- to nine-lobed terminal leaf and three- to five-lobed lateral leaflets. Flowers are 6-in. flattened heads of pale pink in June. They are rather short-lived, lasting only about two weeks. Plants require constantly moist soils. 'Elegans' has white flowers with red stamens, while 'Nana' is only 10 in. tall. Propagate by crown divison in spring. Zone 3.

**F. purpurea** (pur-pur-*ee*-uh).
JAPANESE MEADOWSWEET.
This species grows 2 to 4 ft. high, with brilliant rose-pink flowers in broad, showy sprays in July. It likes some shade, plenty of moisture and a rich soil. Effective in the border and at stream sides, it is very similar to *F. palmata*. Propagate by crown division in early spring. Zone 3.

**F. rubra** (*rue*-bruh).
QUEEN-OF-THE-PRAIRIE.
From the eastern and central U.S., a plant of breathtaking beauty when in full bloom during late June and early July. Its plumes of dark pink florets, 6 to 9 in. across, are borne on sturdy stems 6 to 8 ft. high, above decorative foliage. It makes a memorable combination with blue delphiniums. 'Venusta' has bright deep-pink to carmine flowers. Zone 3.

**F. ulmaria** (ul-*mah*-ree-uh).
QUEEN-OF-THE-MEADOW.
From Asia and Europe. A 3- to 5-ft. plant more useful in smaller gardens than are the taller species. Leaves are hairy and whitish beneath. Flowers in 4- to 6-in. creamy-white panicles. 'Aurea' is grown for its golden-yellow foliage. 'Flore-plena' is a double that stays in bloom longer than the single forms. Divide plant crowns in spring. Zone 3.

**F. vulgaris** (vul-*gay*-ris).
DROPWORT.
(Syn. *F. hexapetala*.) Native to Europe and Asia. This ferny-leaved plant grows to 2 to 3 ft. high, with tiny whitish flowers in loose, graceful clusters. It blooms in June and early July. Useful in the border and the wild garden, it likes a fairly dry location; otherwise the flower stalks tip over. 'Flore-plena' is a double-flowered form, 18 in. tall and more ornamental than the species. Propagate by crown division. Zone 3.

# Fragaria (frag-*gay*-ree-uh).
STRAWBERRY.
Rose Family (*Rosaceae*).
Native to Northern Temperate regions and high elevations of Western Hemisphere tropics. Several varieties of strawberries make excellent ornamental plants for flower borders. *F. virginiana* (vir-jin-ee-*ay*-nuh) is a low grower that looks good in rock gardens and needs sandy loam. Some West Coast gardeners use the native American wild strawberry, *F. chiloensis*, as ground cover. Plants thrive on slightly acid soils where the soils are well drained and moist. Most prefer full sun but can withstand partial shade some of the day.

**F. frel** (*fral*).
PINK PANDA STRAWBERRY.
A hybrid made by English plant-breeder Dr. Jack Ellis. The original cross of *Potentilla palustris* and *Fragaria grandiflora* was made in 1966. Later, by backcrossing (crossing the hybrid with one of its parents), Dr. Ellis was able to develop pink- and red-flowered seedlings. 'Pink Panda' was selected as the name for one of them to honor the symbol of the World Wildlife Fund (the black-and-white panda); a small donation for each plant sold is made to that organization. 'Pink Panda' is patented and trademarked. It grows 8 to 12 in. tall and has bright green, strawberry-like leaves.

## Fragaria

Pink flowers are produced in the spring and intermittently throughout the growing season. It also produces a few small red strawberry fruits. Propagates easily by runners. Zone 5.

**F. vesca** (*ves*-kuh).
EUROPEAN STRAWBERRY.
FRAISES DES BOIS.
The botanical variety *americana* (a-mer-i-*kay*-nuh) is the American form of this species, which originated in the Alps. It grows 8 in. tall and bears white flowers, followed by bright red fruit. A natural everbearer, it matures some fruit throughout the season from June through fall, and is often used to edge borders. The cultivar 'Albomarginata' has green leaves edged with creamy-white.

## Gaillardia (gay-*lar*-dee-uh).

Composite Family (*Compositae*).
Annuals and perennials, native to North America. Showy, variously colored flowers are produced on sturdy plants with rough, 3- to 6-in. alternate leaves. The florets of the blossoms are indented and are yellow, orange, brownish red or white, with purple centers. They are excellent as cut flowers, and the annuals make good cool-greenhouse plants, flowering in late winter and spring. Light, porous, not too rich, well-drained soil and full sun are required. A good choice for sunny, dry locations, they will bloom all summer if faded flowers are kept picked. Propagate by seeds.

**G. aristata** (a-ris-*tay*-tuh).
BLANKET FLOWER.
A hardy and popular perennial, taller than the annuals, 2 to 3 ft. high. Plants produce long, hairy, graceful leaves and large, brilliantly colored yellow flowers, 3 to 4 in. across. Those raised from seed are variable and often do not flower the first year. Whereas most of the introduced

hybrids live only one or two years, the species is long-lived. Propagate by softwood stem cuttings, by crown division or by seeds. Zone 3.

**G. × grandiflora** (gran-di-*floh*-ruh).
BLANKET FLOWER.
This 2- to 3-ft. species is a cross between *G. aristata*, a perennial, and *G. pulchella*, an annual. From the annual it gained a long flowering period (June-September). Unfortunately, it also lost longevity; it may last only two years unless divided annually. Root-prune every summer with a spade, and in the spring dig up the new plants that arise from the severed roots. The gray-green leaves are 6 in. long and alternate with coarse teeth. At 3 ft. tall, the clumps spread to 2 ft. wide. It is multibranched and can be sprawling unless it is tied up. The daisy-like flowers are 3 to 4 in. across and come in solid colors or multicolors. The center can be yellow, brown or purple, and the petals are solid yellow, red or orange, or a combination with yellow tips and red or maroon toward the center. The flowers are produced abundantly. Plant in full sun in average well-drained soil. Over-fertilization can give the plant too open a habit and make it sprawl. Pick off the dying flowers to promote more blooms. 'Baby Cole' is a dwarf, 6- to 8-in. plant with 2- to 3-in.-diameter yellow, maroon-backed ray flowers; 'Burgundy' has rich wine-red flowers and can be propagated from seed; 'Dazzler' has crimson-red tips and yellow centers, and is propagated from seed; 'Goblin' is a 9- to 12-in. cultivar with 4-in. flowers that have red petals with yellow edges; and 'Monarch Strain' is a seed-propagated color mix. Zone 2.

## Gaura (*gaw*-ra).

Evening Primrose Family (*Onagraceae*).
Native to North America. There are eight species in this genus, most of which are best suited to the warmer areas of the country.

*Gaillardia aristata*
BLANKET FLOWER

*Gaura lindheimeri*
WHITE GAURA

**G. lindheimeri** (lind-*hay*-mer-eye).
WHITE GAURA.
Native to Texas and Louisiana. The 1-in. white flowers, tinged pink, open on a loose panicle. The overall effect is airy and delicate. Plants bloom from July until frosts in the late fall. Pruning back to 8 in. in midsummer encourages a bushier plant with more prolific flowering. Leaves are willowlike, 1 to 3 in. long, alternate and sessile. The thick, deep roots make the plant drought-tolerant. Plant in full sun. Pull mulch away from the roots in winter to discourage voles from feeding on them. Propagate by seeds, or by crown division when the plant is two to three years old. Zone 5.

**Geranium** (jer-*ray*-nee-um).
CRANESBILL.
Geranium Family (*Geraniaceae*).
From temperate regions and low level mountainous tropics, hardy perennials and biennials with roundish, deeply lobed leaves and small but airily effective flowers. This genus should not be confused with *Pelargonium*, which includes the houseplants and window-box plants commonly called geraniums. The true geraniums are easily grown in partial shade and ordinary garden soil, well turned to a spade's depth. The species below are representative of a number the geranium fancier may wish to seek out. Propagate by seeds sown in spring (many available only abroad) or by root division, which is very easy.

## Geranium

Geranium clarkei 'Kashmir White'
CLARK'S GERANIUM

Geranium × 'Johnson's Blue'
MEADOW CRANESBILL

Geranium psilostemon
ARMENIAN GERANIUM

Geranium endressii
ENDRESS' GERANIUM

**G. cinereum** (si-*ner*-ee-um).
GRAY-LEAVED CRANESBILL.
Native to the Pyrenees. This is a low-growing species, 6 in. high, which makes it good for rock gardens or the front of the border. The leaves are deeply lobed into five to seven parts. In early summer the pink to purplish-pink flowers appear; these are 1 in. across with dark veins. Plant in full sun to partial shade in well-drained,

moist soil. 'Album' is a cultivar with white flowers; 'Ballerina' is a hybrid which has 2-in. lilac-pink flowers, with darker centers and purple veining, borne on 4- to 6-in. plants; and 'Splendens' has deep red flowers with dark centers on 5- to 6-in. plants. Zones 5 to 8.

**G. clarkei** (*klar*-key-eye).

CLARK'S GERANIUM.

Native to Nepal. Plants are low-growing with deeply cut leaves. The basal leaves are divided into seven divisions, each deeply, pinnately lobed. The flowers are $1/2$ to $3/4$ in. in diameter and face upward. Propagate by division. 'Kashmir Purple' has deep blue flowers that come true to seed. 'Kashmir White' has white flowers with purplish veins; some of the seed-raised plants from this cultivar are purple. Zones 5 to 8.

**G. dalmaticum** (dal-*ma*-ti-kum).

DALMATION CRANESBILL.

Native to Balkan Peninsula. This is a low-growing species, 4 to 6 in. high, with trailing stems. It spreads by rhizomes but is not invasive. The 2-in. leaves are deeply lobed. In late spring light pink, 1-in. flowers appear, 3 to a stem. The foliage turns red-orange in fall. Plant in full sun in moist, well-drained soil. 'Album', a white-flowered cultivar, is not as hardy as the species. Zone 4.

**G. endressii** (en-*dress*-ee-eye).

ENDRESS' GERANIUM.

Native to the Pyrenees. This species grows to 18 in. tall with leaves to 5 in. across. The leaves are deeply lobed into five parts, each of which is lobed into three parts. The 1-in. rose-pink flowers open above the shiny green leaves from early summer to fall. A good ground cover, it will survive in full sun (in the North) to partial shade. It prefers cool locations and is not particular as to soil. 'Wargrave Pink', a cultivar more popular than the species, is a vigorous

plant with salmon-pink flowers. The flower petals are more notched than the species. Zones 4 to 8.

**G. himalayense** (him-ay-*lay*-ense).

From northern Asia, a lovely perennial, 1 to $2^{1}/2$ ft. high, with deeply lobed leaves, cut into seven divisions. Flowers are violet, $1^{1}/2$ in. across, with purple lines, blooming in May and June. 'Birch Double' (syn. 'Plena') has $1/2$-in. double lavender flowers that persist longer than those of the species; 'Gravetye' has 2-in.-wide bright blue flowers with reddish centers and dark veins; and 'Johnson's Blue' is a hybrid between *G. himalayense* and *G. pratense*. It grows to 18 in. tall and has $1^{1}/2$- to 2-in.-diameter clear blue flowers that are in bloom for a long time. Zones 4 to 8.

**G. ibericum** (eye-*beer*-ih-kum).

A clump-forming plant, to 2 ft. tall, that produces sprays of violet-blue flowers in summer. The foliage is heart-shaped, lobed and hairy. Its hybrid, *G. × magnificum*, has deep blue flowers with deeper blue veins. Zones 5 to 8.

**G. macrorrhizum** (mak-ro-*rise*-um).

BIGROOT GERANIUM.

Native to southern Europe. This plant makes a good ground cover because it competes with shrubs and trees for moisture and shade, and crowds out weeds. Takes full sun where summers are cool enough and partial shade where they are not. The palmately lobed leaves are 6 to 8 in. across, nearly evergreen, aromatic when crushed. Flowers appear in late spring above the foliage on slightly hairy, 8- to 12-in.-long stems. They are 1 in. in diameter and magenta in color. Propagate by division: the roots are easily divided. This is an aggressive but not invasive plant. It prefers a dry soil. 'Album' has flowers with white petals and pink calyxes, while 'Ingwersen's Variety' has pale pink flowers and glossy leaves. Zones 3 to 8.

# Geranium

**G. maculatum** (mak-yew-*lay*-tum).
WILD GERANIUM.
Native to North America. This charming and delicate wild flower may be found along roadsides and on the edge of woodlands. It grows 1 1/2 ft. high, with strongly veined leaves and lavender flowers, which bloom in late April and May. It needs more moisture than do some of the other species. The plants are useful in the wild garden or the rock garden. The foliage takes on scarlet tones in fall. Zone 3.

**G. pratense** (*pray*-tense).
MEADOW CRANESBILL.
Native to northern Europe. One of the taller species of this genus, it can grow from 2 to 3 ft. high and sometimes needs support. The leaves are 3 to 6 in. wide and deeply lobed into seven to nine parts. Blue flowers in late spring, 1 1/2 in. across, do not last very long. Plant in moist, well-drained soil in full sun and provide plenty of water. 'Mrs. Kendall Clarke' has pale blue flowers with rosy-pink veination. Three double forms also exist: 'Plenum Alba', 'Plenum Caeruleum' and 'Plenum Violaceum'. All have 1-in. flowers that persist a little longer than those of the single forms of the species. Zone 5.

**G. psilostemon** (sil-*oh*-ste-mon).
ARMENIAN GERANIUM.
Native to Armenia. A stately plant at 4 ft. tall, this species does need some support. The 6- to 8-in. leaves are palmately lobed into 5 to 7 parts and are evergreen. The 1 1/2- to 2-in. red flowers open in midsummer. There is an interesting black spot at the center of each flower. Plant in partial shade in deep, rich, moist soil. The hybrid 'Ann Folkard' (*G. procurens* × *G. psilostemon*) has magenta flowers with black centers on 18-in. plants. Zone 5.

★**G. sanguineum** (san-*gwin*-ee-um).
BLOOD-RED GERANIUM.
From Europe and Asia, a perennial with branching stems, 1 1/2 to 2 ft. high. The crimson flowers, 1 in. across, above gray-white, deeply cut leaves, bloom from mid-May to mid-July. The most popular plant sold under this species is sometimes labeled 'Lancastriense' or 'Prostratum', but is now properly designated as *G. sanguineum* var. *striatum* (stry-*ay*-tum). It produces light pink flowers over a long period of time on 8- to 10-in. plants. Other cultivars include 'Album', with cream-white flowers; 'Alpenglow', with rose-red flowers; 'Glenluce', with large, 1 1/2- to 2-in., deep rose flowers; and 'Shepherd's Warning', only 4 to 6 in. tall with rose-purple flowers. All are good in the border, rock garden or wild garden. Zone 3.

## Geum (*jee*-um).
AVENS.
Rose Family (*Rosaceae*).
A sizable genus of brilliantly colored and generally adaptable border perennials from temperate and cold regions. The best garden forms are described below. They are easily grown in full sun and ordinary garden soil, well turned to a spade's depth. Propagate by seeds or by division in late summer, the latter preferable for perpetuating the best cultivars.

**G. quellyon** (*kwell*-ee-on).
CHILEAN AVENS.
From Chile, a hardy perennial growing 1 to 2 ft. high, with hairy leaves and brilliant, orange-red flowers, 1 1/2 in. across, in clusters. It makes a fine display in the border for six to eight weeks from late May on. Many of the cultivars in commerce are hybrid crosses of *G. quellyon* and *G. coccineum* (kok-*sin*-ee-um), a species with brick-red flowers. The attractive basal leaves are useful at

the front of the border after the plants have flowered. 'Fire Opal' has intense red, semidouble flowers; 'Lady Stratheden' is a popular plant with yellow semidouble flowers; 'Mrs. Bradshaw' is another popular American cultivar, a scarlet with semidouble flowers; 'Princess Juliana' bears light yellow, semidouble flowers; and 'Red Wings' has orange-red semidouble flowers. Propagate by seeds or by crown division. Zone 5.

**G. rivale** (ree-*vah*-lee).
INDIAN CHOCOLATE.
WATER AVENS.
Native to Eurasia and North America. This species has nodding, bell-shaped, reddish-purple flowers. The foliage consists of three to six pairs of leaflets, with the terminal leaflet twice as large as the laterals. The leaflets are quite hairy and serrated. It prefers moist, boglike soils. Apparently, if the rootstock is boiled it produces a liquid that tastes like chocolate. 'Leonard's Variety' has bell-shaped flowers in coppery, creamy-pink flushed with orange; the flowers hang from attractive reddish stalks. 'Lionel Cox' is somewhat similar but has light yellow blossoms held in brown calyxes. Propagate by crown division. Zone 3.

**Gillenia.** See *Porteranthus*.

**Gypsophila** (jip-*sof*-i-luh).
Pink Family (*Caryophyllaceae*).
Showy, well-branched, tiny-flowered annuals and perennials, mostly from Europe and Asia. Hardy and easily grown, they are invaluable as fillers in the hardy border and for cut flowers. Distinctive for their feathery, light profusion of pink or white florets, they are graceful indoors or out. They rebloom intermittently through the summer. Leaves are small, blue-green and opposite. Plants grow best in full sun and well-drained, slightly sandy loam with added lime, well dug to a spade's

depth. Plant where they are to stand, as they do not transplant easily. For best effect, grow in fairly thick groups. Sow seeds in late fall in warm sections, otherwise in early spring, as soon as the soil can be worked. Hybrids and named varieties are best bought in small sizes. Propagate by seeds or by root sections.

*Geranium sanguineum*
BLOOD-RED GERANIUM

*Geum rivale* 'Leonard's Variety'
WATER AVENS

## Gypsophila

**G. paniculata** (pan-ik-yew-*lay*-tuh).

BABY'S BREATH.

Native to Europe and northern Asia, this is the most familiar species. These tall perennials, to 3 ft., are graceful and feathery in habit. The tiny flowers bloom all summer but are most profuse when the days are longest. There are many cultivars available. 'Bristol Fairy' is the most frequently grown; it has double white flowers on 2-ft. plants, but it is not always easy to overwinter. 'Compacta Plena' grows to 18 in. and is not as double as 'Bristol Fairy'; 'Flamingo' is a vigorous 3- to 4-ft. plant with double pink blossoms; 'Perfecta' is another robust plant with double white flowers; 'Pink Fairy' is a pink cultivar much like 'Bristol Fairy' in form but slightly shorter; 'Pink Star' has large, pink double flowers on 1- to 2-ft. stems; 'Snowflake', a form that does better in hotter climates, has double white flowers on 3-ft. plants; and 'Rosy Veil' is a semidouble, soft pale pink, 15-in. plant. Zone 3.

**G. repens** (*ree*-penz).

CREEPING BABY'S BREATH.

This is a perennial of creeping habit with white flowers, blooming from July to September. It is useful in the rock garden or the border and is more tolerant of acid soils than are other species. 'Alba' has clear white flowers. 'Bodgeri', thought to be a hybrid of *G. repens* 'Rosea' and *G. paniculata*, is a 15-in. plant with double pink flowers. 'Rosea' is a 15-in. cultivar with pink flowers. Zone 3.

## Helenium (hel-*lee*-nee-um).

SNEEZEWEED.

Composite Family (*Compositae*).

Large, sturdy, often coarse annuals and perennials, native to North America, useful for the back of large borders, for naturalizing in the wild garden and for cutting. The small yellow, brown or red flowers in loose clusters bloom in August and

September. Almost all species are of very easy culture and need full sun, a moist location and almost any ordinary garden soil, well dug to a spade's depth. Propagate perennial species by crown division in the spring; they will also grow easily from seed, as do the annuals. Some of the outstanding new cultivars are being produced in Germany.

**H. autumnale** (aw-tum-*nay*-lee).

COMMON SNEEZEWEED.

This eastern North American native has yellow blooms in August and September on sturdy, well-branched plants that are effective when used in groups in large borders. These perennials grow 4 to 5 ft. tall and should stand at least 1½ ft. apart in the border. They will grow rampantly almost anywhere except in extreme heat. Frequent dividing encourages sturdier plants with larger flowers. There are many cultivars, some of them hybrids beween *H. autumnale*, *H. bigelovii* (big-e-*loh*-vee-eye) and *H. hoopesii* (hoo-*pes*-ee-eye). Among them are 'Brilliant', with bronze flowers; 'Bruno', with bronze-red flowers on 3- to 4-ft. plants; 'Butterpat', a good yellow form, 3 to 4 ft. tall; 'Gartensonne', having primrose-yellow flowers with reddish-brown centers on 6-ft. plants; 'Moerheim Beauty', with brownish-red petals around a black center; 'Pumilum Magnificum', which is softer than 'Butterpat', growing to 5 ft.; 'Riverton Beauty', producing golden-yellow ray flowers with bronze centers on 3½- to 4-ft. plants; 'Rubrum', with 2- to 3-in.-wide mahogany flowers on 6-ft. plants; 'The Bishop', one of the shortest, growing 2 to 2½ ft., with yellow flowers; 'Waldhorn', with deep brick-red flowers on 3-ft. plants; 'Wyndley', with 2- to 3-in. coppery-brown flowers on short, 2- to 3-ft. plants; and 'Zimbelstern', whose flowers are yellow brushed with bronze on plants 3 to 4 ft. tall. Zone 3.

**Helianthemum** (hee-lee-*an*-thee-mum).

SUNROSE.

Rock Rose Family (*Cistaceae*).

Hardy European, Asian and African slender-stemmed shrubs of low, spreading, evergreen habit. They are ideal for the dry, sunny, sheltered rock-garden or planted wall. Several stems radiate from the central rootstock, and these bear narrow leaves, 1 to 2 in. long, in pairs. The flowers are

*Helenium autumnale* 'Moerheim Beauty'
COMMON SNEEZEWEED

*Gypsophila paniculata* 'Rosy Veil'
BABY'S BREATH

*Gypsophila repens* 'Rosea'
CREEPING BABY'S BREATH

*Helianthemum nummularium* 'Firedragon'
COMMON SUNROSE

# Helianthemum

borne in terminal racemes in spring and summer. These plants thrive in a moderately rich, somewhat alkaline soil, which may be dry at the surface but should be deep enough to hold the moisture found between and under rocks. Propagate by greenwood cuttings or by seeds.

### H. nummularium (num-mew-*lay*-ree-um).
COMMON SUNROSE.

A low shrub, forming a dense mass of slender stems that spread for 1 ft. or more and reach a height of 8 to 12 in. The clear yellow, single flowers are about 1 in. across. There are several cultivars, some hybrids of *H. apenninum* (a-pen-*nye*-num) and *H. croceum* (kroh-*see*-um). A few examples are 'Ben Nevis', with tawny-gold flowers over green foliage; 'Buttercup', 6 to 10 in. tall, with clear yellow flowers; 'Firedragon', with coppery-red flowers contrasted with gray-green foliage; 'St. Mary's', with large white flowers over green leaves; 'Wisley Pink', a lovely pink-flowered plant with gray-green leaves; and 'Wisley Primrose', a light yellow form with gray-green leaves. Zone 5.

## Helianthus (hee-lee-*an*-thus).
SUNFLOWER.

Composite Family (*Compositae*).

A large, widespread genus, consisting of coarse perennials and annuals, with many species, varying greatly in size and habit of growth. All have alternate leaves and, except for a few cultivars, yellow flowers with center disks of brown, gold or a dark purple. Cheerful and familiar flowers, they are sturdy and attractive to seed-eating birds. They thrive in full sun or light shade and in poor soil; at least some of the species grow well in drought areas. All should have soil well turned to a spade's depth.

### H. angustifolius (an-gus-tif-*foh*-lee-us).
SWAMP SUNFLOWER.

Perennial, found in bogs and swamps of North America. The slender stems, covered with stiff hairs, rise 7 ft. Plants produce narrow, linear leaves to 7 in. long and yellow flower heads, to 3 in. across, with purple centers. Blooming from August to October, this species may be effectively grown in border, bog garden or wild garden, as long as there is plenty of moisture. Propagate by division, cuttings or seeds. Zone 6.

### H. × multiflorus (mul-ti-*floh*-rus).
MANY-FLOWERED SUNFLOWER.

A hybrid resulting from crossing the annual sunflower, *H. annus* (*ay*-nus), with the thin-leaf sunflower, *H. decapetalus* (dee-kap-e-*tay*-lus). The offspring are plants with hairy, coarse leaves up to 10 in. long and 4 to 6 in. wide. Plants are usually 4 to 5 ft. tall. Flowers are single or double, in yellows and orange shades. Cultivars bloom for four to six weeks or longer. A few available are 'Capenoch Star', with single lemon-yellow flowers; 'Flore-plena', with fully double yellow flowers much like dahlias on 5-ft. plants; 'Loddon Gold', with 5- to 6-in.-wide, double, bright yellow flowers on $4^{1}/_{2}$- to 6-ft. plants; and 'Morning Sun', with single yellow flowers contrasted against brown centers on 5-ft. plants. Zone 4.

### H. salicifolius (sal-i-sif-*foh*-lee-us).
WILLOW-LEAVED SUNFLOWER.

This native of the southern Plains States is a late-blooming perennial, to 10 ft. tall. It has slender, willowlike leaves, which make it graceful and attractive in a large border or in the wild garden. The yellow flowers, about 2 in. across, with dark purplish-brown centers, bloom late in the season. Zone 3.

*Helianthus × multiflorus* 'Loddon Gold'
MANY-FLOWERED SUNFLOWER

*Heliopsis helianthoides* subsp. *scabra*
SUNFLOWER HELIOPSIS

## Heliopsis (hee-lee-*op*-sis).

Composite Family (*Compositae*).

Hardy, summer-blooming perennials, quite similar in appearance to sunflowers and native to North America. Plants produce opposite, coarsely toothed leaves and showy yellow flowers. Easily grown in full sun, they are useful in informal borders or the wild garden. Rich soil is best, but not necessary. Propagate by seeds or by root division.

**H. helianthoides** (hee-lee-an-*thoy*-deez).
SUNFLOWER HELIOPSIS.

Smooth-stemmed plant, 3 to 5 ft. high, with dark green, lance-shaped leaves, to 5 in. long, and numerous yellow flower heads, to 2 in. across. Generally, this species is too tall and weedy to be an important garden plant. Its subspecies, *scabra* (*skay*-bruh), is more popular and includes several garden cultivars: 'Golden Plume',

a double-flowered, 3- to 3½-ft. tall plant; 'Golden Greenheart', having double yellow flowers with somewhat green centers; 'Incomparabilis', with 3-in.-wide, semidouble orange flowers; 'Karat', with bright yellow flowers on 3-ft. plants; and 'Summer Sun', which produces 4-in. bright yellow flowers on a 2- to 3-ft. plants. The latter is one of the best cultivars for the southern U.S. Divide every two to three years. Zone 3.

## Helleborus (hel-le-*boh*-rus).

HELLEBORE.

Buttercup Family (*Ranunculaceae*).

Perennials, native to Europe and Asia, with dark green, deeply divided leaves and pretty, single flowers on sturdy stems. The most popular species for use in North America are described below. Their most notable characteristic is late fall, winter or early spring flowering. The blos-

# Helleborus

*Helleborus foetidus*
BEAR'S-FOOT HELLEBORE

*Helleborus orientalis*
LENTEN ROSE

*Helleborus niger*
CHRISTMAS ROSE

soms are long-lasting when cut. Propagate by seeds or by division.

**H. argutifolius** (ar-gew-ti-*foh*-lee-us).
CORSICAN HELLEBORE.
(Syn. *H. corsicus* and *H. lividus* subsp. *corsicus*.). From Corsica and Sardinia. A stemmed species that bears green flowers, its greatest attribute is the gray-green, three-part leaflets that are ornamental much of the year. This species is one of the parents of *H. × sternii* (*ster*-nee-eye), which has beautiful mottled leaves. (Only a very few collectors seem to have these new hybrids.) Propagation of *H. argutifolius* is mainly by seeds, but plants can be divided in spring or fall. Zone 6.

**H. corsicus.** See *H. argutifolius*.

**H. foetidus** (*feh*-ti-dus).

BEAR'S-FOOT HELLEBORE.

Native to western and southern Europe. The foliage on this species is evergreen. Each leaf is deeply lobed into seven to nine narrow segments. The basal mass of dark green foliage gives rise to light green, 18- to 24-in. flower stems, which in turn open up in February to nodding, pale green, bell-shaped flowers, sometimes with a purple rim. The specific name comes from the term "fetid," which implies bad-smelling, and the flowers are indeed somewhat malodorous. After the flower stalks die, cut them back. At this time, the new basal leaves are established and will cover the dead stumps. Plant in partial shade in well-drained soil. It will tolerate dry soils but prefers rich, moist soil with plenty of organic matter. Zone 5.

**H. lividus** subsp. **corsicus.** See *H. argutifolius.*

**H. niger** (*nye*-jer).

CHRISTMAS ROSE.

From Europe and western Asia, this species grows 6 to 12 in. high, with white, pink-flushed flowers, 2 to 3 in. across, above the large, handsome, evergreen leaves. It is greatly sought after because its season of bloom—from November to March—makes it an important outdoor blossom for the winter garden in cool zones.

It needs winter protection from Zone 5 northward, preferably with a glass-topped frame that is removed on warm, sunny days. It dislikes being moved and often takes two to three years after planting to come to bloom. For best results, provide plenty of moisture, being careful, however, that the roots are not soggy, though they must not dry out. Porous soil, rich in leafmold and lime, plenty of shade in hot summer months and sun in winter complete its needs. Mulch with rotted manure in April. Admittedly, this is a

fussy plant, but once established in a location it likes, it will thrive for years and reward the gardener with long-lasting cut flowers through the winter months. Propagate by seeds or by division.

Division requires a special method—do not lift the entire plant, but cut away from the established plant a piece of crown and the attached roots, thus disturbing the parent plant as little as possible.

There are several botanical varieties, subspecies and cultivars of Christmas rose. The variety *altiflorus* (al-ti-*floh*-rus) has 3- to 4-in. flowers with red spots, while the foliage is larger and more toothed; the subspecies *macranthus* (ma-*kran*-thus) has flowers tinged with rose, and leaves that are small and spiny; 'Potter's Wheel' is a cultivar with large, white, rounded flowers with a green eye and can be propagated only vegetatively. Zone 3.

**H. orientalis** (or-ee-en-*tay*-lis).

LENTEN ROSE.

Quite similar to *H. niger* in appearance and culture, except that the flowers range from white, pink, maroon or purple fading to green, and several appear together on a branched, leafless stem. This species blooms from March to May. Sturdier and more colorful than the more familiar Christmas rose, this plant deserves a place in the garden. There are many fine varieties and hybrids. *H. atrorubens* (at-row-*rue*-benz) is a closely related species with rich plum-purple flowers. Propagation is by seeds or by division in spring or fall. Zone 4.

★★**Hemerocallis** (hem-er-oh-*kal*-lis).

DAYLILY.

Lily Family (*Liliaceae*).

Mostly hardy, mostly herbaceous perennials, native from central Europe to China and Japan. Some have tuberous roots. Several of the first

# Hemerocallis

*Hemerocallis* 'Janice Brown'
DAYLILY

*Hemerocallis* 'Siloam Bertie Ferris'
DAYLILY

*Hemerocallis fulva* 'Kwanso Variegata'
DAYLILY

hybridized cultivars spread by underground runners; most of the newer cultivars remain in tight clumps. While these do best in a deeply dug, well-fertilized, sunny bed or border, they tolerate a wide range of conditions—poor or dry soil, boggy soil, high shade or northern exposure. With their high tolerance, daylilies are among the gardener's most useful perennials. Species daylilies are experiencing something of a renaissance, but it is the continued introduction and improvement of the newer cultivars that has made this genus so popular. See the related essay on pages 20-21.

The plant produces a fountain of roughly 1-in.-wide, strap-shaped foliage. Flowers are borne one, two or a few at a time on a tall, naked scape over a three- to six-week period. Basically, the blossoms resemble a trumpet lily, but the petals and sepals may be very broad, even completely overlapping, or they may be ribbonlike (these are the so-called "spider-flowering" kinds) and reflexed.

**H. altissima** (al-*tis*-i-muh).
PURPLE MOUNTAIN DAYLILY.
Native to China. The specific name implies a tall plant; in good soils *H. altissima* reaches 7 ft. in height. The flowers are light yellow, fragrant and night-blooming. Many plants sold under this name, however, are diurnal (flowering by day and closing at night) and not true to the species type. 'Autumn Minaret' is a tall, diurnal-flowering hybrid made by crossing *H. altissima* and *H. fulva* (*ful*-vuh). Zones 4 to 9.

**H. × aurantiaca** (aw-ran-ti-*ay*-kuh).
ORANGE DAYLILY.
Native to China and Japan. The flowers are a burnt orange and borne on 3-ft. scapes in midsummer. It is a coarse plant with evergreen foliage. The plant representing this species is believed to be a hybrid and probably a single clone. The heirloom cultivars 'Miranda' and 'Sir Michael Foster' share a common ancestor in *H. × aurantiaca*, which was crossed with *H. citrina* and *H. lilio-asphodelus*, respectively. Zones 7 to 10.

**H. citrina** (si-*try*-nuh).
CITRON DAYLILY.
A true spider (the flower features ribbonlike petals in which the length is five times the petal width) that is pale yellow, highly fragrant and nocturnal. The foliage is a deep blue-green and each leaf bends near the top. A wonderful plant for the evening garden, its flowers open at about 6:00 P.M. and close as the sun rises the next morning. The parent of many of today's spiders. Zones 4 to 9.

**H. coreana** (kor-ee-*ay*-nuh).
KOREAN DAYLILY.
Vigorous plants growing from 15 in. to 3 ft. tall. Flowers range from pale gold to deep orange. Some are spiderlike, while others have somewhat wide petals. The foliage usually goes dormant in late fall. Primary bloom season is late July and August. This species has recently become more available because of plant-collecting trips to Korea by the U.S. National Arboretum. Zones 4 to 9.

**H. dumortieri** (dew-mor-tee-*air*-ee).
EARLY DAYLILY.
From Japan, this species is distinguished from other daylilies by its unbranched scapes with two to four brown-backed buds in pairs. The flower color is a rather strong orange. Clumps produce many scapes, which bend outward, producing a skirt of flowers on the outside of the leaves in May. Zones 4 to 9.

**H. flava.** See *H. lilio-asphodelus*.

## Hemerocallis

*Hemerocallis lilio-asphodelus*
LEMON DAYLILY

*Hemerocallis multiflora* 'Golden Chimes'
MANY-FLOWERED DAYLILY

**H. fulva** (*ful*-va).
TAWNY DAYLILY.
Native to Japan. This is one of the most frequently seen plants in the United States. It is a robust grower that spreads by rhizomatous underground shoots. It is a triploid, meaning it has 33 chromosomes rather than the normal 22, and does not set seeds. Its flowers are borne in early summer and are a rusty orange. Plants grow 4 ft. tall and form a "colony" of several feet after a few years. Because of its rhizomatous nature it is useful for holding soils on highway embankments. Most of the plants appear to be one cultivar, 'Europa'. There is also a triploid double form, 'Kwanso', which masquerades under several different cultivar names, including 'Florepleno', 'Green Kwanso' and 'Variegated Kwanso'. The variegated form reverts to the green form easily unless the green shoots are judiciously rogued. Propagate by division. Zone 3 to 9.

**H. lilio-asphodelus** (lil-ee-o-as-foh-*del*-us).
LEMON DAYLILY.
(Formerly *H. flava*.) Native to east Asia and one of the most useful landscape species of this genus, the lemon daylily grows to 3 ft. tall, producing lemon-yellow, fragrant blossoms in late spring. A large clump scents the air for several feet. The flowers are diurnal (opening by day and closing at night) and often last two or more days during cool weather. New plants should not be started from seed, as this usually produces weak and inferior specimens. Plants can be easily propagated from the underground rhizomes. Zones 3 to 9.

**H. minor** (*my*-nor).
DWARF DAYLILY.
Native to eastern Siberia. Foliage is grasslike on plants seldom more than 15 in. tall. Scapes produce only two to three flowers at their tips. The yellow or gold flowers have extended bloom

periods—they start opening between 3:00 and 10:00 P.M. one day, are fully open from 10:00 A.M. to 2:00 P.M. the second day and close between 2:00 and 11:00 A.M. the third day. Clumps stay in bloom about two weeks. Established plants may rebloom in late summer. *H. minor* is one of the first daylilies to become dormant, often by early fall when the days begin to shorten. Zones 2 to 8.

**H. multiflora** (mul-ti-*floh*-ruh).
MANY-FLOWERED DAYLILY.
From China, heavily branched plants with up to 75 to 100 3-in. flowers in late summer or early fall. Scapes grow to 40 in. tall but often bend with the weight of flowers and seeds. Flowers are orange or cadmium-yellow. Cultivars of this species are 'August Pioneer', a chrome-orange flushed fulvous; 'Golden Chimes', a 36-in. shrublike plant whose 2-in. gold flowers have brown backs; 'Thumbelina', a clear orange; and 'Tinker Bell', an orange. Zones 4 to 9.

**H. thunbergii** (thun-*ber*-gee-eye).
THUNBERG'S DAYLILY.
Native to northern China, Korea and Japan. It has 4-in., yellow, fragrant flowers borne on 3-ft. scapes. The flowers open in the afternoon between 2:00 and 10:00 P.M. and close between 1:00 and 10:00 P.M. the second day. This species is the parent of many early cultivars. Only a few specialists list it in their catalogs. Zones 4 to 9.

# Heuchera *(hew-ker-uh).*
ALUMROOT.
Saxifrage Family (*Saxifragaceae*).
As many as 50 to 75 species native to North America. They have a pretty habit of growth, with basal clusters of lobed, generally heart-shaped leaves, often evergreen, from which rise slender stems, 1 to 2 ft. high, with spires of tiny,

bell-shaped florets, $1/3$ in. across, in white, pink, red or greenish white. Many of the improved cultivars are crosses of *H. sanguinea*, *H. americana* and *H. micrantha*. The plants are most effective in the rock garden or at the top of a low wall, where the delicacy and grace of the bloom can be seen and appreciated. If used in the border, they are best planted in large groups. The cut flowers are long-lasting. Partial shade or full sun and a well-drained, humusy soil with plenty of moisture are needed. Propagate by crown division or offsets in the spring.

**H. americana** (ah-mer-i-*kay*-nuh).
AMERICAN ALUMROOT.
An attractive wild flower of the eastern U.S., resembling foamflower (*Tiarella cordifolia*) but with taller flower stems, $1 1/2$ to 2 ft. high, set near the top, with loose, pyramidal clusters of small greenish-white or greenish-purple florets. The foliage of this species is coppery-purple in winter. It blooms in June and July. The leaves of 'Sunset' have purple veins radiating out in an interesting pattern from their centers. 'Garnet Red' has green leaves in summer and garnet foliage in the cooler weather of fall, winter and spring. Zone 4.

**H. micrantha** (my-*kran*-thuh).
SMALL-FLOWERED ALUMROOT.
A native of the West Coast of the U.S., with small, white flowers on stems 2 ft. high, making an airy effect. It can be distinguished from other species by its flower petals, which are twice as long as the sepals. It has been crossed with other species to make the hybrid *H. × brizoides* (briz-*oy*-deez), which has pale pink florets in a delicate spray and is very effective in the rock garden. 'Palace Purple' is a cultivar often listed under *H. micrantha* var. *diversifolia* (dye-ver-si-*foh*-lee-uh). It originated at Kew Gardens in England from seeds obtained from America. Its foliage is ivy-shaped

## Heuchera

*Heuchera micrantha* 'Palace Purple'
SMALL-FLOWERED ALUMROOT

*Hibiscus moscheutos* 'Southern Belle'
COMMON ROSE MALLOW

*Heuchera sanguinea*
CORALBELLS

and deep purple, but the flowers are of little consequence and are usually removed. 'Palace Purple' is often grown from seed and is therefore somewhat variable. Specialists have selected many purple-leaved forms. 'Montrose Ruby' is a hybrid of *H. americana* and *H.* 'Palace Purple'; it has dark purple leaves mottled silver. *H. micrantha* is not as hardy in the eastern U.S. as are some of the other alumroots. Zone 5.

**H. sanguinea** (san-*gwin*-ee-uh).
CORALBELLS.
Best known of the various species, this is a hardy, graceful and long-lived species. With its low mat of rounded, persistent leaves it makes an especially good edging plant. It needs excellent drainage and full sun in the North, shade in the South. Coralbells prefer soils that are not acid. They are useful in the cool greenhouse for winter forcing, as well as outdoors. A few of the cul-

tivars, mostly hybrids with other species, are 'Bressingham Blaze', with scarlet blooms; 'Chatterbox', which produces large pink flowers; 'June Bride', a white; 'Mt. St. Helens', with brick-red flowers; 'Raspberry Regal', which produces masses of bright raspberry flowers; 'Red Spangles', a red; and 'Shere Variety', with deep pinkish-red flowers. Zone 3.

**H. villosa** (vil-*loh*-sa).
HAIRY ALUMROOT.
The five- to seven-lobed leaves are triangular and very deeply cut. The leaves and flower stems are hairy. This species flowers after the others. The 3-ft. airy panicles produce whitish-pink flowers. It is more successful in the heat of the South than many others. Zone 6.

## Heucherella (hew-ker-*rell*-uh).
FOAMY BELLS.
Saxifrage Family *(Saxifragaceae)*.
A bigeneric hybrid resulting from the crossing of *Heuchera* species and *Tiarella cordifolia*, the native foamflower. It is known only in the single species below.

**H. tiarelloides** (tye-uh-rel-*oy*-deez).
FOAMY BELLS.
Plants produce pink or sometimes white or coral-red flowers on 1 1/2-ft. stems in spring. Daintier than most of the related heucheras, this species has smaller, mottled leaves. The plants are stoloniferous and make a good ground cover for shade. They bloom in spring and again in fall. 'Bridget Bloom' is a named cultivar with shell-pink flowers that persist for up to eight weeks. Propagate by crown division in spring. Zone 3.

## Hibiscus (hye-*bis*-kus).
Mallow Family *(Malvaceae)*.
Nearly two hundred species of herbs, shrubs and trees native to tropical and temperate regions around the world. The leaves are palmately veined, lobed and sometimes parted. The flowers are mainly bell-shaped and often very large. The temperate sorts die to their bases in winter and reappear from heavy stems above ground or slightly below in late spring. The most common ornamental types used in perennial gardens are often hybrid crosses of *H. coccineus* (kok-*sin*-ce-us), *H. militaris* (mil-i-*tay*-ris), *H. moscheutos* and *H. palustris* (pa-*lus*-tris).

**H. moscheutos** (mus-*kay*-tus).
COMMON ROSE MALLOW.
A marshland native of the eastern and central U.S. Leaves are lanceolate to ovate, toothed and either unlobed or slightly three- to five-lobed. Plants grow 4 to 5 ft. tall. Flowers are white, pink or rose, usually with a crimson center, and 6 to 8 in. across. Bloom time is from early August into fall. Most cultivars listed under this species are hybrids with other native species. 'Cotton Candy' is pink with a small crimson center; 'Lord Baltimore' is by far the most popular, with bright red flowers on robust plants; 'Snow Queen' is white with a small crimson center; 'Southern Belle' is a seed cultivar producing flowers in white, pink or red shades on 4-ft. plants; the closely related 'Disco Belle' is a strain with similar colors but is only 1 1/2 to 2 ft. tall. Propagate by crown division or by seeds. Zones 4 to 9.

## ★ ★Hosta (*hoss*-tuh).
PLANTAIN LILY.
Lily Family *(Liliaceae)*.
Useful, sturdy, long-lived perennials from China and Japan that are sometimes erroneously identified as *Funkia*, an old generic name. There

## Hosta

*Hosta fortunei* 'Albo-marginata'
Fortune's Hosta

*Hosta undulata*
Wavy Hosta

*Hosta sieboldiana* var. *elegans*
Siebold Hosta

*Hosta ventricosa aureomaculata*
Blue Hosta

are twenty to thirty species, depending on how they are "lumped" or "split" by taxonomists. Plants have decorative, heavy clumps of beautiful green leaves, above which spikes of white or lavender funnel-shaped flowers appear in mid-summer to fall. For further information about gardening with hostas, see the related piece on pages 26–27.

**H. fortunei** (for-*too*-nee-eye).
FORTUNE'S HOSTA.
From eastern Europe, named for the plant collector Robert Fortune (1812-1880). Large plants with striking foliage, they produce distinctly winged petioles up to 14 in. long. The blades are cordate or cordate-oval, up to 12 in. long and 7 to 8 in. wide, with 8 to 10 pairs of veins. Flowering scapes grow to 30 in. Flowers are funnel-shaped, pale mauve or light violet. Most plants represented in this species are of European origin and not directly from Japan as is often thought. 'Albo-marginata' (*al*-boh-mar-jin-*ay*-tuh) is a fine, showy, white-edged cultivar. Zones 3 to 8.

**H. lancifolia** (lan-si-*foh*-lee-uh).
LANCE-LEAF HOSTA.
From Japan, a slender-leaved garden plant producing purple flowers on tall scapes in late summer that is often used as an edging plant or a ground cover. Petioles are grooved and red-dotted at the base. It grows 12 to 14 in. tall. The plain green leaves are 4 to 7 in. long and 1 in. wide. The leaves have five to six pairs of veins. Zones 3 to 8.

**H. plantaginea** (plan-ta-*jin*-ee-uh).
FRAGRANT HOSTA.
Native to China. Glistening, lime-green leaves help separate *H. plantaginea* from all other hostas. Its evening-opening, large white flowers are highly fragrant and borne near the end of summer (August–September). Petioles are 10 in. long and winged, with overlapping edges on the upper portion. Blades are cordate at the base, up to 11 in. long and 10 in. wide, and have 6 to 9 pairs of veins. The cultivar 'Grandiflora' (gran-di-*floh*-ruh) has slightly larger flowers and narrower leaf blades. 'Aphrodite' is a double form with petaloid stamens. Zones 3 to 9.

**H. sieboldiana** (see-bold-ee-*ay*-nuh).
SIEBOLD HOSTA.
From Japan, this is perhaps the best-known species in America. In its native habitat its foliage ranges in color from green to glaucous-blue. Mature clumps can be more than 3 ft. tall and 5 ft. wide. Petioles are 24 in. long. Blades are ovate-cordate, up to 18 in. long and 12 in. wide, and have 14 to 18 veins. Scapes are often just below the foliage and bear funnel-shaped, almost white flowers. The variety *elegans* (*el*-e-ganz) has more glaucous foliage and is more seer-suckering than the species. It was discovered in the Georg Arends' nursery in Germany about 1905. 'Frances Williams', the most popular cultivar, is a bud sport of *H. sieboldiana* var. *elegans*. Its leaves have creamy-beige edges. Zones 3 to 8.

**H. sieboldii** (see-*bold*-ee-eye).
Small to medium clump-forming hostas from Japan. Petioles are almost flat, up to 10 in. long, winged and spotted purple. Blades, 6 in. long and 2$^{1}/_{2}$ in. wide, are lanceolate-elliptic with clear white margins and have three pairs of veins. Flowering scapes reach 20 in. in height. The flowers are funnel-shaped, clear mauve with deep violet stripes and white lines, and bloom in late summer. 'Alba' is a green-leaved, white-flowered form. 'Kabitan' is now considered a form of this species; it has strong yellow leaves and is stoloniferous. Zones 3 to 8.

## Hosta

**H. tardiflora** (tar-di-*floh*-ruh).

LATE-FLOWERING HOSTA.

From Japan, a late-flowering creeping hosta. Petioles are longer than the leaf blades, up to 10 in., and are purple-tinted at the base and not winged. Blades are lanceolate to narrow-elliptic, 6 in. long and $2^1/2$ in. wide, with five pairs of veins. Flowering scapes are held slightly above the 12-in. mound of foliage. Scapes have twenty-five or more light violet, funnel-shaped flowers. It blooms in late summer with asters, liriopes and colchicums. Zones 3 to 8.

**H. tokudama** (tok-ah-*dah*-muh).

TOKUDAMA HOSTA.

Native to Japan. Slow to increase but one of the most beautiful hostas because of its glaucous foliage and heavy substance, this was originally considered a species but is now thought to be a garden hybrid. Petioles are broad, grooved and about 8 in. long. Blades are cordate or orbicular. The upper surface is puckered. Plants grow to 12 in. and have flower scapes about the same height; flowers are bell-shaped and almost white. 'Flava-circinalis' is larger than other forms of *H. tokudama*; its leaf margins are bright chartreuse-yellow. 'Aurea-nebulosa' has yellow centers and irregular margins of glaucous-blue. Zones 3 to 8.

**H. undulata** (un-dew-*lay*-tuh).

WAVY HOSTA.

Native to Japan, this species is used extensively to edge borders and walks. Several forms exist, the best of which have creamy-white leaves that are twisted and curled. All forms of this species are sterile (perhaps an indication that it does not deserve species status). Petioles are 5 in., winged, striped greenish-white and purplish-dotted at the base. Blades vary from ovate-oblong to lanceolate-elliptic, are 4 to 6 in. long and 2 in. wide, and have 7 to 9 pairs of veins. Leaf edges are wavy. Flowers are pale violet. The different variegated selections in this group are unstable. Zones 3 to 8.

**H. ventricosa** (ven-tri-*koh*-suh).

BLUE HOSTA.

A large clump-forming species native to China. Glossy green leaves provide a nice background for blue flowers in midsummer. It is the only hosta known to exhibit apomixis (the ability to produce viable seeds without cross-pollination); because of this feature, it is much propagated from seed. Petioles are 16 in. long, broad and have rose-purple dots. Blades are shiny green, ovate or cordate, 9 in. long and 7 in. wide, with 7 to 9 pairs of widely spaced veins. Flower scapes are 3 ft. tall and bear 20 to 30 urn-shaped, deep blue flowers. 'Variegata' (var-ee-*gay*-tuh), known in America as 'Aureomarginata', has creamy-white, irregular margins. Zones 3 to 9.

## Houttuynia (hoo-too-*in*-ee-uh).

Lizard-tail family *(Saururaceae)*.

From east Asia, water plants or plants for continuously moist soils. The leaves are green, 2 to 3 in. long with stipules united to petioles, somewhat heart-shaped and malodorous when crushed. Plants reach 18 in. in moist sites and are quite invasive.

**H. cordata** (kor-*dat*-ah).

CHAMELEON PLANT.

From Japan south to the mountains of Java and Nepal. It has alternate green leaves, which are somewhat heart-shaped, and grows 12 to 15 in. tall. White flowers appear in early summer and are $1/2$ in. long on 1- to 2-ft. spikes. 'Chameleon' is a recent import from Korea with leaves decorated with white, pink and red colors; it is 6 to 9 in. tall. It spreads by underground stems to make a ground-cover mat and needs wet or moist

*Houttuynia cordata*
CHAMELEON PLANT

*Iberis sempervirens*
EVERGREEN CANDYTUFT

soils. In the South its foliage dies down in late summer. Propagate by digging up the mat of plants and selecting shoots with pieces of roots. Zones 5 to 8.

## Iberis (eye-*beer*-is).

CANDYTUFT.

Mustard Family *(Cruciferae)*.

Annuals and perennials native to the Mediterranean region. The perennials are low-growing, narrow-leaved plants, some evergreen and all nearly indispensable in wall and rock gardens and for the front of spring borders. Full sun and ordinary garden soil, well turned to a spade's depth, are required. Propagate perennials by seeds a year before blooms are desired, by cuttings or by root divisions.

**I. jucunda.** See *Aethionema coridifolium*.

**I. sempervirens** (sem-per-*vye*-renz).

EVERGREEN CANDYTUFT.

From southern Europe, possibly the best of the perennials. Plants provide a cheerful May bloom of fragrant, shiny white flowers in dense heads above evergreen, slender foliage in a thick, dark green mat, 1 ft. high. They may be used as low clipped hedges or as edging in formal gardens. This species is very attractive to honeybees, long-lived, dependable and often reblooms when clipped back after flowering. The cultivar 'Autumn Snow' is 8 to 10 in. tall with large flowers and blooms in both spring and fall; 'Little Gem' is only 5 to 8 in. tall with small flowers; 'Purity' has lustrous green leaves and is a heavy-flowering plant; 'Pygmaea' is a low prostrate form; and 'Snowflake' is 8 to 10 in. tall and bears 2- to 3-in.-wide heads of pure white flowers. Plants propagate easily from 2-in. shoot cuttings. Zones 3 to 9.

## Inula (*in*-yew-luh).

Composite Family *(Compositae)*.

Tall, showy but rather coarse perennials, native mostly to Europe and Asia. Plants produce long, handsome, basal leaves and vivid yellow, daisylike flowers. The species below is a decorative background plant for the border, wild garden or herb garden. Easily grown in ordinary garden soil and sun.

### I. ensifolia (en-si-*foh*-lee-uh).
SWORDLEAF INULA.

Native to Europe and Asia. This 2-ft.-tall, branching, compact plant has 4-in. swordlike leaves. The yellow daisy flowers open in late spring. They are 1 to 2 in. wide, held singly on each stem, and the blossoms will last up to six weeks in cool summer areas. Plant in full sun in moist, well-drained soil. *I. ensifolia* is short-lived in the southeastern U.S. 'Golden Beauty' is an 18- to 24-in. cultivar with 2-in.-wide daisy flowers. Propagate by seed or by crown division. Zones 3 to 8.

## Kirengeshoma (keer-en-gay-*show*-muh).
YELLOW WAXBELLS.
Saxifrage Family *(Saxifragaceae)*.

From Japan, a shrublike plant with erect, purplish stems. The leaves are maplelike and opposite. Flowers are borne in axillary clusters (usually three flowers per cluster). It thrives in moist, rich soils in partial shade.

### K. palmata (pal-*may*-tuh).
YELLOW WAXBELLS.

The leaves are palmately lobed into seven to ten parts and are coarsely toothed around the margins. The basal leaves are 6 in. wide, while the upper ones are considerably smaller. The bell-shaped yellow flowers are 1¹/₂ in. long and waxy. The seedpod has three-pointed horns. The vari-

ety *koreana* (kor-ee-*ay*-nuh) is slightly taller with more open flowers. It is also thought to be hardier. Propagate by crown division after three to five years. Zones 5 to 7.

## Knautia (*naw*-tee-uh).
Teasel Family *(Dipsacaceae)*.

Native to North Africa, Europe, the Caucasus and western Siberia. Leaves are opposite, pinnatifid and toothed at the tips. Flowers are small, forming dense bracts. Plants prefer well-drained soil and full sun.

### K. macedonica (mah-ze-*don*-i-cuh).
CRIMSON PINCUSHION.

(Syn. *Scabiosa rumelica*.) Very much like the scabiosas, but the flower heads are crimson colored. The stems are much divided to produce multiple pincushion flower heads on twisting stems. Flowers are up to 2 in. across in the first or second week in June. Plants perform best in full sun and well-drained soil. In warmer climates they are short-lived. Propagate by crown division or by small shoot cuttings. Zones 5 to 8.

## Kniphofia (nip-*hoh*-fee-uh).
RED-HOT-POKER.
TORCH LILY.
TRITOMA.
Lily Family *(Liliaceae)*.

Mostly hardy perennials, native to Africa, with slender leaves and pyramidal spires of yellow and red, down-turned, tubular flowers all summer. Flower stems reach 3 to 4 ft. high. Well-drained soil and some shade are needed. In the colder zones the roots should be lifted for the winter and stored in a frost-free location in boxes of moist sand. Plant out in early spring. Propagate in spring by crown division, offsets or seeds.

*Inula ensifolia* 'Golden Beauty'
SWORDLEAF INULA

*Knautia macedonica*
CRIMSON PINCUSHION

*Kirengeshoma palmata*
YELLOW WAXBELLS

*Kniphofia uvaria* 'Little Maid'
TORCH LILY

# Kniphofia

**K. uvaria** (yew-*vay*-ree-uh).

COMMON TORCH LILY.

This is the familiar species, growing 3 to 4 ft. high. Blossoms are yellow at the base of the spire, shading to bright red at the top. There are several improved cultivars, all very showy when planted in masses. Many of the modern-day cultivars are hybrids with other species. Among them are 'Buttercup', a 3-ft. light yellow; 'Candlelight', a 3-ft. light yellow; 'Jenny Bloom', a 2$^1$/$_2$-ft. cream and coral; 'Little Maid', a 2$^1$/$_2$-ft. ivory or primrose-white; 'Pfitzeri', a 2$^1$/$_2$-ft. deep orange; 'Springtime', a 3-ft. plant with red upper flowers tipped with yellow and lower flowers muted yellow; 'Wrexham Buttercup', a 4-ft. pure yellow; and 'Yellow Hammer', a 3-ft. dark yellow. Zones 5 to 9.

## Lamium (*lay*-mee-um).

Mint Family *(Labiatae).*

Somewhat weedy herbs of European origin. The leaves are opposite, the stems square. The plant thrives in partial shade. It is easily propagated by division of the plants in spring or by seeds.

**L. maculatum** (mak-yew-*lay*-tum).

SPOTTED DEAD NETTLE.

A perennial with trailing stems to 1$^1$/$_2$ ft. long and dark green, oval leaves to 2 in. long, blotched with white along the midrib. Light purplish-red flowers are produced throughout the summer. This species has naturalized in the eastern U.S. Among the cultivars are 'Album', which has creamy-white flowers and pale green leaves; 'Aureum', pink flowers and golden leaves with a broad white midrib; 'Beacon Silver', rosy-pink flowers with silvery leaves edged in green; 'Chequers', deep mauve-pink flowers and leaves with a silver center; 'Roseum', pink flowers; and 'White Nancy', which is a white-flowered form like 'Beacon Silver' but a stronger grower. Zones 3 to 8.

## Lathyrus (*lath*-i-rus).

Pea Family *(Leguminosae).*

Hardy and half-hardy annuals and perennials, widely distributed over almost all parts of the Northern Temperate Zone, much cultivated and hybridized. Leaves are blue-green and alternate, and the plants usually produce climbing stems, which support themselves by tendrils. The characteristic pealike flowers, often brilliantly colored and sometimes fragrant, are pretty in the garden and especially lovely in cut flower arrangements. All species sprout easily from seed sown outdoors in very early spring, but their cultural needs vary from seashore sand to rich, deep loam. Special forms are propagated by division of older clumps.

**L. vernus** (*ver*-nus).

SPRING VETCHLING.

This is a non-climbing relative of the sweet pea *L. odoratus* (oh-door-*ay*-tus). The branches reach 1 to 1$^1$/$_2$ ft. tall. Each leaf is made up of two to three pairs of shiny, pointed leaflets. The racemes of $^3$/$_4$-in., nodding, reddish-purple, pealike flowers appear in late spring to early summer. The foliage disappears after flowering is complete. This species is deep-rooted, so give it deep, rich, moist soil, in full sun. There are three botanical varieties: *albiflorus* (al-bi-*floh*-rus), with creamy-white flowers; *cyanus* (sigh-*ay*-nus), with light blue flowers; and *roseus* (roh-zee-us), with pink blossoms. The cultivar 'Variegatus' has pink and white flowers. Zones 4 to 7.

## Lavandula (lav-*van*-dew-luh).

LAVENDER.

Mint Family *(Labiatae).*

Herbs or shrubs of the Old World, with opposite aromatic leaves and dense spikes of attractive blue, lilac or violet flowers. Lavenders are good plants for the rock garden or flower border in well-drained, rather light soils. Propagate by seeds sown in spring or summer, by softwood or hard-wood cuttings made in August or September, or by careful division of clumps in early spring.

★ **L. angustifolia** (an-gus-ti-*foh*-lee-uh).
COMMON LAVENDER.
ENGLISH LAVENDER.
The foliage is evergreen, 2$^1$/$_2$ in. long, $^1$/$_4$ in. wide, on a square stem. The flowers are borne in terminal spikes, 3 to 4 in. long, made up of whorls of small lavender flowers which open in summer. Both the flowers and the foliage contain aromatic oils that are used in many different ways. The plant has a shrubby habit, growing to 3 ft. tall if left unpruned. It can be shaped to form a hedge or other form and responds well to this treatment, putting on good vigorous growth when pruned in spring. Plant in full sun in well-drained soil. 'Hidcote' has deep purple flowers and grows 18 in. tall; 'Jean Davis' has lavender-

*Lavandula angustifolia* 'Hidcote'
COMMON LAVENDER

*Lamium maculatum*
SPOTTED DEAD NETTLE

*Lavandula stoechas* subsp. *pedunculata*

# Lavandula

white flowers and is 10 to 15 in. tall; and 'Munstead Dwarf' has lavender flowers on 12-in. plants. Zones 5 to 9.

**L. stoechas** (*stek*-ess).
FRENCH LAVENDER.
SPANISH LAVENDER.
From central Spain and the mountains of Portugal, small shrub about 12 in. tall, with silver, hairy leaves and spikes of fragrant, dark purple flowers borne from showy, large, purple bracts. This tender perennial does well outdoors year-round in mild climates and makes an excellent pot plant in the North in a sunny, cool, moist atmosphere. The subspecies *pedunculata* (pe-dunk-yew-*lay*-tuh) has longer flower stalks (up to 10 in.). Zones 8 to 9.

# Leucanthemem. See *Chrysanthemum*.

# Liatris (lye-*ay*-tris).
BLAZING-STAR.
GAY-FEATHER.
Composite Family *(Compositae)*.
A tall North American perennial, up to 6 ft. high, with handsome purple or white blooms in spikes or sometimes panicles in August and September. Flowers open from the top down. Plants of this genus are among the hardiest of the available choices for the perennial border. A light but fairly rich soil is desirable for best blooms, but these plants will survive poor soil and extremes of heat, cold and drought. Propagate by seeds in early spring or by crown division, also in spring.

**L. pycnostachya** (pik-noh-*stak*-ee-uh).
KANSAS GAY-FEATHER.
Native from Wisconsin to Louisiana and Texas. Small purple flower heads, 1 in. across, in dense spikes, 1¹/₂ ft. long, are produced on plants 3 to

5 ft. tall. The flowers remain on the plant in good condition for a long time. The plants are showy in a wild garden or a large border, and best when massed. Zones 3 to 9.

**L. scariosa** (scar-ee-*oh*-suh).
TALL GAY-FEATHER.
This species is often mislabeled in nurseries by names such as *L. saspelaus*. This clump-forming plant is native to meadows in the eastern U.S. Plants grow to 3 ft. tall. The leaves are 5 in. long and 1 in. wide, and are held alternately on the stout, erect stems. The flower spikes are at the end of each stem. Anywhere from twenty-five to fifty rose, lavender or white flowers make up a spike. The spike opens from the top down starting in summer and going on into fall. Plant in full sun to partial shade in light soils. 'September Glory' bears purple flowers that all open about the same time. 'White Spire' is similar to

*Liatris spicata*
SPIKE GAY-FEATHER

'September Glory' but has white flowers. Zones 3 to 9.

**L. spicata** (spy-*kay*-tuh).
SPIKE GAY-FEATHER.
Native from Maine to Florida and west to Louisiana. Growing 3 to 4 ft. tall, with very large lower leaves, up to 1 ft. long, plants produce heavy spikes 15 in. long, bearing lavender and white florets, $1/2$ in. across. This is the best species for garden cultivation. The variety *montana* (mon-*tay*-nuh), native to Virginia and North Carolina, grows only 10 to 20 in. tall. 'August Glory' has purple-blue flowers on 3- to 4-ft. plants. 'Floristen White' has cream flowers on 3-ft. plants and performs well in the warmer zones. 'Kobold' (syn. 'Gnome') displays lilac-purple flowers in midsummer on $2^1/2$-ft. plants. Zones 3 to 9.

# Ligularia (lig-yew-*lay*-ree-uh).
GOLDEN-RAY.
LIGULARIA.
Composite Family *(Compositae)*.
Closely related to *Senecio*, these easily grown, tall perennials from Europe and Asia make fine foliage effects in the border or indoors as houseplants. Although they are grown primarily for their interesting foliage, they have pretty sprays of small orange and yellow flowers in July and August. Their primary requirement is plenty of water. Outdoors, they are excellent for the back of the border or in the wild garden. Sun or partial shade and ordinary garden soil, well turned to a spade's depth, are required. Indoors they need a basic potting mixture and not too much heat. They do well in a cool greenhouse or near a cool window in the house. Plants grown indoors may be plunged (right in the pot) into the garden during the summer, preferably in a shady spot. Propagate by cuttings or by division.

**L. dentata** (den-*tay*-tuh).
BIGLEAF LIGULARIA.
The basal rosette of this species bears alternate, 1-ft.-wide, kidney-shaped, coarse leaves on 1-ft. stalks. These leaves have coarsely pointed teeth, are dark green above and purple below, and are leathery-looking. They form attractive mounds up to 4 ft. high. The flower stalk is purple and branched with 2- to 5-in., coarse, orange, daisy-like flowers appearing in July and August in large heads held well above the foliage. Plant only in a cool, moist place with full sun or partial shade. A large amount of soil moisture is necessary to keep the foliage from wilting in the hot summer sun. Plants prefer a spot where the roots can be in constant contact with water, such as a streambank or pond edge, but do not allow the crown to be covered with water, especially in winter. Plant in very rich soil with lots of organic matter. 'Desdemona' is more compact than the species and has deeper purplish foliage in spring; during the warmer part of the summer the upper surfaces of the leaves are green and the bottoms purple; golden-yellow flowers. 'Othello' has smaller flowers than 'Desdemona' and is not as compact. 'Greynog Gold' is a hybrid of *L. dentata* and *L. veitchiana*; its flowers are bright orange on plants to 5 to 6 ft. tall. Zones 5 to 8.

**L. stenocephala** (sten-oh-*sef*-a-luh).
NARROW-SPIKED LIGULARIA.
The foliage is light green, 1 ft. long and triangular, with coarse teeth on the margins, and forms a basal mound up to about 4 ft. tall. The flower stems are a dark purple, almost black, and reach a height of about 5 ft. The yellow, $1^1/4$-in. daisy flowers are clustered around the top 2 ft. of the stem, ending in a point. Like *L. dentata*, this species prefers a very moist location with deep, rich soil high in organic matter. Plant in full sun, but light afternoon shade will help to keep the

## Ligularia

*Ligularia dentata* 'Desdemona'
BIGLEAF LIGULARIA

*Linaria purpurea*
PURPLE TOADFLAX

*Limonium latifolium*
SEA LAVENDER

*Linum perenne*
GARDEN FLAX

leaves from wilting in the hot summer sun. 'The Rocket' is the cultivar most often offered. It is more compact than the species, growing 18 to 24 in. tall. Zones 5 to 8.

## Limonium (lye-*moh*-nee-um).

SEA LAVENDER.
SEA PINK.
STATICE.
Plumbago Family *(Plumbaginaceae).*

(Often listed as *Statice*.) A large genus, mostly from the Mediterranean region. It comprises annuals and perennials, all easily grown and of great value in dried arrangements for their light airiness. The plants are very useful in the rock garden, mixed borders and the cutting garden. They grow well near the seacoast, as their common names imply, and are salt-tolerant. The colors range from white and shades of yellow to pink and lavender. Sow seeds indoors in early March and transplant outdoors in May if very early bloom is wanted. Otherwise, sow seeds outdoors in April where plants are wanted for midsummer bloom. Full sun and a deeply dug, well-drained, porous but not too rich soil are required. When the blossoms are wanted for drying, they ought to be cut as soon as good color shows.

### L. latifolium (lat-i-*foh*-lee-um).

An outstanding perennial from Bulgaria and southern Russia, $1\frac{1}{2}$ to $2\frac{1}{2}$ ft. tall, with an airy blue-and-white flower cluster and large, oval leaves, 6 to 9 in. long. The large sprays of bloom make elegant displays in July and August. 'Blue Cloud' has lighter blue flowers than the species; 'Collier's Pink' has pink flowers; 'St. Pierre' is a taller form with loose sprays of flowers; and 'Violeta' has dark violet-purple flowers. A dry, not too rich soil is required. Thin to stand 1 ft. apart. Zones 4 to 9.

## Linaria (lye-*nay*-ree-uh).

TOADFLAX.
Figwort Family (*Scrophulariaceae*).

This large genus of annuals and perennials, native to the Northern Temperate Zone, includes several familiar wild flowers—for example, the yellow-and-orange butter-and-eggs, *L. vulgaris*, seen commonly along roadsides. The flower clusters at the ends of the stems are often showy. All species are easily grown in ordinary garden soil and full sun. The plants are useful in borders, the rock garden, and the cutting garden. Propagate by crown division.

### L. purpurea (pur-pur-*ee*-uh).

PURPLE TOADFLAX.

The short, narrow, lance-shaped, opposite leaves are gray-green. Numerous stems about 3 ft. tall end in racemes of purple snapdragon-like flowers about $\frac{1}{3}$ in. long. They appear in summer and bloom for a long time. Plant in full sun in a light, well-drained, ordinary garden soil. 'Canon Went' is a pink cultivar, while 'Yuppee Surprise' is a light lavender hybrid that blooms over a long period of time. Zones 4 to 10.

## Linum (*lye*-num).

FLAX.
Flax Family (*Linaceae*).

Native mostly to temperate or subtropical regions. There are many graceful species, both annual and perennial, with red, blue, yellow or white blossoms and small, narrow, blue-green alternate leaves. (Golden flax has broad leaves.) The blooms last only a day but are followed the next morning by a new crop of flowers. The plants are attractive in the border and, in the case of the smaller species, excellent in the rock garden, where their delicate habit of growth is best displayed. Ordinary golden soil, well turned to a spade's depth, good drainage and full sun are required. The perennials can all be propagated by crown division or grown from seed; the later plants, of course, will not bloom until the next spring.

**L. flavum** (*flay*-vum).

GOLDEN FLAX.

Abundant yellow flowers, 1 in. across, on this perennial from central Europe add warmth and brightness to the border. The plant is 1 to 2 ft. tall, and it blooms all summer. The cultivar 'Compactum' is a superior 6- to 9-in. plant. Zones 5 to 8.

**L. perenne** (per-*ren*-ee).

GARDEN FLAX.

A graceful perennial native to Europe, with sky-blue flowers, 1 in. across. It grows to $1^{1}/_{2}$ ft. and is excellent in the border or the rock garden. Its delicate habit and long summer bloom make it a favorite with many gardeners. Plants sometimes die out over winter, but the species self-sows. The plants need a light soil and cannot tolerate too much moisture. Space at least 8 in. apart in the border for effective display. The variety *album* (*al*-bum) is a whitish (not pure white) form. The subspecies *alpinum* (al-*pye*-num) is not as floriferous as the species but is shorter at 8 to 12 in. The subspecies *lewisii* (lew-*iss*-ee-eye), or prairie flax, has sky-blue flowers $1^{1}/_{2}$ in. across and blooms abundantly. It is perennial, native to western North America and stockier than the species. A closely allied species, *L. austriacum* (aus-tri-*ak*-um), from southern Europe, is somewhat more perennial in southern zones. All of these bloom in late June or July. Zones 4 to 9.

## Liriope (li-*rye*-oh-pee).

LILYTURF.

Lily Family *(Liliaceae)*.

Low-growing perennials from Asia. *Liriope* and its species are often confused with, or used synonymously with, species of the related *Ophiopogon*

genus; the difference is that the flowers have inferior ovaries in *Ophiopogon*, superior ones in *Liriope*. Often used as ground covers because of their heavy matlike growth, lilyturfs produce grass-like leaves and profuse little lavender or white flowers. They thrive in sun or shade in ordinary garden soil, well turned to a spade's depth. Where not hardy, they are often grown in a cool greenhouse as a low edging or under benches. Propagate by seeds or by division of plants in early spring.

★ **L. muscari** (mus-*kay*-ree).

BLUE LILYTURF.

Leaves are 1 to $1^{1}/_{2}$ ft. long. Pretty clusters of lavender flowers on spikes that are the same height as the grass-green leaves bloom in late summer. Today lilyturf is one of the predominant ground cover and edging plants in the southeastern U.S. One of the best plants for gardens is the variety *variegata* (var-ee-*gay*-tuh), with creamy-white margins. Plantsmen usually divide the various cultivars of *L. muscari* into green or variegated forms. Some of the best of the green-leaved types are 'Lilac Beauty', with vigorous green leaves and lilac flowers displayed well above the foliage; 'Majestic', with large, deep lilac flowers; and 'Munroe's White', a slow-growing white-flowered cultivar. Variegated types include 'Gold Banded', with wide leaves having a yellow band down the middle and lavender flowers; 'John Burch', with variegated foliage and cockscomb-shaped lavender flower spikes; 'Silver Midget', an 8-in.-tall plant with narrow white bands on short leaves; and 'Silver Sunproof', with nearly white leaves in full sun, but more green and yellow leaves in partial shade. Zones 6 to 9.

*Liriope muscari*
BLUE LILYTURF

*Lobelia cardinalis* 'Queen Victoria'
SCARLET LOBELIA

**Lobelia** (loh-*bee*-lee-uh).
Bellflower Family *(Campanulaceae)*.
Perennials and annuals, native mostly to tropical and warm temperate regions, all with showy flowers of irregular structure. Some are suited to the wild garden (especially the native species), others are useful in the border or as container plants. Propagate perennials by crown division in the fall or spring.

**L. cardinalis** (kar-din-*nay*-lis).
CARDINAL FLOWER.
SCARLET LOBELIA.
This beautiful wild flower of the eastern U.S. is found in shallow water along the banks of streams, in either partial shade or full sun. If its roots are in water, it stands full sun well and thrives. A perennial, it grows 2 to 4 ft. tall with brilliant red blossoms, 1 to 1¹/₂ in. long, blooming in a spike along a stiff stem in late July or August. The dark green, oblong, coarsely toothed, alternate leaves are up to 4 in. long. It may succeed in a moist, rich soil, with some shade, but is often temperamental about establishing itself. It is best used as a poolside plant or in a bog garden. Several hybrids have been developed by crossing *L. cardinalis* with *L. splendens* (*splen*-denz) and *L. siphilitica*. 'Queen Victoria' is the most popular hybrid, with brilliant red flowers displayed above bronze foliage on plants 3 to 5 ft. tall. Zones 3 to 9.

**L. siphilitica** (sif-il-*lit*-ik-uh).
BLUE LOBELIA.
GREAT LOBELIA.
Blue, purplish or occasionally white flowers, 1 in. long in a graceful spike, make this hardy perennial, native to the U.S., a very pretty garden flower. It puts on a fine display if grown in a moist, slightly acid soil and is good next to the pool or in the bog garden. Plants grow to 3 ft. tall and ought to be set out 15 in. apart. Bloom is

## Lobelia

in August and September. White forms of this species are common in the wild. 'Blue Peter' is a superior English garden cultivar. Hybrids have been introduced from crosses of *L. siphilitica*, *L. cardinalis* and *L.* 'Queen Victoria'. These are tetraploids (a botanic distinction that denotes plants in which chromosomes are produced in fours, rather than the usual twos) with large flowers, thick leaves and thick stems. 'Brightness' produces bright cherry-red flowers above purplish-red foliage on plants $3^{1}/_{2}$ ft. tall; 'Oakes Ames' has scarlet flowers and dark green foliage on $2^{1}/_{2}$-ft. plants; and 'Wisley' has scarlet flowers and green leaves and also grows $2^{1}/_{2}$ ft. tall. Zones 4 to 8.

## Lupinus (lew-*pye*-nus).

LUPINE.

Pea Family *(Leguminosae)*.

The lupines are a large genus native to North and South America and the Mediterranean region. There are annuals, perennials and so-called tree lupines. All are hardy and have colorful spikes of bloom, although differing in habit of growth. They can be grown from seed, although germination is slow. It is best to sow seeds where the plants are desired and then thin to correct distances, since they do not transplant well. The perennial lupines may also be propagated by division of the clumps in early spring, but this must be done with care because of their reluctance to be moved. They will grow almost anywhere in well-drained soil and sun.

Sow in ordinary garden soil that has been deeply dug and enriched with rotted manure or compost. The humus-rich soil will hold the moisture the lupines love. Seeds may also be planted singly in peat pots in a cool greenhouse or a cold frame. Soaking the seeds in warm water overnight may hasten sprouting. Filing through the tough outer seed husk will aid germination.

In May, plant out the peat pots, 3 ft. apart, where the lupines are to grow. Although they prefer full sun, they will tolerate some shade. They do not, however, like hot summers (above 85°F) and for this reason grow especially well in the Pacific Northwest. These hybrids bloom largely in June in dense clusters of flowers covering two-thirds of the tall spikes. Their colors are breathtaking shades of lavender, blue, pink, red, white, dark yellow, orange and bicolor blends of these colors.

The tree lupines are native to warm climates, Zone 7 and south, where they grow to a height of 5 to 6 ft. They thrive in well-drained, ordinary garden soil in a sheltered, sunny place. Prune in February or March, cutting back one-third to one-half of the previous year's growth.

### L. arboreus (ar-*boh*-ree-us).

TREE LUPINE.

A shrubby perennial, native to California, 4 to 8 ft. tall, with handsome compound leaves that grow at the end of the stem—a palmate form characteristic of the whole genus. The fragrant blossoms, in a loose, attractive spike, are usually yellow, though there are purple and white varieties, and appear in May. Plants are especially attractive when trained on a garden wall or trellis in the sun. Zones 7 to 9.

### L. perennis (per-*ren*-is).

WILD LUPINE.

The common wild lupine, found in open woods of eastern North America, is a most charming and perennial wild flower. The long-stalked leaves have eight narrow, light green leaflets, and the dense spikes of pealike flowers are generally blue but sometimes white or pink. The pods or seeds should not be eaten. It grows about 2 ft. tall and blooms in early summer. A dry, sandy soil and sun are needed. It is suitable for either the border or the wild garden, although, like all lupines, it is not easy to transplant. Zones 4 to 9.

# Lupinus

*Lupinus* 'Russell Hybrid'
LUPINE

*Lupinus arboreus*
TREE LUPINE

**L. polyphyllus** (pol-if-*fill*-us).
WASHINGTON LUPINE.

A large perennial, native to western North America. It grows 5 ft. tall and has long, showy spikes of blooms all summer—usually a purple-and-blue combination. Woolly seedpods follow the flowers. There are yellow, white, pink and blue varieties. The variety *moerheimii* (moor-*hye*-mee-eye) is lower and more compact. Refinement of this species gave rise to the enormously colorful group known as Russell lupines, upon which most garden displays depend. The Russell lupines are especially beautiful hybrids that caused a sensation on their introduction in the 1940s because of their wide range of colors and density of bloom. The strain was developed over the years, and named for George Russell, a railroad–crossing guard at a quiet spot in Yorkshire, England. The nature of his post gave him time to tend to

*Lupinus polyphyllus*
WASHINGTON LUPINE

## Lupinus

his garden, and there, beside the tracks, he bred flowers that are now grown around the world.

Like the other lupines, they resent being moved and are best grown from seed planted directly at the back of the border (since they grow about 3 ft. tall) in July. Russell lupine cultivars popular today include 'Gallery Hybrids', 15- to 18-in. plants in blue, pink, red and white; 'Minarette', 18- to 20-in. plants in mixed colors; 'My Castle', 2 to 3 ft. plants in mixed colors; and 'The Governor', 2- to 3-ft. plants with blue and purple flowers. Zones 4 to 8.

### Lychnis (lik-nis).
CAMPION.
CATCHFLY.
Pink Family (Caryophyllaceae).
A large genus of annuals, biennials and perennials native throughout the Northern Temperate Zone. Many have truly beautiful flowers with bright colors: white, red, pink, blue and purple. All have opposite leaves. Most of the species are grown as annuals, the biennials and perennials being started indoors in March, the hardy annuals sown outdoors in April. Perennial species may also be propagated by division. All grow best in full sun or light shade in moderately rich, well-drained soil, well turned to a spade's depth. They are fine plants in the border as well as useful all summer as cut flowers. With their long season of bloom (late June to frost) and their ease of culture, their popularity is understandable.

**L. × arkwrightii** (ark-rye-tee-eye).
ARKWRIGHT'S CAMPION.
This 1-ft.-tall perennial is a hybrid of L. × haageana with L. chalcedonica. It produces loose heads of star-shaped scarlet flowers that bloom most of the summer. Plants are somewhat short-

*Lychnis chalcedonica*
MALTESE-CROSS

*Lychnis coronaria* 'Alba'
MULLEIN-PINK

lived, lasting two to three years. 'Vesuvius' is a cultivar with vermilion flowers. Zone 4.

**L. chalcedonica** (chal-see-*don*-i-kuh).
JERUSALEM-CROSS.
MALTESE-CROSS.

A perennial from Russia and Siberia. Growing to 2 to 3 ft. tall, it is occasionally seen as an escape along roadsides in the eastern U.S. The type has glowing scarlet flowers, 1 in. across, in a loose cluster. There are white, pink and rose-colored varieties, as well as some doubles. Zones 3 to 9.

**L. coronaria** (kor-oh-*nay*-ree-uh).
DUSTY MILLER.
MULLEIN-PINK.
ROSE CAMPION.

A grayish-leaved, woolly, hardy perennial from southern Europe, about $1^1/2$ to $2^1/2$ ft. tall. The solitary crimson flowers on this short-lived perennial are displayed all summer, but the principal attraction of the plant lies in its gray foliage. The cultivar 'Alba' has white blossoms, while the variety *astrosanguinea* (as-troh-san-*gwin*-ee-uh) bears carmine-red flowers. 'Abbotswood Rose' is a compact cultivar with pink flowers. 'Oculata' has white flowers with a cerise eye. Zone 4.

**L. flos-jovis** (*floss-joh*-vis).
FLOWER-OF-JOVE.

One of the gray, woolly-leaved plants that are so pleasant in August heat and so effective in moonlight. A perennial from the mountains of southern Europe, it grows 1 to $1^1/2$ ft. tall and has densely clustered, small pink flowers, each $^1/2$ in. across, which bloom in June and July. It is a sturdy and useful plant for the floral border or the rock garden. 'Hort's Variety' bears rose-pink blossoms. Zones 5 to 9.

**L. × haageana** (hah-jee-*ay*-nuh).
HAAGE CAMPION.

A hardy perennial of good, compact form, with large flowers—red, crimson, salmon or white—in groups of two or three. Each bloom is up to 2 in. across. Of hybrid origin, this plant grows 1 ft. tall and blooms in June and July. It may be treated as an annual if started early indoors, since it usually flowers the first year from seed. Thin in the border to stand 6 in. apart. This is another fairly short-lived campion: two to four years. Zone 5.

**L. viscaria** (vis-*kay*-ree-uh).
GERMAN CATCHFLY.

(Sometimes listed as *Viscaria viscosa*). A hardy perennial from Europe and Asia, $^1/2$ to $1^1/2$ ft. tall, with slender leaves in a compact tuft and clusters of small red, white, pink or striped red-and-white flowers, which bloom in May or June. There is a sticky spot on the stem under each flower cluster, which gives the plant its common name. There are two botanical varieties: *alba* (*al*-buh), white, and *flore-plena* (*floh*-re-*plee*-nuh), a double rose-pink. Zones 3 to 8.

# Lysimachia (lye-sim-*may*-kee-uh).
LOOSESTRIFE.
Primrose Family *(Primulaceae)*.

Widely distributed in temperate and subtropical regions, a large genus of perennials, most of which are too weedy to be useful in the cultivated garden. The species below are exceptions. Ordinary garden soil, well turned to a spade's depth, full sun and adequate moisture are needed. Propagate by seeds or by division in spring or fall.

**L. clethroides** (kleth-*roy*-deez).
GOOSENECK LOOSESTRIFE.
JAPANESE LOOSESTRIFE.

A sturdy, easily grown, graceful perennial with pretty, nodding spikes of small, white, star-shaped

## Lysimachia

florets on stems 2¹/₂ to 3 ft. tall in late June and July. It is good in the border and useful as a cut flower. This species can be invasive. Zones 3 to 8.

**L. nummularia** (num-yew-*lay*-ree-uh).
CREEPING JENNY.
MONEYWORT.
A persistent, pervasive, low creeper, 1 to 2 in. tall, with dark green, small, round leaves. Abundant, small, bright yellow, cup-shaped flowers bloom during June and July. It grows in sun or partial shade. 'Aurea' is a golden-leaved cultivar and a better choice as a ground cover. Its fragrant flowers bloom from June through August. Suitable for edgings or hanging baskets but perhaps too rampant for small rock gardens. This species may be propagated by rooted joints. Zones 3 to 8.

**L. punctata** (punk-*tah*-ta).
YELLOW LOOSESTRIFE.
Native to Europe and western Asia. Plants grow to 2 ft. tall and 1 ft. wide. ³/4-in.-wide yellow flowers are borne in whorls in the upper leaf axils from May to September. The centers of the flowers have a small brownish circle. This species is best planted in areas with cooler summers. Propagate by cuttings or seeds. Zone 4.

## Lythrum (*lith*-rum).
LOOSESTRIFE.
Loosestrife Family *(Lythraceae)*.
Native to North America and the Old World, perennials and annuals of easy cultivation. The species described below are the most familiar and the handsomest of the native or naturalized species. It is a sturdy, bushy plant that makes a fine display from June to August, especially when planted in masses. It thrives in full sun, plenty of water and ordinary garden soil, well turned to a spade's depth. Several states have

placed *Lythrum* on their noxious weed list because of its self-seeding habit in bogs and wetlands. Propagate by crown division.

**L. salicaria** (sal-ik-*kay*-ree-uh).
PURPLE LOOSESTRIFE.
WILLOW HERB.
From Europe, a beautiful, purple-flowered perennial of sunny, wet meadows. The small flowers, ³/4 in. across, grow in dense spikes on plants that are 2 to 5 ft. tall. It is useful in the wild garden but must not be allowed to crowd out other flowers. Some popular cultivars are 'Firecandle', with intense rosy-red flowers; 'Robert', with deep pink flowers on 2-ft. plants; 'Roseum Superbum', a very vigorous 3- to 5-ft. plant with large 1-in. flowers; and 'The Beacon', with rose-red flowers on 3¹/2-ft. plants. This is a particularly durable species for gardens in the Northern Temperate Zone, where winter cold is dry and persistent. Zone 3.

**L. virgatum** (vir-*gay*-tum).
WAND LOOSESTRIFE.
From Asia Minor. This plant is very similar to *L. salicaria* but tends to be more diminutive. The leaves are lance-shaped, 4 in. long, on branching stems up to 3 ft. tall. The flowers are borne on short stalks in racemes and open all summer and into the fall. Plant in full sun in a moist, well-drained soil. Cultivars of this species include 'Dropmore Purple', a rosy-purple form 2¹/2 ft. tall; 'Morden Gleam', a rose-flowered plant 2 to 3 ft. tall; 'Morden Pink', a compact type with pink flowers that is male-sterile but will bear seeds if planted with *L. salicaria* cultivars; 'Pink Spires', a deep pink form about 3 ft. tall; 'Purple Spires', which differs from 'Pink Spires' by having rose-purple flowers; 'Rose Queen', only 18 in. tall with pink flowers; and 'The Rocket', a deeper pink form 2 ¹/2 ft. tall. Zones 3 to 9.

**Macleaya** (mak-*lay*-uh).

Poppy Family *(Papaveraceae)*.

Native to Asia, very tall, picturesque, shrubby perennials, persistent and spreading, and needing plenty of space. They are useful in the very large border or wild garden. Rich soil and full sun are needed. Propagate by seeds or by suckering shoots.

**M. cordata** (kor-*day*-tuh).

PLUME POPPY.

(Formerly *Bocconia cordata*.) From China and Japan. This is the most familiar species, 5 to 8 ft. tall, with large, roundish leaves, 6 to 8 in. across. Leaves are deeply lobed, gray-green on top and whitish underneath. Small creamy-pink florets with showy stamens in long graceful plumes appear in June and July. Seed heads are attractive into fall. The plant has a lush tropical appearance.

*Lythrum salicaria* 'Firecandle'
PURPLE LOOSESTRIFE

*Lysimachia punctata*
YELLOW LOOSESTRIFE

*Macleaya cordata*
PLUME POPPY

## Macleaya

Its tendency to spread may make it troublesome, so ideally it would do best planted in a confined border by itself, where it cannot crowd out other plants and where its own splendid display is best appreciated. This species is sometimes confused with the inferior *M. microcarpa* (my-kroh-*kar*-puh), which has bronzy flowers and seedpods that (unlike those of this species) are not ornamental, and is an invasive grower. Zones 3 to 8.

**M. microcarpa.** See *M. cordata.*

## Malva (*mal*-vuh).

MALLOW.

Mallow Family *(Malvaceae).*

Hardy annuals, biennials and perennials, native to Europe, North Africa and Asia. All have pink or white flowers in the leaf axils, and alternate leaves. Some are weedy plants. Propagate by seeds or by crown division.

**M. alcea** (al-*see*-uh).

HOLLYHOCK MALLOW.

A 2- to 3-ft. species that is native to Europe but is naturalized in the U.S. The flowers are dark rose to white and 2 in. across. 'Fastigiata' is usually more available than the species. Plants of this cultivar are more upright and display 2-in.-diameter flowers. Zones 4 to 8.

**M. moschata** (mos-*kay*-tuh).

MUSK MALLOW.

A sturdy and long-lived perennial from Europe, 2 ft. tall, with characteristic lobed leaves and pretty pink flowers, sometimes white, 1 to 2 in. across, that appear in summer. These plants can be found along roadsides in many parts of the U.S. They are often subject to somewhat disfiguring rust and leaf-spot diseases. There are two cultivars: 'Alba', which is white, and 'Rosea', a pink. Zones 3 to 5.

## Meconopsis (mee-koh-*nop*-sis).

Poppy Family *(Papaveraceae).*

A sizable genus of poppylike annuals, biennials and perennials from Europe and Asia, all with yellow juice in their stems. Often difficult to establish, they require special soil preparation and carefully chosen situations in order to persist. They need cool summers to thrive. Prepare well-drained soil that is porous and rich, made slightly acid with leafmold and peat, by adding extra sand to ensure good drainage. The plants need abundant water during the spring and summer, and protection from winds and hot sun. In fact, they enjoy partial shade. Given these conditions, they will thrive and add greatly to a border. Propagate by root division or by seeds, sown where plants are wanted, since like most poppies they are not easily transplanted. Seeds can be started indoors, one or two to a small pot, and the seedlings set out with as little root disturbance as possible.

**M. baileyi.** See *M. betonicifolia.*

**M. betonicifolia** (bet-on-iss-if-*foh*-lee-uh).

BLUE POPPY.

BLUE POPPY OF TIBET.

(Syn. *M. baileyi.*) A tall perennial, 5 to 6 ft., with lavender-blue flowers to 2 in. across, in heavy, handsome, flattish clusters. It blooms in June and July. The lobed, grayish leaves are up to 6 in. long. It flourishes on the northwest coast of the U.S., especially in Washington, but does not do as well elsewhere in the U.S. Zones 7 to 8.

**M. cambrica** (*kam*-bri-kuh).

WELSH POPPY.

Native to Europe and England. The 8-in. leaves are ferny and a bright green color. Single lemon or orange, $2^{1}/_{2}$ in.-flowers are carried above the foliage on slender, hairy stems. Plants self-seed freely. Zones 6 to 9.

*Malva moschata*
MUSK MALLOW

*Meconopsis betonicifolia*
BLUE POPPY

**Megasea.** See *Bergenia*.

**Mertensia** (mer-*ten*-see-uh).

BLUEBELLS.

Borage Family *(Boraginaceae)*.

Native to Asia, Europe and North America. There are several species, but only *M. virginica* is widely grown. The roots are thick and fleshy, leaves gray-green or bluish and alternate. The blue-pink flowers are loosely branched in one-sided clusters presenting a drooping effect. Plants prefer moist, rich soils and are easy to grow. Propagate by seeds sown immediately when ripe.

**M. virginica** (vir-*jin*-i-cuh).

VIRGINIA BLUEBELLS.

A beloved native American plant from New York to Minnesota and south to Alabama and Tennessee. The obovate leaves are 6 in. long. The 1-in. flowers are fragrant, pink in bud and blue

*Meconopsis cambrica*
WELSH POPPY

## Mertensia

*Mertensia virginica*
VIRGINIA BLUEBELLS

when open. Ferns make good companion plants because they fill in the empty spaces left when the bluebells die down in summer. The plants prefer light shade. 'Alba' is a white cultivar and 'Rubra' a pink. Zones 3 to 9.

## Monarda (moh-*nar*-duh).
HORSE-MINT.
Mint Family *(Labiatae)*.
Native to North America, aromatic perennials of sturdy habit, growing in strong clumps. The showy, clustered flowers are white, lavender, pink or red, blooming at the top of the leafy stems. They are very attractive to honeybees, butterflies and hummingbirds. They grow so vigorously and spread so rapidly that they may need restraining in the garden. Some species are often seen along roadsides. They make fine plants for the herb garden, the larger border and the wild garden. Plant where they will get full sun or very light

*Monarda didyma* 'Cambridge Scarlet'
SCARLET BEE BALM

*Myosotis scorpioides*
FORGET-ME-NOT

shade. They thrive in ordinary garden soils. Cutting back the blossoming stems after flowering often brings a second crop of blooms. Propagate by seeds or by root division in the spring.

**M. didyma** (*did*-i-muh).
BEE BALM.
OSWEGO TEA.
SCARLET BEE BALM.
Handsome, bright red florets, 2 in. long, in thick clusters bloom on leafy square stems, $1^1/2$ to 3 ft. tall, from mid-June to early September. Plants are striking in the border or when planted in large groups beside a pool or brook. There are many cultivars available. 'Adam' produces cerise flowers on compact plants. 'Cambridge Scarlet' is the most popular cultivar, with scarlet flowers on robust plants growing 3 ft. tall. 'Croftway Pink' produces soft pink flowers; 'Gardenview Red' was selected for its rose-red flowers and resistance to powdery mildew. 'Mahogany' has dark burgundy flowers on 3-ft. plants. 'Marshall's Delight' is a hybrid from the Manitoba Research Station in Canada and is somewhat more resistant to powdery mildew; its 2-in. blossoms are a bright pink. 'Snow White' displays creamy-white flowers on 3-ft. plants. 'Violet Queen' has hairy leaves and deep purple flowers. Zones 4 to 9.

**M. fistulosa** (fiss-tew-*loh*-suh).
BERGAMOT.
WILD BERGAMOT.
A showy native, distributed from Maine to Florida and west to the Mississippi River. It often makes beautiful lavender patches of color along the roadside and in moist meadows. It likes full sun and plenty of water. A tall plant, $1^1/2$ to $3^1/2$ ft., it thrives in cultivation and is very useful in the wild garden. It should, however, be planted with care, since it may crowd out other plants. A white variety is available. Zones 3 to 9.

**Myosotis** (mye-oh-*soh*-tiss).
FORGET-ME-NOT.
Borage Family *(Boraginaceae)*.
Annuals, perennials and biennials, native to Europe and America; the perennials are almost always grown as annuals. One of the most beautiful of the early spring flowers, growing in matlike clusters, the blossoms of sky-blue, pink and white halted only by the heat of summer. Few spring flowers are as valuable or as pretty as edging plants, as an underplanting in the bulb garden, in the cutting garden, for naturalizing in the wild garden, in moist woodlands and beside pools and small streams. It is also useful in the cool greenhouse. Partial shade and an acid soil give best results, but these flowers are adaptable to many soils and often to full sun. Plants self-sow abundantly once established. Blooms appear in January and February on the West Coast and in other warm areas, later in the spring in regions where it is cooler. Propagate by seeds sown in spring for quick bloom or in fall for earliest bloom, or by division.

**M. palustris.** See *M. scorpoides*.

**M. scorpioides** (skor-pee-*oy*-deez).
(Syn. *M. palustris*.) The true European perennial forget-me-not, free-flowering in spring. The tiny flowers are blue, occasionally pink, with a yellow eye. This is a prostrate plant with stems as much as 18 in long. The variety *semperflorens* (sem-per-*floh*-renz) is more compact than the species; it continues to bloom into summer and is therefore especially useful. Zones 3 to 8.

**Nepeta** (*nep*-e-tuh).
CATMINT.
Mint Family *(Labiatae)*.
Aromatic herbs, both annual and perennial, native to Europe, Asia and Africa. Flowers are blue or white, in clusters or spikes. The stems

are square and the leaves opposite. Most are grown as edging plants. They are easily grown and are propagated by seeds or by division.

### N. × **faassenii** (fahs-*sen*-ee-eye).
FAASSEN'S MINT.

This species is a cross of *N. mussinii* and *N. nepetella*. The gray foliage is opposite, 1¹/₂ in. long, coarsely toothed and pubescent. The surface of the leaves has a crinkled appearence, and when crushed the leaves are aromatic. Each square stem has an open raceme of purple, ¹/₂-in., two-lipped flowers. In flower the plant mounds up to 2 ft. tall. The first flowers open in late spring to early summer and continue through to fall. If the plants are cut back by one-third to one-half after the first flush of flowering is over, they will rebloom in the fall. The flowers are sterile, so plants will not self-sow. Plant in full sun in well-drained, ordinary garden soil. 'Dropmore' is a cultivar with thicker gray-green leaves and lavender-blue flowers. 'Six Hills Giant' is sometimes considered a hybrid of *N. × faassenii*; it grows to 3 ft. and is 3 ft. wide. 'Variegata' has leaves edged with creamy yellow. Zones 4 to 8.

### N. **mussinii** (muss-*seen*-ee-eye).

This plant is similar to *N. × faassenii* but is not as good a garden plant. It tends to sprawl and the flowers do not last as long. Also, the plant self-sows, and overcrowding can thus be a problem. The 1-in.-long foliage is gray and coarsely toothed and has a crinkled appearence. When crushed, the foliage is aromatic. The flowers are blue, in open racemes at the end of each stem. These sprawling mounds are about 1 ft. tall. Plant in well-drained, ordinary garden soil in full sun. 'Blue Wonder' is a 12- to 15-in. cultivar with 6-in. flower spikes. 'Snowflake' is a cream and white selection. Zone 3.

*Nepeta × faassenii* 'Six Hills Giant'
FAASSEN'S MINT

*Oenothera missouriensis*
OZARK SUNDROPS

**Nipponathemum.** See *Chrysanthemum*.

**Oenothera** (ee-noh-*thee*-ruh).
EVENING PRIMROSE.
Evening-primrose Family *(Onagraceae)*.
A large, wide-ranging American genus of annuals, biennials and perennials. All are easily grown in ordinary garden soil and full sun. For the perennials that are not reliably winter-hardy, seeds should be planted every year. Plants are useful in the border, the rock garden and the wild garden. Propagate annuals and biennials by seeds, perennials by root division.

**O. missouriensis** (miz-oor-ee-*en*-sis).
OZARK SUNDROPS.
From the south-central U.S., probably the most decorative of all the species. Large yellow blossoms, 4 to 6 in. across, are produced in showy abundance on this low-growing, spreading, 8- to 10-in.-high perennial. Blooms open in late afternoon during June and July. It can be propagated by crown division or by cuttings. Its habit of growth makes it an especially effective plant in the rock garden. Zones 4 to 8.

**O. speciosa** (spee-see-*oh*-suh).
SHOWY PRIMROSE.
From the south-central U.S., a day-blooming, hardy perennial. Large flowers, 1 to 3 in. across, range in color from white to deep pink. It grows 1½ to 2 ft. tall and blooms freely in May and June. Due to its stoloniferous habit, it can be invasive. The plants bloom from seed the first season. Zones 5 to 8.

**O. tetragona** (tet-ra-*goh*-nuh).
SUNDROPS.
Native to eastern North America. This hardy, shrubby perennial has red stems and blooms during the daylight hours. It grows to 3 ft. high, with bright yellow blossoms, 2 in. across, in showy clusters, produced in a continuing abundance during June and July. It likes a dry, well-drained soil and full sun. The variety *fraseri* (*fray*-zer-eye) has lemon-yellow blooms, and reddish-purple foliage, especially in spring. 'Fireworks' has bright red buds and purplish leaves. 'Yellow River' has large, 2-in. flowers on 18-in. plants. Zones 5 to 9.

★ ★**Paeonia** (pay-*oh*-nee-uh).
PEONY.
Peony Family *(Paeoniaceae)*.
Popular, long-lived, hardy perennials of both herbaceous and shrubby tree forms native to Eurasia and western North America. Peonies are grown in temperate regions for their showy single or double blossoms in shades of rose, pink, white and yellow, which appear in late May and early June. Foliage of the herbaceous types is decorative, with compound leaves that last well until first frosts and are erect on strong stems. In the herbaceous cultivars the entire plant gives a bushy effect, ranging from 1½ ft. to 3½ ft. in height. The flowers are excellent for cutting and are long-lasting. For more information on growing peonies, see the related essay on pages 22–23.

**P. albiflora.** See *P. lactiflora*.

**P. anomala** (a-*nom*-uh-luh).
UNUSUAL PEONY.
From eastern Russia and Central Asia, an early-flowering peony with large, to 4 in., rose flowers, single in form. The flower petals are obovate, the stamens yellow. Each flower has three to five pistils. Zones 2 to 9.

## Paeonia

*Paeonia lactiflora* 'Mrs. Franklin D. Roosevelt'

**P. lactiflora** (lak-ti-*floh*-ruh).
COMMON GARDEN PEONY.
(Formerly *P. albiflora.*) Native to China, it is often used as a rootstock for grafting tree peonies. The plants have 3- to 4-in. blooms with eight or more petals that are particularly showy, in colors of white or pale pink. There is a center of yellow stamens and four to five red pistils. The foliage is dark green and the leaflets lance-shaped. Most of the herbaceous peonies have *P. lactiflora* as one of their parents. There are thousands of cultivars available. Since 1923 the American Peony Society has selected certain cultivars for their outstanding performance by awarding them Gold Medals. Some of the most popular hybrids of this group are 'Bu-te', a white Japanese; 'Bowl of Cream', a creamy-white double; 'Burma Ruby', a bright red single; 'Cytherea', a rose-pink semidouble; 'Dolorodell', a salmon-pink full double;

*Paeonia lactiflora* 'Sky Pilot'

'Kansas', a red double; 'Miss America', a blush-pink, fading white semidouble; 'Moonstone', a blush-pink double; 'Mrs. Franklin D. Roosevelt', a soft light-pink double; 'Nick Shaylor', a blush-pink double; 'Red Charm', a rich red double; 'Walter Mains', a dark red Japanese; and 'Westerner', a pink Japanese.

### P. obovata (ob-oh-*vah*-tuh).
OBOVATE PEONY.

From Siberia and China, an elegant single-flowered peony passed from one gardener to the next via seeds. The foliage is a soft gray-green sometimes flushed with copper. Each stem produces one pristine cup-shaped flower followed by brilliant blue seeds. The botanical variety *alba* (*al*-buh) is most often grown. It is pure white and offset by yellow stamens. Zones 5 to 8.

### P. officinalis (o-fis-i-*nay*-lis).
COMMON PEONY.

From Europe. This red–flowered species was commonly grown in European gardens before the new hybrids were developed. The solitary crimson flowers are 4 to 5 in. across, with yellow stamens and two to three woolly white carpels. 'Alba Plena' has double white flowers. 'Rubra Plena' has double deep red flowers. Zones 3 to 9.

### P. tenuifolia (ten-yew-i-*foh*-lee-uh).
FERNLEAF PEONY.

A European species with elegant, finely cut foliage. Flowers are deep crimson or purplish, 2 to 3 in. and bloom in early May. A larger-blooming double form, 'Rubra Plena', is also available. Zones 4 to 8.

### P. wittmanniana (wit-mann-ee-*ay*-nuh).
WITTMANN'S PEONY.

This native of the Caucasus grows to 3 ft. and has flowers to 4 in. across. The lovely single flowers are yellow with some white. Zones 5 to 8.

## Papaver (pap-*pay*-ver).
POPPY.

Poppy Family *(Papaveraceae)*.

Native to Europe, Asia and North America. Some of the loveliest and most exciting perennial, biennial and annual flowers for borders belong to this genus. The various species range from 6 in. to 4 ft. tall. The basal leaves of poppies are generally hairy and die down soon after flowering. The flowers have shimmering silky petals in shades of white, cream, pink, yellow, orange and red (there are blue poppylike flowers, but these belong to the genus *Meconopsis*). The most popular species are the dramatic and strongly colored perennial Oriental poppies, *P. orientale*; the smaller pastel-hued annual Shirley or corn poppies, *P. rhoeas* (*ree*-as); and the hardy, large-flowered and fragrant Iceland poppy, *P. nudicaule*, (new-di-*kaw*-lee), which is also a perennial.

Perennial and annual species have similar cultural requirements. Poppies need well-drained soil, generally on the light and sandy side. Most may be propagated by seeds, though the perennials may be increased by root division and from root cuttings. Seeds sown in late summer in warmer climates will produce handsome flowers in the spring; in cooler regions they may be planted on the snow or directly in the soil of the border in late winter or early spring. Full sun is required. Annual and perennial poppies do not respond well to transplanting and should, whenever possible, be planted where they are to flower. Most poppies make excellent vase flowers. Sear the stem with a lighted match the moment it is

## Papaver

cut; this stops the flow of milky juice from the stem and helps the blossoms last longer in water.

**P. orientale** (or-ee-en-*tay*-lee).
ORIENTAL POPPY.
Native to the Mediterranean and Persia. This is the most dramatic of all the poppies. Huge, silky blooms, 4 to 8 in. wide, ranging from white to darkest red, are produced on stately stems 24 to 48 in. tall with gracefully arching, feathery foliage. The species has been much hybridized, and striking single- and double-flowered cultivars and strains are available. Plant Oriental poppies in full sun in ordinary garden loam that has been well worked. Propagate by seeds, by division or by root cuttings. Plants propagated by cuttings or division retain the characteristics of the original hybrid, while those raised from seed may not.

Starting Oriental poppies from seed is not difficult. Plant them in sandy soil in a cold frame in early spring or out-of-doors in May. The soil must be finely worked and the seeds planted sparsely in shallow drills, then tamped. Seedlings should be left undisturbed until fall and then planted in their permanent location. The Oriental poppy has thick but rather fragile roots and is difficult to transplant when older. It is slow to establish itself but will increase in size and bloom annually if left undisturbed. Root cuttings can be taken after the foliage has died down late in the season. Lift the root and divide into cuttings 3 to 4 in. long. Set the cuttings in the soil horizontally and cover with 1 in. of fine earth, or set them vertically and top with 1/2 in. of soil. Keep them moist in the cold frame for several weeks, and protect from severe frosts through the winter. Plants will be rooted and ready to transfer to permanent beds in mid-spring.

Some of the most attractive cultivars include 'Bonfire', a brilliant red; 'Cedar Hill', an early light pink; 'China Boy', with 8- to 10-in. blos-soms that are white with an orange border; 'Doubloon', a double orange; 'Fatima', a white with pink edges; 'Helen Elizabeth', a salmon-pink; 'Juliane', a pink, free of spots; 'Karine', a clear pink with red spots; 'May Queen', an older, fully double orange-vermillion, which is somewhat floppy; 'Perry's White', a white with good substance; 'Pinnacle', ruffled white and scarlet flowers; 'Raspberry Queen', a raspberry-pink; 'Show Girl', a clear pink with a white base and ruffled; 'Snow Queen', a white with black spots; 'Suleika', a deep red with bluish spots; 'Turkenlouis', a fiery orange-red with a deeply fringed edge; and 'Withery', an unusual lavender color. Zones 4 to 9.

## Patrinia (pa-*tree*-nee-uh).

Valerian Family *(Valerianaceae)*.
Native to east and central Asia. Most species are slightly rhizomatous or stoloniferous. The basal leaves are simple to pinnatifid. Flowers are yellow or white, usually very small and in cymes or panicles. Plants in flower have a doglike odor.

**P. gibbosa** (gib-*bose*-uh).
Native to Japan. The stems of this plant reach 2 to 2 1/2 ft. in height, with broad, shiny, pinnately cut, opposite leaves about 6 in. long. In summer the 3- to 4-in. clusters of tiny yellow flowers open and last through late summer. Plant in moist, peaty soil in a shady wooded location. It can take full sun if the soil is moist enough. Zones 5 to 9.

**P. scabiosifolia** (scab-ee-oh-si-*foh*-lee-uh).
A plant recently introduced into American gardens by the U.S. National Arboretum. Small yellow flowers, somewhat like the herb dill, are produced in August and September. The seeds are also decorative. Plants reach 5 ft. or taller and grow on a wide range of soil types. Many

*Papaver orientale*
ORIENTAL POPPY

*Papaver orientale* 'Bonfire'
ORIENTAL POPPY

seedlings are produced by the mother plants. Zones 5 to 9.

## Penstemon (pen-*stee*-mon).

BEARD-TONGUE.

Figwort Family *(Scrophulariaceae)*.

A large and diverse genus of perennials, practically all North American. Nearly every region has adapted kinds. Some excel naturalized in open, sunny places. Some are for rock gardens. Bloom season for most comes immediately following iris time. In practice, penstemon species are usually thought of in two broad groups: Eastern and Western. The first stands humid summer heat, high moisture much of the year and perennial garden conditions. The second needs sharp drainage and light, dry air, as in the West. Today there are also many perennial hybrids much more widely adapted than the untamed species, in a great range of colors and types.

*Papaver orientale* 'May Queen'
ORIENTAL POPPY

# Penstemon

Penstemons have blue, purple, red, pink, yellow or white flowers that are funnel-, bell- or tube-shaped, with two lips (three–parted and two–parted above) and five stamens, the fifth being bearded and usually sterile. Flowers are commonly borne on stiff spikes rising from foliage rosettes or mounds that sometimes are evergreen. The plants need much sun, reasonably moist soil during the spring growth season and ordinary garden soil. Few are long-lived (with a few exceptions, like the Elfin series, which is longer-lived than most), but many will self-sow to perpetuate themselves. Most are readily increased by crown divisions taken in spring, summer or fall; they also grow well from seed planted outdoors in fall, winter or early spring in a preferably sterile planting mix, lightly covered. To lengthen the life of the clumps, cut off the seed stalks before they ripen and allow plenty of room between plants. Newly set seedlings of perennial types usually bloom their second season. Some kinds are subject to leaf-spot diseases and are helped by occasional fungicide sprays.

Only a few penstemons are widely available as plants from nursery sources. Some of the easiest to grow are those with the prefix "prairie" from the North Platte Experiment Station in Nebraska. Many more, however, are listed as seeds from specialists or in plant–society exchanges—and most penstemons are easy to grow from seed. Today's best garden penstemons are probably the hybrids grown from seed. Both hybrids and species are highly variable.

**P. barbatus** (bar-*bay*-tus).
BEARDED PENSTEMON.
A fairly long-lived, much-used perennial with glossy, narrow green foliage and stiff stems, up to 4 ft., bearing open panicles of scarlet shark's-head tubular flowers. It grows well in the East although western in origin. The variety *coccineus* (kok-*sin*-ee-us) grows 15 to 18 in. tall and has scarlet flowers, while the variety *torreyi* (torr-ee-eye) differs only in that it does not have a "beard" on the flower stamen. Some frequently offered cultivars are 'Bashful', a 12- to 14-in. plant with orange flowers; 'Crystal', an 8- to 12-in. plant with white flowers; 'Prairie Dawn', with pale pink flowers; 'Prairie Dusk', with rose–purple flowers; 'Prairie Fire', with deep purple flowers; 'Rose Elf', with shell-pink flowers; and 'Twilight', a seed-propagated form with a mix of colors. Zones 2 to 8.

**P. campanulatus** (kam-pan-yew-*lay*-tus).
HAREBELL PENSTEMON.
This species is seldom seen in the U.S.; however, hybrids of *P. campanulatus* and *P. hartwegii* (hart-*wej*-ee-eye) are now commonly grown. The species has narrow, sharply toothed leaves, 3 in. long, and tubular flowers. The plant is identified by its bearded staminode (one stamen that does not bear pollen). 'Evelyn' has pale pink, 1-in. tubular flowers on an 18-in. plant. 'Garnet' has wine-colored flowers, which open in late summer, on a 20-in. plant; it is not particularly winter-hardy. Zones 4 to 7.

**P. digitalis** (dij-i-*tay*-lis).
FOXGLOVE PENSTEMON.
Native to the eastern and central U.S. Stem leaves grow to 7 in. long and are toothed. Flowers are borne in open panicles and are 1 in. across, white or flushed with purple. 'Husker Red' has deep red-bronze leaves and white flowers. Zones 3 to 9.

**P. × gloxinioides** (gloks-in-ee-*oy*-deez).
GLOXINIA PENSTEMON.
These are hybrids of *P. hartwegii* (hart-*wej*-ee-eye), which bears deep scarlet flowers, and *P. cobae* (koh-bay-ee), with reddish-purple to white flowers. The individual flowers are 2 in. wide. Most cultivars lack winter hardiness. 'Firebird'

*Penstemon barbatus* var. *coccineus*
BEARDED PENSTEMON

*Penstemon campanulatus* 'Garnet'
HAREBELL PENSTEMON

has deep red flowers, while 'Sour Grapes' is a grape-purple. Zones 8 to 9.

**Perovskia** (per-*roff*-skee-uh).
RUSSIAN SAGE.
Mint Family *(Labiatae)*.
Deciduous herbs and subshrubs from Turkestan to northeast Iran. They have opposite leaves and small whorls of flowers. They need a sunny spot in well-drained soil. Propagate by softwood cuttings, under glass.

★ **P. × superba** (sue-*per*-buh).
RUSSIAN SAGE.
Most of the plants in the U.S. are a single clone from a cross of *P. atriplicifolia* (a-trip-li-si-*foh*-lee-uh) and *P. abrotanoides* (ab-row-tan-*oy*-deez). The foliage is gray-green, with white hairs on the leaves, and the plant has square stems. Each 1½-in. leaf is coarsely toothed. The flowers appear in

*Perovskia × superba*
RUSSIAN SAGE

spires that are openly branched and about 1 to
$1^1/2$ ft. long. Each tubular flower is light blue.
Flowers open in mid to late summer, and flowering lasts well into fall. The plant is shrublike and
grows to 5 ft. tall. Cut back the stems to the
ground each spring. Plant in full sun in well-
drained garden soil. Newer cultivars include
'Blue Haze', with pale blue flowers and nearly
entire leaves; 'Blue Spire', with bright blue
flowers and finely dissected leaves; and 'Longin',
a hybrid selection 3 to 4 ft. tall with a more
upright plant habit.  Zones 4 to 9.

## Phlomis (*floh*-miss).

Mint Family *(Labiatae).*
Herbaceous perennials and shrubby evergreens
from the Mediterranean region and Asia. The
herbaceous ones have square stems. They bloom
in early summer with clusters of purple, yellow
or white flowers. The shrubs will tolerate poor
soil. Both kinds are good for the wild garden.

**P. fruticosa** (frew-ti-*koh*-suh).
JERUSALEM SAGE.
An erect shrub, growing to 4 ft., with dense yellow or white woolliness. It resembles sage with
its gray-green wrinkled leaves, but the leaves are
larger than those of sage—up to 5 in. long and
$1^3/4$ in. wide. The yellow flower heads have
twenty to thirty florets. Propagate by division in
fall or spring. Zones 4 to 8.

## Phlox (flox).

Phlox Family *(Polemoniaceae).*
Annual or perennial herbaceous plants of North
America, with lance-shaped leaves, opposite or
alternate. The flowers are in loose panicle clusters
atop stiff to willowy erect stems. Each flower has
five petals with a long, narrow tube. Colors range
from whites to pinks, dark reds and maroons, and
some lavender-purples. Orange, cream, buff and

*Phlomis fruticosa*
JERUSALEM SAGE

*Phlox maculata* 'Omega'
MEADOW PHLOX

salmon shades are common in some species and garden strains.

Phlox can be garden assets if a few simple rules are followed. They grow best in an open site where the soil is well drained. Plant, if possible, on a cool site with bright light. Too-brilliant, hot sun often fades bright pink phlox. Divide plants every three to five years. Fill planting holes with topsoil mixed with a generous amount of leafmold and peat moss. Allow only five to six stems per clump on *P. paniculata*; thinning the clump reduces the possibility of powdery mildew. Pinch back one or two stalks in each clump in spring to ensure some bloom after the main phlox season. Removing dying flowers and pinching out green seedpods will also encourage phlox to extend its season of bloom. The tall cultivars may need staking; do this early, before wind or rain has beaten them out of shape.

Water phlox during droughts. Once the roots become bone-dry, the plants may never recover during the season. Soak the soil rather than sprinkling the tops, because the latter can cause the foliage to mildew. A summer mulch is important in hot climates. Sprays to reduce powdery mildew should be applied just before the plants flower and two to four weeks later.

Large perennial species require root division every few years and can be propagated by cuttings, by crown division or by selecting 2-in. sections of root and planting 1 in. deep.

**P. divaricata** (di-var-i-*kay*-tuh).
WOODLAND PHLOX.
Native to eastern North America and one of the favorites for garden use. It is a low, spreading plant about 18 in. high, with soft blue flowers borne profusely from late spring into early June, and is often found wild in woodlands. The variety *laphamii* (laf-*am*-ee-eye) is from the western U.S. and has purple-blue flowers with a magenta eye. 'Dirgo Ice' is an 8- to 12-in.-tall plant with blue flowers; 'Fuller's White' is also a dwarf plant (8 to 12 in. tall) with white flowers; and 'Chattahootchee' is a hybrid between *P. divaricata* var. *laphamii* and *P. pilosa* having blue flowers with red-purple eyes. Zones 3 to 9.

**P. maculata** (mak-yew-*lay*-tuh).
MEADOW PHLOX.
WILD SWEET WILLIAM.
Native to eastern North America and often wild in fields and woodlands where there are open, sunny patches. It is 2 to 3 ft. tall with conical panicles of red, maroon or purple, loosely shaped, and stiff erect stems. The foliage is thick, leathery and glossy. It flowers two weeks before *P. paniculata*. Cultivars include 'Alpha', with lilac–pink flowers on 3-ft. plants; 'Dirgo', white flowers with pink eyes on 3-ft. plants; 'Miss Lingard', also called 'Wedding Phlox', with pure-white flowers on 2- to 4-ft. plants; 'Omega', white flowers flushed violet with a deeper violet eye on 2½-ft. plants; and 'Rosalinde', dark pink flowers on 3-ft. plants. Zones 3 to 9.

★**P. paniculata** (pan-ik-yew-*lay*-tuh).
GARDEN PHLOX.
From eastern North America, the tall, herbaceous border phlox. There are numerous named cultivars that grow to 4 ft. and produce brilliant, showy flower panicles from white to dark red with wide variation in between. Plants can best be shown in mixed borders in an open, sunny site, but aeration is most important, especially where mildew is a problem. Mature plantings should be divided every three to four years to keep clumps thriving. Remove faded flower heads to prevent any reseeding and reverting to the species type.

Among the popular pink cultivars are 'Bright Eyes', pink with a crimson eye; 'Dresden China', pastel-pink with a rose eye; and 'Eva Cullum', clear pink with a darker eye. Purple and lavender cultivars include 'Ann', a late-bloomer with large lavender flower heads; 'Franz Schubert', lilac with a darker eye; and 'Progress', pale violet with a darker eye. In salmon and red shades are 'Fairest One', salmon-pink with a dark red eye; 'Othello', deep red; 'Sandra', bright salmon-red and mildew-resistant; 'Sir John Falstaff', salmon-pink; and 'Starfire', cherry-red.

Cultivars with variegated leaves are 'Harlequin', green leaves edged white with fuchsia-colored flowers; and 'Norah Leigh', creamy-white leaves with green centers and lavender flowers. White cultivars include 'David', large white flowers on a mildew-resistant plant; 'Mt. Fuji', clear white flowers on 4-ft. plants; and 'White Admiral', clear white flowers on late-blooming plants. Zones 4 to 8.

**P. stolonifera** (stoh-lon-if-*er*-uh).
CREEPING PHLOX.
From eastern North America, a creeping ground cover with purple flowers; one of the most shade-tolerant species. Plants produce both flowering and sterile shoots. The flower petals are usually unnotched. 'Blue Ridge' has blue-lilac flowers; 'Bruce's White' has white flowers with yellow eyes; 'Pink Ridge' has mauve-pink flowers; and 'Sherwood Purple' has purple-lilac flowers that are very fragrant. Zones 2 to 8.

**P. subulata** (sub-yew-*lay*-tuh).
GROUND PINK.
MOSS PINK.
Native to eastern North America, a mat-forming phlox that often carpets rock gardens and slopes with tiny pink flowers in early May. It prefers full sun. The small green leaves are evergreen. Many garden cultivars and hybrids are available. 'Apple Blossom' is flush-pink with a deeper eye; 'Blue

Hills' is light blue; 'Crimson Beauty' is red; 'Millstream Jupiter' is blue; 'Venus' bears pink flowers; and 'White Delight' is pure white. Zones 2 to 9.

## Physalis (*fiss*-a-lis).
Nightshade Family (*Solanaceae*).
There are nearly 100 species in this genus, but only one, *P. alkekengi*, is of importance to gardeners. Most are creeping plants. The flowers are axillary and not too showy. The calyx becomes large and bladderlike.

**P. alkekengi** (al-ke-*ken*-jee).
CHINESE-LANTERN.
Native to Japan. This species is grown in gardens for the bladderlike orange structures surrounding the fruit. They look much like small Chinese lanterns. The leaves are broad-based and 2 to 3 in. long. Plant in full sun on sites that can supply constant moisture. To dry, collect the lanterns immediately after they enlarge and take on the orange color. 'Gigantea' has fruits up to 8 in. wide. 'Pygmaea' grows 12 to 15 in. tall. Zones 3 to 9.

## Physostegia (fye-so-*stee*-jee-uh).
FALSE DRAGONHEAD.
OBEDIENT PLANT.
Mint Family (*Labiatae*).
Hardy, persistent, decorative, native American perennials, blooming from July to September. Plants produce slender spikes of pink, purple or white, two-lipped, tubular florets. The individual florets can be twisted to a different position and will stay put, accounting for the common name obedient plant. Rich, moist soil and full sun or light shade give best results. Good border plants when in large clumps, they are also fine for the wild garden and make long-lasting cut flowers. Propagate by crown division or by seeds.

*Phlox paniculata* 'Franz Schubert'
GARDEN PHLOX

*Physalis alkekengi*
CHINESE-LANTERN

*Phlox paniculata* 'Starfire'
GARDEN PHLOX

*Physostegia virginiana* 'Vivid'
OBEDIENT PLANT

# Physostegia

**P. virginiana** (ver-jin-ee-*ay*-nuh).

Obedient Plant.

Native to the eastern U.S., an easily grown, interesting perennial, graceful from July to September, depending on the cultivar. Long spires of bloom are produced on stems 3 to 4 ft. high. The species has individual purplish-pink florets that are 1 in. long. The leaves are slender, toothed and blue-green, in basal clusters and along the stems. White and light pink cultivars are available. Botanical varieties include *alba* (*al*-buh), which is pure white, 20 in. and blooms from mid-July to September; and *grandiflora* (gran-di-*floh*-ruh), which has larger rose flowers on $3^{1}/_{2}$-ft. plants from August to October. Cultivars include 'Summer Snow', a white, $2^{1}/_{2}$-ft. plant that blooms from July to September; 'Variegata', a handsome white variegated plant with rose flowers; and 'Vivid', a dark pink, 20-in. dwarf that blooms from mid-July to October and is a long-lasting cut flower. All are sturdy and effective. Zones 2 to 9.

## Platycodon (plat-i-*koh*-don).

Balloon Flower.

Bellflower Family (*Campanulaceae*).

There is only one species, a showy perennial from eastern Asia. Long–lived and hardy, it needs plenty of water, full sun and a loose, porous soil. The roots are often used as a vegetable crop in Asian countries. Propagate by seeds or by division in late spring.

**P. grandiflorus** (gran-di-*floh*-rus).

Plants grow $1^{1}/_{2}$ to $2^{1}/_{2}$ ft., with fine, blue, pink or white blossoms that are 3 in. across when fully open and plumply balloon-shaped when in bud. Blooms appear in July and August. When well grown, this plant is distinctive and well branched, but often needs staking. It is especially effective in the mid-border, or, in its dwarf forms, in the rock

garden. Shoots appear very late in spring; mark clumps so they are not harmed by early cultivation. The botanical variety *mariesii* (mar-*reez*-ee-eye) is shorter than the type, growing to only 18 in., and needs no staking. It has dark blue or white flowers. A double variety, *plenus* (*plee*-nus), is worth growing. There are also several cultivars. Two frequently offered are 'Apoyama', a 15- to 18-in. plant with violet flowers, and 'Shell Pink', a seed-propagated selection with pink flowers on 18- to 24-in. plants.

## Plumbago larpentiae.

See *Ceratostigma plumbaginoides*.

## Polemonium (pol-e-*moh*-nee-um).

Phlox Family (*Polemoniaceae*).

Easily grown, hardy, spring-flowering perennials, mostly from North America. The individual flowers, usually blue, bloom in graceful clusters and resemble the common garden phlox. They last well when cut. A rich, porous, well-drained soil and light shade are needed. Propagate by seeds sown in spring or by crown division in late summer.

**P. caeruleum** (see-*rew*-lee-um).

Jacob's-ladder.

Found wild in moist woods in the U.S., a moundlike plant for the perennial border, with yellow-anthered blue florets, 1 in. across, in showy clusters. Flower stems are 1 to $2^{1}/_{2}$ ft. high. Blooms appear in May and June. The variety *album* (*al*-bum) has white flowers. Zones 2 to 7.

**P. reptans** (*rep*-tanz).

Creeping Polemonium.

Native to eastern North America, this plant is a wild flower through much of the eastern and midwestern woodlands. It grows only 1 ft. tall and has a shallow rhizome, but it does not

*Platycodon grandiflorus*
BALLOON FLOWER

*Polemonium caeruleum*
JACOB'S-LADDER

spread as the common name implies. Each leaf is made up of seven to fifteen leaflets. The variety *alba* (*al*-buh) bears white flowers, while the cultivar 'Blue Pearl' grows 8 to 10 in. tall and has blue flowers.

## Polygonatum (poh-lig-oh-*nay*-tum).
SOLOMON'S-SEAL.
Lily Family (*Liliaceae*).
Lovely spring-blooming wild flowers native to the whole North American continent, found along damp roadsides and in rich, half-shady woods. They make fine plants for the rock garden or the wild garden. Deep, rich, humusy soil and partial shade are needed. Propagate by seeds or by root division.

### P. biflorum (bye-*floh*-rum).
SMALL SOLOMON'S-SEAL.
Native to eastern North America. It grows 3 ft. tall, with arching, graceful, leafy stems. Greenish-white tubular flowers, in twos, are suspended from the axils of the paired leaves. It is easily grown and attractive in the rock garden, as well as effective for flower arrangements. Zones 3 to 9.

### P. commutatum (kom-mew-*tay*-tum).
GREAT SOLOMON'S-SEAL.
Found from the U.S. to Mexico. Plants may reach 5 to 6 ft. in height and form colonies equally as wide. They are excellent for the edges of moist woodlands. In spring, $3/4$-in. yellow-green to whitish-green flowers are produced in 3- to 8-flowered clusters in the leaf axils. Zones 3 to 7.

### P. odoratum (oh-door-*ah*-tum).
FRAGRANT SOLOMON'S-SEAL.
Native to Europe and Asia. The stems of this $1^1/2$- to 2-ft. plant are unbranched and arching. Each leaf has two bell-shaped, 1-in. white flowers

## Polygonatum

*Polygonatum odoratum*
FRAGRANT SOLOMON'S-SEAL

*Polygonum bistorta* 'Superbum'
SNAKEWEED

*Polygonum affine* 'Dimity'
HIMILAYAN FLEECE FLOWER

*Porteranthus trifoliata*
BOWMAN'S-ROOT

dangling from the axil. The lancelike leaves are alternate; there are eight to twelve on each stem. These plants grow well in wooded areas. Plant in partial shade. Garden performance is best when there is bright light and rich, moist soil. The variety *thunbergii* (thun-*ber*-jee-eye) is a larger plant than the species. Stems grow 3 ft. tall and have 6-in. leaves. A cultivar, 'Variegata', has green leaves with white margins. It is attractive with ferns and bleeding-hearts. Zones 3 to 9.

## Polygonum (poh-*lig*-oh-num).
FLEECE FLOWER.

KNOTWEED.

Buckwheat Family (*Polygonaceae*).

Annuals and perennials from Europe and Asia. They vary in hardiness, but all are easily grown in full sun or light shade and ordinary garden soil, well turned to a spade's depth. Plants have alternate leaves and produce small pink or white flowers; the angled stems are curving and jointed. They are useful in borders or the wild garden, but they are vigorous growers and should be kept under control. Propagate perennials by seeds or by division. In addition to the exotic garden species listed below, many polygonums grow natively, particularly in wet meadows and along streams. While ornamental in their native habitat, these are not suitable for garden use.

### P. affine (a-*fee*-nee).
HIMALAYAN FLEECE FLOWER.

Native to the Himalayas. The 6- to 9-in. tall plants are for the front of the border or can be used as a ground cover. The green leaves are 4 in. long and turn bronzy in winter. The rose flowers appear in 2- to 3-in. spikes on upright stalks. Plants enjoy cool, moist areas. Full sun is necessary for them to stay compact. 'Darjeeling Red' is a vigorous cultivar with deep pink flowers. 'Donald Lowndes' is 8 to 10 in. tall and carries double salmon-pink

flowers. 'Superbum', sometimes listed as 'Dimity', is a more-vigorous form and starts with blush-white flowers, which turn to crimson; winter foliage is bronzy-brown. Zones 3 to 7.

### P. bistorta (biss-*tor*-tuh).
SNAKEWEED.

From Europe to Asia, a sturdy perennial with pink or white clusters of tiny florets on upright stems, $1\frac{1}{2}$ to 2 ft. tall. The flowers are long-lasting and make good cut flowers. Leaves are medium green with a prominent white midrib. Plants bloom in August and early September. 'Superbum' has larger flowers than the species and is the form usually offered in commerce. Zones 3 to 8.

## Porteranthus (por-ter-*an*-thus).
BOWMAN'S-ROOT.

INDIAN-PHYSIC.

(Syn. *Gillenia*.) There are two species native to eastern North America. Leaves are three-parted, sessile or short-stalked. The flowers are white or pinkish with five delicate, narrow petals borne in loose, flat-topped corymbs.

### P. trifoliata (tri-fo-lee-*ah*-ta).
BOWMAN'S-ROOT.

From Ontario to Georgia and west to Missouri. In summer, masses of starry little white flowers cover the trifoliate leaves. The wine-colored, tubular sepals persist after the petals fall. Plants are usually about 2 ft. tall, but some grow to 4 ft. They enjoy cool, moist woodland areas with bright light. Propagate by seeds. Zone 4.

## Primula (*prim*-yew-luh).
PRIMROSE.

Primrose Family (*Primulaceae*).

A large and extermely varied genus of beautiful spring-blooming perennials from Europe and Asia,

## Primula

found in cool or alpine regions. Primroses combine well with daffodils and tulips and are a mainstay of the spring rock garden. They make a splendid underplanting beneath deciduous trees before the leaves open and are very effective in the wild garden, especially when planted in groups or masses.

The English primroses and their hybrids are lower-growing than the Asiatic species. All need rich soil, plenty of water all summer (amounts vary with the species) and partial shade after flowering is over. The damp, cool sections of the West Coast are ideal for primroses, which do well under trees tall enough to filter the sunlight in spring and shade the plants from midsummer heat. Some species are at their best beside woodland streams and ponds. Others are grown commercially under glass.

While primroses depend for their greatest garden value on some of the named horticultural strains, the following species and hybrids are representative of the most beautiful and adaptable.

**P. denticulata** (den-tik-yew-*lay*-tuh).
DRUMSTICK PRIMROSE.
A hardy Himalayan species, 12 to 15 in. high, with dense clusters of white or lavender florets above basal rosettes of broad, handsome, spatulate leaves. Plants bloom in May and June. Most need protection from the winter sun. The variety *alba* (*al*-buh) is a white-flowered form. The variety *cachemiriana* (kash-em-mihr-ee-*ay*-nuh) has fine, dark purple flowers and decorative, gray-green, powdery leaves. 'Ronsdorf Strain' is a seed-propagated cultivar in a mix of white, purple and rose. Propagate this species by seeds or by division. Zones 5 to 8.

*Primula japonica*
JAPANESE PRIMROSE

*Prunella × webbiana*
SELF-HEAL

**P. japonica** (jap-*pon*-i-kuh).

JAPANESE PRIMROSE.

From Japan, a sturdy, showy, vigorous plant with flower stems 1 to 2 ft. high, topped by heavy, whorled, candelabra clusters of purple or white flowers, 1 in. across, and with basal clusters of leaves. It blooms in June and July. It naturalizes readily in wet but well-drained shady locations and is excellent in the border. Extensive hybridizing has produced many fine colors— white and all shades of red and rose, as well as striped and bicolored blooms. It usually makes a late start in spring. 'Bartley Strain' is pale pink and considered one of the finest; 'Miller's Crimson' has bright red flowers; and 'Postford White' has large white flowers. Zones 5 to 7.

**P sieboldiana** (see-bole-*dee*-ah-nah)

SIEBOLD PRIMULA.

Plants are covered with fine hairs. Flowers are 1 to 1½ in. wide and are held well above the foliage. The foliage often goes dormant in summer; because of this feature it survives the hot summers of the northeastern U.S. 'Alba' is a white-flowered cultivar; 'Akatonbo' has dark rose, lacy flowers; and 'Sumina' produces large blooms in blue. Propagate by seeds or by division. Zones 5 to 8.

## Prunella (proo-*nell*-uh).

Mint Family (*Labiatae*).

(Sometimes listed as *Brunella*.) Low-growing, hardy perennials from Europe and Asia. The leafy stems creep and root, forming dense mats from which the flower spikes grow in summer. Purple, violet, pink or white flowers bloom in dense, elongated heads with leafy bracts. Useful in the rock garden, *Prunella* is also a good ground cover for almost any location, thriving in poor soil and partial shade. It can become a pest in the lawn, however, and should be used with care. Propagate by division or by seeds.

**P.** × **webbiana** (web-ee-*ay*-nuh).

SELF-HEAL.

A plant of hybrid origin, very similar to *P. grandiflora* (gran-di-*floh*-ruh); probably a hybrid of *P. grandiflora* and *P. grandiflora* var. *pyrenaica* (pye-ren-*ay*-i-kuh). This hybrid species has blunter leaves and a shorter growth habit, but the flower is the same as that of *P. grandiflora*. Plant in full sun to partial shade in moist soil. Do not allow plants to dry out. 'Little Red Riding Hood' is 6 in. tall and has red spikes; 'Loveliness' has lavender flowers; 'Pink Loveliness' produces pink flowers; and 'White Loveliness' is a white-flowered form. Zones 5 to 8.

## Pulmonaria (pull-moh-*nay*-ree-uh).

LUNGWORT.

Borage Family (*Boraginaceae*).

European perennials with spotted, hairy leaves and pretty, funnel-shaped flowers in clusters. Plants are easily grown in sun or partial shade, in ordinary garden soil with ample moisture. They need dividing every three or four years for best bloom. Roots can become infected with the root-knot nematode. Propagate by seeds or by division.

**P. angustifolia** (an-gus-ti-*foh*-lee-uh).

BLUE LUNGWORT.

The leaves and flowers emerge at the same time. Leaves are dark green, hairy and unspotted. They arise mostly from the plant base, but some appear along the flower stem. The flower stem grows to about 1 ft. tall. In early spring the pink buds open to form a cluster of nodding, blue, trumpet-shaped flowers. This plant makes a good ground cover. Plant in full to partial shade in average garden soil that is cool and moist. It will tolerate full sun but the foliage looks shabby by the end of the season. 'Azurea' has lovely blue flowers; 'Mawson's Blue' produces violet-blue flowers; and 'Munstead's Blue' bears pure blue flowers. Zones 2 to 8.

**P. longifolia** (lon-ji-*foh*-lee-uh).
LONG-LEAVED LUNGWORT.
Native to western Europe, 10 in. high and 20 in. wide. The foliage is five to six times as long as wide. It is more adaptable in areas that have hot summers, and its deep blue flowers are displayed a little later than those of other species. 'Bertram Anderson' has purple-blue flowers and dark green leaves spotted silvery green. Zones 3 to 8.

**P. rubra** (*rue*-bruh).
RED LUNGWORT.
Native to southeastern Europe. Its salmon-red flowers are a distinct departure from the blue lungworts. The foliage is light green and is evergreen in milder climates. 'Bowle's Red' has red flowers and spotted leaves; 'Redstart' is a more compact plant with darker red flowers; and 'Salmon Glow' bears salmon flowers. Zones 4 to 7.

★ **P. saccharata** (sak-kar-*ray*-tuh).
BETHLEHEM SAGE.
Native to Italy and France. Plants grow up to 1½ ft. and produce pink, tubular flowers that turn blue as they mature. The leaves are three times as long as wide and are white-spotted. An early bloomer, it flowers in late April and May and is pretty in the wild garden or the spring border. The soil should be light and porous, and ample moisture should be available. Propagate by division.

The variety *alba* (al-buh) has white flowers and can be raised from seed. 'Highdown' is taller than the species and has blue flowers earlier in the season; 'Margery Fish' is more vigorous than the species; 'Mrs. Moon' has large, silver-spotted leaves and pink flowers that turn blue, and is the most commonly offered clone; and 'Sissinghurst

White' has large white flowers and white coalescing spots. Zones 3 to 8.

## Ranunculus (ra-*nun*-kew-lus).
BUTTERCUP.
CROWFOOT.
Buttercup Family (*Ranunculaceae*).
A large genus of pretty perennials, widely scattered over Europe and North America, with yellow or, occasionally, pink or white blossoms. Most are easily grown in ordinary garden soil, well turned to a spade's depth. They require full sun and plenty of moisture. They are useful in the perennial border, the wild garden or the rock garden. Propagate by seeds (germination is likely to be slow and irregular) or by division.

**R. aconitifolius** (ak-oh-nye-ti-*foh*-lee-us).
ACONITE BUTTERCUP.
Native to the Alps, this buttercup grows 2 to 3 ft. high, with clusters of white blooms, 1 in. across. The flowers are held well above the deeply cut, palmate foliage, which is thick near the base. Blooms appear in May and June. The variety *flore-pleno* (*floh*-re-*plee*-noh) is a double white, while *luteo-plenus* (*lew*-tee-oh-*plee*-nus) is a pretty double yellow. Zones 5 to 8.

**R. acris** (*ay*-kris).
COMMON BUTTERCUP.
Native to Europe. This is the familiar buttercup seen growing wild in fields and by roadsides. Though not a native to the U.S., it has naturalized so extensively as to be considered indigenous. Several golden-yellow, shining, cup-shaped blossoms, 1 in. across, appear on each slim-stemmed plant, 2 to 3 ft. high. Leaves are divided into three to seven sections (usually five). The double variety, *flore-pleno* (*floh*-ree-*plee*-noh), is sometimes grown in borders, in the rock garden or in the wild garden, and does not spread as

rapidly as the species. Even less invasive is the variety *stevenii* (stee-*ven*-ee-eye), which has single and semi-double yellow flowers on plants sometimes reaching 3 to 4 ft. Zones 3 to 7.

**R. montanus** (mon-*tay*-nus).
MOUNTAIN BUTTERCUP.
This native of the European Alps is a dwarf, to 6 in., with 3- to 5-parted leaves and lovely 1-in.-wide golden-yellow flowers in spring. It spreads rapidly to make a good ground cover. 'Molten Gold' has larger golden-yellow flowers than the species. Zones 5 to 8.

# Rheum (*ree*-um).
RHUBARB.
Buckwheat Family (*Polygonaceae*).
Perennial herbaceous herbs native to Asia and grown for their striking foliage and flowers. The species *rhabarbarum* (ra-*bar*-bar-um) is garden rhubarb, grown for the edible stalk. The ornamentals have long-stalked leaves that are divided, finger-fashion, and numerous flowers in clusters appear at the end of a central stalk. Propagate by rooted pieces in early spring.

**R. palmatum** (pal-*may*-tum).
ORNAMENTAL RHUBARB.
Growing to 5 ft., this species has leaves that are light green above, purplish below, heart-shaped at the base and palmately lobed. Flowers stalks are 2 ft. tall with crimson flowers. It requires constant moisture and some shade during the hottest part of the day. Japanese beetles may damage the foliage. 'Astrosanguineum' has new leaves with dark purple coloring; the flowers are a deep cherry-red, followed by attractive fruit. 'Bowle's Variety' is similar but has rose-red flowers. Zones 4 to 7.

*Ranunculus aconitifolius*
ACONITE BUTTERCUP

*Rheum palmatum* 'Atropurpureum'
ORNAMENTAL RHUBARB

## Rheum

**R. rhubarbarum.** See *Rheum*.

## Rodgersia (rod-*jer*-see-uh).

Saxifrage Family (*Saxifragaceae*).

Native to Japan and China, a small group of herbaceous perennials grown for their handsome foliage and plumelike flower spikes. They need a deeply worked soil into which a generous portion of moisture-holding peat moss or compost has been worked, and are most successful in a location free of direct midday sun. They are particularly effective massed in groups on a moist bank. Propagate by seeds or by crown division in spring before new growth starts.

**R. aesculifolia** (ees-kew-li-*foh*-lee-uh).
FINGERLEAF RODGERSIA.
Native to China. Plants eventually grow 5 to 6 ft. tall and 6 ft. wide. Basal leaves are composed of seven 6- to 10-in.-long leaflets that are coarsely toothed. The leaves look like those of horse-chestnut trees. The petioles are covered with brown hairs. Flower panicles are 1½ to 2 ft. long and bear creamy-white flowers. Zones 5 to 6.

**R. pinnata** (pin-*nay*-tuh).
FEATHERLEAF RODGERSIA.
Native to China. The basal foliage is pinnately compound, but because the leaves are close together can have the appearance of being palmately compound. At the end of the long petioles are five to nine leaflets, each about 8 in. long with serrations around the edges. Leaf diameter is 12 to 16 in. Each vein is impressed into the leaf surface, giving the surface a crinkled appearance. The plant forms a rounded mound with the flower heads standing above the foliage. Each flower stalk is 3 to 4 ft. tall with a dense, branched panicle of pale pink to rose-red, tiny, petalless flowers appearing in late spring. These panicles resemble those of astilbes. A single plant

*Rodgersia pinnata*
FEATHERLEAF RODGERSIA

*Rudbeckia fulgida*
ORANGE CONEFLOWER

can grow quite large, up to 5 ft. wide, spreading by thick rhizomes. Plant in cool, moist, highly organic soil, such as on a streambank or pond edge. Give full sun to partial shade; in full sun, it must have constant moisture or the leaf edges turn brown. Cultivars include 'Alba', with creamy-white to yellow flowers; 'Elegans', rose-pink flowers; 'Rose', rose flowers; 'Rubra', rose-red flowers; and 'Superba', with bronze-purple leaves less coarse than the species and with long-lasting rose-red flowers. Zones 5 to 7.

### R. podophylla (pod-oh-*fill*-uh).
BRONZELEAF RODGERSIA.

Native to China and Japan. This species is valued for its foliage, which reaches 3 to 4 ft. in height from a fleshy perennial rootstock, and has leaves that are bright green when young and become bronze as they mature. It differs from *R. aesculifolia* by having only five leaflets. Blooms of feathery cream plumes appear in summer. Zones 4 to 6.

### R. tabularis (tab-yew-*lay*-ris).
SHIELDLEAF RODGERSIA.

Native to China and Korea. Leaves are large, circular and lobed (not compound). The petioles attach to the middle of the leaves. Both sepals and petals are found on the flowers, which distinguishes it from other *Rodgersia* species, which do not have flower petals. Zones 5 to 7.

## Rudbeckia (rud-*bek*-ee-uh).
CONEFLOWER.

Composite Family (*Compositae*).

(Sometimes listed as *Echinacea*.) Annual, biennial and perennial plants, all native to North America. Though coarse in habit, they are sturdy, especially useful for their August and September bloom, and good in the border, the wild garden or the cutting garden. All the species have raised, conelike centers, and some have two-colored petals. Color generally ranges from pale yellow to orange, with some red tones and some bronze shades. Ordinary garden soil, well turned to a spade's depth, and full sun are the only cultural requirements. They are easily grown from seed, or, in the case of the perennials, by crown division.

### ★ R. fulgida (*full*-jih-duh).
ORANGE CONEFLOWER.

Native to North America. The foliage is entire and hairy. The dense, dark green, basal leaves give rise to 30-in. flower stems topped by 2- to 3-in. daisylike flowers with golden-orange ray flowers and black or dark brown disk flowers. Flowers appear from July to September. The flower centers or cones are attractive all winter and can be used in dried-flower arrangements. Each plant produces a large quantity of blossoms, which cover the entire plant with bloom. These plants are slightly rhizomatous, but the growth is slow and noninvasive. Plant in full sun in well-drained, average garden soil. There are four botanical varieties of this species: *compacta* (kom-*pak*-tuh), which grows 15 to 18 in. tall with smaller flowers; *deamii* (*deam*-ee-eye), with large basal leaves on 24-in. plants and more flowers than the species; *speciosa* (spee-see-*oh*-suh; syn. *R. newmanii*), growing 18 in. tall with 2$^{1}/_{2}$-in. flowers and deep ray petals; and *sullvantii* (sull-*van*-tee-eye), with its popular cultivar 'Goldsturm' bearing 3- to 4-in., deep yellow flowers on 30-in. plants. Zones 3 to 9.

### R. laciniata (las-in-ee-*ay*-tuh).
CUTLEAF CONEFLOWER.

From North America, a familiar, tall-growing perennial, to 9 ft., usually seen in the cultivar 'Golden Glow', a 5- to 7-ft. double with light yellow flowers in late summer, grown in almost every farmhouse garden. The lobed leaves and flowers, 4 in. across, make a fine display in

## Rudbeckia

August and September. Plants are of very easy culture. The species has single yellow flowers tinged with green and grows wild from the East Coast to the Midwest. Zones 3 to 9.

**R. newmanii.**  See *R. fulgida* var. *speciosa*.

**R. nitida** (*nit*-id-uh).
Shining Coneflower.
From the southern U.S., a perennial form, 4 ft. tall, with 6-in. lance-shaped leaves and drooping yellow ray flowers. The center disk is 2 in. tall, greenish and columnar. Two cultivars are commonly grown: 'Autumn Sun', a 5-ft. plant with drooping yellow flower petals displayed from August to October; and 'Goldquelle', with double yellow flowers on 3-ft. plants blooming from July to October. Zones 4 to 10.

**R. triloba** (try-*loh*-buh).
Three-lobed Coneflower.
Native to the U.S. These 24-in. plants carry many small 1¹/₂-in. yellow flowers with purplish-black cones in the center. Flowers are flat and round and open about the same time as *R. fulgida* var. *sullvantii* 'Goldsturm'. The species name comes from the 3-lobed basal leaves. With the increased interest in native plants, this one is again appearing on sales lists. The variety *nana* (*nay*-nuh) is a shorter plant and blooms earlier. Zones 3 to 10.

## Salvia (*sal*-vee-uh).
Sage.
Mint Family (*Labiatae*).
A large genus, native to many parts of the temperate zones and the tropics. It includes annuals, biennials and perennials, as well as shrubs and the kitchen herb called sage, *S. officinalis*. Almost all have small flowers in showy spikes and are square-stemmed, as are all mints. Full sun, ample moisture and a fairly rich garden soil, well turned to a spade's depth, are required. They are grown from seed, started indoors in February, outdoors in late April or early May. Perennials can also be propagated by root division or by cuttings. Most sages are grown in borders for their decorative properties, but some are grown commercially and in herb gardens for their pungent leaves, used as seasonings for meats and sausages and for sage tea. Plants are well adapted to the cool greenhouse.

**S. azurea** (a-*zoo*-ree-uh).
Azure Sage.
Native to the southeastern U.S. Plants grow 3 to 4 ft. tall and produce spikelike blue flowers in the fall when few other plants are in bloom. The variety *grandiflora* (gran-di-*floh*-ruh; syn. *S. pitcheri*) has paler green leaves and paler blue flowers. On rich garden soils it may need staking. *S. uliginosa* (ewe-lig-i-*noh*-suh) is a similar, less hardy South American species that thrives on wet sites. Propagate by seeds, by division or by terminal cuttings. Zones 5 to 9.

**S. nemorosa** (nem-oh-*roh*-suh).
Wood Sage.
Native to southeast Europe. Several good garden cultivars are juggled from species to species. The hybrid clone 'Superba' is such an example. It is a bushy plant with many erect, branching spikes and violet-blue flowers. The large crimson-purple flower bracts add further dimension to the spikes. Two other cultivars, 'East Friesland' and 'Lubeca', are very similar, growing 18 in. tall. If the flower spikes are cut after the first bloom, plants will flower again. 'Lubeca' blooms two weeks longer than 'East Friesland'. The cultivar 'May Night' is also similar but 6 in. taller. It is considered a hybrid of *S. pratensis* and *S. nemorosa* and is usually listed under the hybrid designation *S. × sylvestris* (sil-*ves*-tris). Slugs are attracted to these cultivars and need to be controlled.

*Salvia officinalis*
GARDEN SAGE

Propagate by crown division or by tip cuttings. Zones 5 to 9.

### S. officinalis (o-fis-i-*nay*-lis).
GARDEN SAGE.
From Spain west to the Balkan Peninsula and Asia Minor, a familiar perennial garden herb with grayish, hairy leaves, used for flavoring. When grown commercially it is treated as an annual. Its purple or white flowers make an attractive display in early summer. The plant grows 24 to 36 in. tall. 'Albiflora' bears white flowers; 'Purpurascens' has reddish-purple leaves and purple flowers; and 'Tricolor' has white, purple-tipped, variegated leaves and purple flowers. Zones 4 to 9.

### S. pratensis (pray-*ten*-sis).
A hardy, 3-ft. perennial with red-spotted, wrinkled foliage and blue, sometimes rose or white flowers. It is very often considered the same as *S. haema-*

*todes* (hee-ma-*toe*-deez). If spent blooms are removed, another bloom flush usually results. The variety *alba* (*al*-buh) is a white-flowered form, while the variety *tenorii* (ten-*or*-ee-eye) has deep blue flowers. Cultivars include 'Atroviolacea', with dark violet flowers; 'Indigo', with blue flowers on well-branched plants; 'Rosea', with rose-purple flowers; and 'Variegata', with light blue flowers streaked white. Propagate by cuttings. Zones 3 to 9.

## Sanguinaria (san-gwin-*ay*-ree-uh).
Poppy Family (*Papaveraceae*).
Native to the woods of the eastern U.S. and Canada. The only species is a low, spring-blooming perennial with red sap. The handsome, deeply lobed leaves, which begin unfolding at the same time as the flowers, are carried singly on stems that grow directly from the root and continue to grow after the flowers are gone. The small, white, starry flowers are borne singly. It grows best in a light soil with plenty of decayed plant material, in partial to full shade. It needs abundant moisture and does well in the rock or wild garden. Propagate by seeds or by root division.

### S. canadensis (kan-a-*den*-sis).
BLOODROOT.
It grows 6 to 8 in. tall with white flowers 1¹/2 to 2 in. across. The rich dark green leaves, one of

*Sanguinaria canadensis*
BLOODROOT

the most attractive features of the plant, may reach a diameter of 8 to 10 in. by late spring. A double cultivar, 'Multiplex', is available, one of the few double-flowered plants that retain most of the simple loveliness of single-flowered forms. Zones 3 to 8.

## Sanguisorba (san-*gwi*-sor-buh).

Rose Family (*Rosaceae*).

Tall, hardy perennials native to Europe, Asia and North America. Plants produce alternate, compound, boldly toothed leaves and small spikes of minute flowers in late summer. They are easily grown in the summer border or the herb garden. Japanese beetles sometimes damage the foliage. Propagate by seeds or by root division in early spring.

### S. canadensis (kan-a-*den*-sis).
CANADIAN BURNET.

A slender, erect plant native to marshes and wet meadows of North America. It grows up to 6 ft. tall. The compound leaves have ten to fifteen oblong, finely toothed leaflets. The spikes of the tiny white florets are about 6 in. long. It needs moist soil similar to that of its native habitat. Plant in full sun in the North and shade in the South. It can be grown in the wild garden. Propagate by seeds or by division. Zones 3 to 8.

### S. obtusa (ob-*too*-suh).
JAPANESE BURNET.

From Japan, a graceful plant reaching 3 to 4 ft. in height and displaying 4- to 6-in.-long pink, slightly nodding, bottlebrush blossoms. The leaves are gray-green and made up of seven to thirteen leaflets. They do best in moist soils. The variety *albiflora* (al-bi-*floh*-ruh) has white flowers. Propagate by seeds or by division. Zones 4 to 8.

### S. officinalis (o-fis-i-*nay*-lis).
BURNET.

An herb growing to 5 ft., with 7 to 13 leaflets to each leaf. The 1-in. dark purple flowers grow on 1-in. spikes. Native to Europe and Asia, it has become naturalized in North America. 'Rubra' is an improved color form. Zones 4 to 8.

## Santolina (san-toh-*lye*-nuh).

Composite Family (*Compositae*).

From the Mediterranean region, gray-leaved, low-growing, evergreen shrubs with inconspicuous flowers and aromatic leaves. The plants are useful in the rock garden, in the herb garden and as a low, clipped hedge at the front of a border. Ordinary garden soil, good drainage and full sun are needed. Propagate by cuttings rooted in sand.

### S. chamaecyparissus (kam-ee-sip-*ar*-iss-us).
LAVENDER COTTON.

This is a very attractive plant and the most common species in cultivation. It is shrubby with many small branches, 1 to 2 ft. high, and cool-looking in the brightest sun because of its grayness. In moonlight its coral-like branches reflect the moon's rays. The small, pale yellow, inconspicuous florets, $1/2$ in. across, bloom in July and August. In addition to its garden uses, lavender cotton is very effective indoors in winter arrangements, where it is appreciated for its form and its continuing fragrance. It has long been used in knot gardens, where its grayness provides a contrast to green hedges. The dwarf cultivar 'Nana' is popular for bedding. Zones 6 to 8.

### S. virens (*vye*-renz).
GREEN LAVENDER COTTON.

Native to the Mediterranean region. It has a spreading form with narrow, linear green leaves and cream-toned flowers on 18-in.-tall plants. Plants are excellent for edging. Zones 6 to 8.

*Sanguisorba canadensis*
CANADIAN BURNET

*Santolina chamaecyparissus*
LAVENDER COTTON

**Saponaria** (sap-oh-*nay*-ree-uh).

SOAPWORT.

Pink Family (*Caryophyllaceae*).

Annuals and perennials from the Old World, in many colors and sizes. White, pink, rose and scarlet flowers are all included in the species listed below. Many are fragrant. All last very well when cut. The plants are showy, easily grown and effective in the border and the rock garden. For annuals, sow seeds in early spring where plants are wanted, or start indoors in late February to set out in May. They prefer full sun and a porous garden soil. Since the season of bloom is short, make successive sowings for a longer season. Perennials can be propagated by seeds or by root division.

**S. ocymoides** (oh-sim-*moy*-deez).

ROCK SOAPWORT.

From the European Alps, a creeping perennial 5 to 8 in. tall, with flowers in shades of pink and rose in loose clusters. Of very easy culture, it is especially suited to trailing over rocks. Several varieties have larger and more abundant blooms than the species. The variety *splendens* (*splendenz*), with rose flowers, is considered the best garden selection. Zones 2 to 7.

**S. officinalis** (o-fis-i-*nay*-lis).

BOUNCING BET.

Native to southern Europe, a familiar and very pretty perennial used in early gardens; it was brought to America from England. Pink or white flowers in clusters, each 1 in. across, are borne on plants 2 to 3 ft. tall and are long-lasting when cut. It needs full sun. Hardy and long-lived, it can be used in large borders, in front of shrubbery and in the wild garden. It spreads by underground stolons, which can be reset. 'Rosea Plena' is a double, very fragrant, 2-ft. plant that flowers for

# Saponaria

*Saponaria officinalis*
BOUNCING BET

*Scabiosa caucasica*

twelve or more weeks. In moist, rich soils it needs support. Zones 3 to 10.

## Saxifraga. See *Bergenia*.

## Scabiosa (skay-bee-*oh*-suh).
PINCUSHION FLOWER.
SCABIOUS.
Teasel Family (*Dipsacaceae*).
Native to Europe, Asia and Africa. Most are hardy perennials, but one annual is a great favorite of flower arrangers. Plants come in good shades of white, pink, yellow, blue and very dark reds and purples. They last well when cut and are easily grown in ordinary garden soil, well turned to a spade's depth, and full sun. These are good plants for the border and the cutting garden.

★**S. caucasica** (kaw-*kas*-ih-kuh).
Native to the Caucasus Mountains, a lovely perennial scabious, with pale blue, white or lavender flowers and grayish foliage. Long-blooming, from early July until frost, it is sturdy, well branched and hardy. Plant in full sun in the North and in shade in the South. It often blooms the first year from seed if started early. Propagate also by division or by cuttings. 'Butterfly Blue'™ (the trademarked name is protected in the U.S. by Iverson's Perennial Gardens of Long Grove, Illinois) is reportedly a cross of *Knautia* and *S. columbaria* (kol-um-*bar*-ee-uh). It produces 2-in. blue flowers on 18-in. plants during most of the summer. 'Clive Greaves' is a large-flowered, prolific clone with lavender-blue flowers. 'Loddon White' is also a large-flowered clone but has creamy-white flowers. 'Moerheim Blue' is another large plant with dark blue flowers. Zones 3 to 7.

**S. rumelica.** See *Knautia macedonica*.

# Sedum (*see*-dum).

STONECROP.

Orpine Family (*Crassulaceae*).

Tough, hardy, ubiquitous, drought-resistant perennials, mostly of the Northern Temperate Zone, that may well be called the backbone of an easy–maintenance rock garden. They are enormously useful in an endless variety of situations— beside steps, on walls and at the front edge of borders. They are mostly low spreaders, with succulent, often evergreen leaves and clusters of small, star-shaped, white, yellow, red, pink or, rarely, blue flowers. There are also some tender succulents in this extensive genus that make attractive greenhouse subjects or pot plants for the home. All thrive in full sun and almost any well-drained soil. Division of plants in summer or fall is the easiest means of propagation. Leaves that fall to the ground often root themselves. Plants can also be propagated by seeds or by cuttings.

**S. acre** (*ak*-ree).

GOLD-MOSS STONECROP.

GOLDEN-CARPET.

A species from Europe and Asia with slim, trailing stems, covered with fleshy, pointed, bright green leaves about $^1/_8$ in. thick. Clusters of yellow flowers appear at the ends of the stems in early summer. It grows vigorously in cracks of rocks or concrete where the water supply is almost nonexistent. In competition with more delicate plants, therefore, it can be a pest, so it is best reserved for spots where nothing else will grow. If it overgrows a wall, simply pull it out by the handful. It yields easily, and remaining plants will be undisturbed. The variety *majus* (*may*-jus) is larger than the species, while the variety *minus* (*my*-nus) is more compact. The cultivar 'Aureum' displays golden-tinted shoot tips in spring; flowers are a paler yel-

low than the species. 'Elegans' has silvery shoot tips. Zones 3 to 8.

★ **S.** 'Autumn Joy'.

AUTUMN JOY SEDUM.

Of hybrid origin and considered one of the finest perennial plants in commerce. The spring foliage emerges a soft blue-green and is handsome all summer. Individual leaves are fleshy, toothed and 2 to 3 in. long. Pink flowers appear in early fall (late August to early September), gradually turning to salmon-bronze and finally coppery-red in November. It is generally believed that the Arends Nursery of Germany made the cross, *S. telephium* (tel-e-*fye*-um) × *S. spectabile* (circa 1955), that produced 'Autumn Joy'. 'Indian Chief' may be the same plant. Propagates easily by division or by cuttings. Zones 3 to 10.

**S. cauticola** (kaw-ti-*koh*-lum).

A Japanese species with floppy stems, about 6 in. long, that grow from the root. Blue-green leaves, about 1 in. long, are rounded at the tip. Purple-rose flowers appear in flat-topped clusters in early fall. A hybrid of *S. cauticolum* and *S.* 'Autumn Joy' produced 'Ruby Glow', which bears ruby flowers on 12-in. plants. Zones 6 to 9.

**S. floriferum** (floh-*rif*-er-um).

FLORIFEROUS SEDUM.

From China, a low-growing (6-in.) plant with alternate leaves, $1^1/_2$ in. long and toothed at the ends. The yellow flowers are $^1/_2$ in. wide. Some taxonomists feel that it is a hybrid between *S. hybridum* (hye-*brid*-um) and *S. kamtschaticum*. 'Weihenstephaner Gold' is a front-of-the-border or ground cover plant with profuse yellow flowers in early summer and red fruit capsules later in the season. It makes a tight plant mass, 6 in. tall. The foliage is burgundy in the fall and winter. Zones 3 to 8.

## Sedum

*Sedum acre*
GOLD-MOSS STONECROP

*Sedum* × 'Vera Jameson'
VERA JAMESON STONECROP

*Sedum* 'Autumn Joy'
AUTUMN JOY SEDUM

*Sempervivum tectorum*
COMMON HOUSELEEK

**S. kamtschaticum** (kam-*chat*-i-kum).

KAMCHATKA STONECROP.

A hardy Asian species with slender stems, 6 to 12 in. high, from a central rootstock. The dark green leaves, about 1½ in. long, have coarse edges. Loose clusters of orange-yellow flowers appear in late summer. The cultivar 'Variegatum' has leaves edged with cream. Zones 3 to 8.

**S. sieboldii** (see-*bold*-ee-eye).

SIEBOLD STONECROP.

One of the best-known and most satisfactory garden perennials, from Japan. Slender stems spread 6 to 8 in. from the central root. The almost perfectly circular blue-green leaves have a narrow red edge. It looks like a very dwarf eucalyptus. Dense clusters of pink flowers appear in autumn. The cultivar 'Medio-variegatum', with soft cream-yellow variegation, is unusually striking and good as a houseplant. Propagate by stem cuttings in spring. Zones 3 to 8.

**S. spectabile** (spek-*tab*-i-lee).

SHOWY STONECROP.

Another dependable Japanese species, this is a strong-growing perennial to 2 ft. with flat, light green leaves, 2 in. across, 3 in. long and slightly notched. Huge clusters of light pink flowers appear in late summer at the top of the stems. It thrives in sun or partial shade in the garden or a container. Propagate by division in spring. Two fine cultivars are 'Carmen', with salmon-colored flowers on 18- to 24-in. plants, and 'Meteor', with purplish-red flowers on 18- to 24-in. plants. Zones 3 to 10.

**S. spurium** (*spew*-ree-um).

TWO ROW STONECROP.

An Asian species that produces mats of shoots 6 in. high. Rounded, sometimes evergreen leaves, 1 in. long and slightly notched at the tips, appear in two rows, as the common name implies. Loose sprays of pale pink, white or crimson flowers appear in late summer. 'Dragon's Blood' is the most popular cultivar, with purplish-bronze foliage and dark starry flowers. Zones 3 to 8.

**S.** × 'Vera Jameson'.

VERA JAMESON STONECROP.

Of hybrid origin, an outstanding sedum cultivar growing 8 to 10 in. tall and about as wide. The leaves are glaucous-purple and the flower heads dusky pink. The origin of this cultivar (circa 1972) is not well documented; it is possibly a cross of 'Ruby Glow' and *S. maximum* cv. 'Atropurpureum'. It is useful for the front of borders or as a ground cover. Propagate by division or by tip cuttings. Zones 4 to 9.

## Sempervivum (sem-per-*vye*-vum).

Orpine Family (*Crassulaceae*).

These are evergreen perennials of the Old World, consisting of a rootstock topped by a tight cluster of mostly incurving, fleshy leaves forming an almost globular rosette. Clusters of white, pink, yellow or purple flowers are borne on stems that grow out of the centers of the leaf rosettes. Plants succeed in any well-drained, moderately fertile soil, preferably in full sun, although most kinds will tolerate light shade. Propagate by seeds or by offsets.

**S. tectorum** (tek-*toh*-rum).

COMMON HOUSELEEK.

HEN-AND-CHICKENS.

OLD-MAN-AND-WOMAN.

Grows up to 1 ft. tall, producing bright green leaves that have red-purple pointed tips and form rosettes 3 to 4 in. across. Spreading clusters of purplish-pink flowers appear in early summer. A plant of many uses, it makes a fine ground cover and also does well as a houseplant. The variety *cal-*

## Sempervivum

*careum* (kal-*care*-ee-um) has smooth leaves and brown-purple tips, while the variety *cupreum* (*koo*-pree-um) has larger rosettes that take on coppery colors in cool seasons. Zones 3 to 8.

### Sidalcea (sye-*dal*-see-uh).
FALSE MALLOW.

MINIATURE HOLLYHOCK.

Mallow Family (*Malvaceae*).

Perennials native to western North America with deeply lobed, blue-green leaves and sprays of pink, purplish or white blooms. Ordinary, well-drained garden soil and full sun are needed. The plants are good in the border and are easily grown, either from seed or crown division. Divide at least every three years for best flowering.

### S. malviflora (mal-vee-*floh*-ruh).
CHECKERBLOOM.

WILD HOLLYHOCK.

Native to California. Pretty, satiny, rose-pink blossoms, 2 to 3 in. across, are produced on plants that grow to 3 ft. This perennial thrives on the West Coast but is adaptable to almost any location in full sun. Blooms appear in June and July and last well when cut. It is a good plant for the mixed border. Named cultivars include 'Brilliant', 2 to 2¹/2 ft. tall with carmine-red flowers; 'Elsie Heugh', 2 to 3 ft. tall with pale pink, fringed flowers; 'Loveliness', 2¹/2 ft. tall with shell-pink flowers; and 'William Smith', 3 ft. tall with salmon-rose flowers. Zones 5 to 7.

### Silene (sye-*lee*-nee).
CAMPION.

CATCHFLY.

Pink Family (*Caryophyllaceae*).

A large genus of annuals, perennials and biennials found almost everywhere in the world's temperate zones. Many of the species are hardy and long-lived. The plants are widely grown for the

border, the rock garden and the wild garden. They bloom all summer but are not useful as cut flowers. Full sun and ordinary garden soil are needed. Propagate the perennials by seeds sown in place, by crown division in spring or by cuttings in midsummer.

### S. vulgaris (vul-*gay*-ris).
BLADDER CAMPION.

From Europe, northwest Africa and temperate Asia, a variable species with both smooth and hairy-leaved types. Leaves are 1 to 2 in. long and ovate. The plants are erect, 1 to 2 ft. tall. Flowers can be white or red. They have inflated, veined calyxes and deeply notched petals. The subspecies *maritima* (mare-i-*tee*-muh), which is from northern Europe and known by the common name of sea campion, has trailing stems that form a light green mat. The white, double form, 'Flora Plena' (*floh*-re *plee*-nuh), is preferred to the species. Zones 4 to 9.

### Sisyrinchium (sis-ir-*rink*-ee-um).
BLUE-EYED GRASS.

Iris Family (*Iridaceae*).

Low-growing perennials native to America, with grasslike leaves in strong clumps and small, but attractive, blue or yellow flowers. As wild flowers they are often found in wet meadows. They are easily grown in ordinary garden soil, but most species need steady moisture. Propagate by seeds or by root division.

### S. striatum (stry-*ay*-tum).
ARGENTINE BLUE-EYED GRASS.

Native to Argentina and Chile. Creamy-yellow flowers are borne on upright spikes, usually with nine to twelve flowers per spike. Each of the 1-in. flowers is darker in the center and striped with purple on the back sides. The foliage is 1 in. wide. Plants form large clumps that can be

*Sidalcea malviflora*
CHECKERBLOOM

*Sisyrinchium striatum*
ARGENTINE BLUE-EYED GRASS

divided. After flowering the leaves often turn yellow. Zones 4 to 8.

## Smilacina (smy-la-*sye*-nuh).

FALSE SOLOMON'S-SEAL.
Lily Family (*Liliaceae*).
Native to North America and Asia, handsome, perennial wild flowers of sunny, damp roadsides and the moist edge of woodlands. They are easily grown in moist, partly shady places. Propagate by division.

**S. racemosa** (ra-se-*moh*-suh).
FALSE SOLOMON'S-SEAL.
This native North American plant, which grows to 3 ft., is often found with the true Solomon's-seal but has very different blossoms—plumy, fragrant, closely packed clusters of tiny greenish-white florets at the end of each stem. The clusters are 3 to 5 in. long. Blooms appear in May and

*Smilacina racemosa*
FALSE SOLOMON'S-SEAL

## Smilacina

June. The alternate, blue-green, wavy-edged leaves, 6 in. long, ascend the flower stem and resemble the leaves of the true Solomon's-seal. Very attractive, spotted, pinkish-red fruit clusters appear during summer. A beautiful spring flower that is effective in the rock garden and the wild garden, it also combines well with ferns. Zones 3 to 7.

## Solidago (sol-i-*day*-goh).

GOLDENROD.

Composite Family (*Compositae*).

Native mostly to North America. The beautiful and familiar goldenrods of fields and roadsides are members of a large genus that has been unjustly maligned as the cause of hay fever, because it blooms at the same time as ragweed (*Ambrosia*), the true culprit. English gardeners have produced several fine, hardy hybrids. Propagate by seeds or by crown division.

**S. canadensis** (kan-a-*den*-sis).

CANADIAN GOLDENROD.

(Syn. *S. reflexa*.) Native to North America. Of the species, this is the showiest and the most frequently cultivated. Reaching 5 to 6 ft. in height with narrow, toothed 5-in. leaves and large, attractive sprays of tiny yellow flowers, it blooms from late July to October or until hard frost. It makes a strikingly handsome display in the large border and the wild garden and is much grown and admired in England. Hybridizers have relied heavily on this species to produce garden forms. It has been crossed with the European species, *S. virgaurea* (vir-*gaw*-ree-uh), to produce some of the tall cultivars. An intergeneric cross of *S. missouriensis* (miss-or-ee-*en*-sis) and *Aster ptarmicoides* (*as*-ter tar-mi-*koy*-deez) produced X *Solidaster luteus* (*soh*-li-das-ter *lew*-tee-us). This intergeneric species has been crossed with *S. brachystachys*

*Solidago canadensis*
CANADIAN GOLDENROD

*Spigelia marilandica*
INDIAN PINK

(brak-i-*stay*-kis) to produce shorter clones. Some of the hybrid goldenrod cultivars commonly available are 'Baby Gold', 2 to 2$^1$/$_2$ ft. tall with large racemes of bright yellow flowers; 'Cloth of Gold', 18 to 24 in. tall with deep yellow flowers on a dense plant; 'Crown of Rays', 2 ft. tall with large panicles of yellow flowers; 'Goldenmosa', 2$^1$/$_2$ ft. tall with yellow flowers in August; and 'Golden Thumb', 1 ft. tall with yellowish-green foliage and yellow flowers. Zones 4 to 9.

**S. reflexa.** See *S. canadensis*.

**S. sempervirens** (sem-per-*vye*-renz).
SEASIDE GOLDENROD.
A handsome, sturdy species, 4 to 8 ft. high, with smooth, lance-shaped leaves and large, leafy clusters of yellow florets. As its common name implies, this plant does well in seaside gardens, even in salt marshes, but it will also grow in any sandy loam. It blooms in late summer and fall. Zones 4 to 9.

**S. sphacelata** (spay-seh-*lay*-tuh).
FALSE GOLDENROD.
Plants are 2 ft. tall. The basal and larger leaves are broadly ovate and 3 to 6 in. long, with petioles 3 to 9 in. long. Flower heads are golden yellow and 2$^1$/$_2$ in across. 'Golden Fleece' is a recent cultivar, 18 in. tall, producing golden flowers from mid-August to October. Zones 4 to 9.

**Spigelia** (spy-*jee*-lee-uh).
SPIGELIA.
Logania Family (*Loganiaceae*).
Native to the southeastern U.S. Leaves are opposite and entire. The flowers are tubular and upright. They are good plants for shady borders and rock gardens. Propagate by crown division or by seeds.

**S. marilandica** (mare-i-*lan*-di-kuh).
INDIAN PINK.
Flowers in early summer are 2 in. long and 1 in. wide. The outside of the flower is red and the inside yellow. Leaves are opposite and 4 in. long. Plants grow best in moist soils. Zones 6 to 9.

**Spiraea.** Some species that are often listed under this genus actually belong to *Filipendula*.

**S. aruncus.** See *Aruncus dioicus*.

**Stachys** (*stay*-kis).
BETONY.
Mint Family (*Labiatae*).
A large genus of widely scattered annuals and perennials, found in temperate zones. A few are cultivated for ornamental use. Plants produce grayish leaves and colorful flowers in spikes. They are easily grown in full sun and ordinary garden soil, well turned to a spade's depth. Propagate by seeds in spring or by root division in fall. Zone 4.

**S. byzantina** (biz-an-*tee*-nuh).
LAMB'S-EARS.
(Syn. *S. lanata* and *S. olympica*.) Found from Caucasus to Iran. It grows to 1$^1$/$_2$ ft. high, with large, gray, woolly leaves, 5 to 8 in. long, in tufts at the base of the plant. It is attractive and cool-looking in daylight and shimmers in moonlight, when the plants have an almost luminous quality. The inconspicuous purple flowers are borne in thickly clustered gray spikes, 15 to 18 in. long, and may be used fresh or dried in arrangements.

Very hardy and long-lived once established, it is fine for edging borders or paths, in clumps at the front of the border and as a bedding plant. 'Cotton Ball' produces flower spikes, but they are abortive and instead produce cotton bobbles on the stems. 'Sheila McQueen' is more compact

# Stachys

than the species, but its leaves are larger and less woolly. 'Silver Carpet' was selected because it does not flower; it does not, however, overwinter as well in the garden as does the species. Propagate by seeds, or in the case of the cultivars by crown division in early spring. Zones 4 to 8.

**S. lanata.**  See *S. byzantina.*

**S. officinalis** (o-fis-i-*nay*-lis).
COMMON BETONY.
The leaves, which are 4 to 5 in. long, hairy and wrinkled with scalloped edges, arise from mats of square stems.  Purple flower spikes rise about 1$^{1}$/$_{2}$ to 2 ft. tall, and are composed of three whorls of $^{1}$/$_{2}$-in. tubular flowers.  They bloom in late spring. Plant in full sun to partial shade. They respond well to rich, moist but well-drained soils. The variety *alba* (*al*-buh) has creamy-white flowers, while the variety *rosea* (*roh*-zee-uh) bears rose-colored flowers. Propagate by crown divison. Zones 4 to 8.

**S. olympica.**  See *S. byzantina.*

## Statice.  Some species that are often listed under this genus actually belong to *Limonium.*

## Stokesia (stoh-*kee*-zee-uh).
STOKES' ASTER.
Composite Family (*Compositae*).
There is only one species, a hardy perennial native to the southeastern U.S., with pretty, aster-like flowers and abundant foliage. A good garden plant, it is useful for cutting and in the perennial border. Full sun and well-drained, slightly sandy garden loam are needed. Propagate by seeds or by crown division in spring.

**S. cyanea.**  See *S. laevis.*

**S. laevis** (*lee*-vis).
STOKES' ASTER.
(Syn. *S. cyanea.*) Native from South Carolina to Florida and Louisiana.  It grows 1 to 1$^{1}$/$_{2}$ ft. high, with lavender-blue flowers, 2 to 4 in. across, blooming in midsummer. The plant has branched, purplish, hairy stems. Leaves are 6 to 8 in. long and evergreen. It enjoys well-drained soil and filtered sunlight. Winter mulch is necessary in colder zones. There are many cultivars. 'Alba' has white flowers borne more sparingly than those of the species; 'Blue Danube' has lavender-blue flowers up to 5 in. across; 'Blue Moon' has silvery-blue heads; 'Blue Star' is a large-flowered type; 'Klaus Jelitto' has 3$^{1}$/$_{2}$- to 4-in. blue flowers and large leaves; 'Lilacina' has lilac flower heads; 'Lutea' has pale yellow flowers; 'Rosea' is a pink-flowered form; 'Silver Moon' has pure-white flower heads; and 'Wyoming' has deep blue flowers. Zones 5 to 9.

## Teucrium (*too*-kree-um).
GERMANDER.
Mint Family (*Labiatae*).
Herbs, subshrubs and shrubs, widely distributed in warm and temperate regions of the world, with opposite leaves and small spikes or heads of flowers. The species below is suited for the rock garden or border plantings in well-drained soil. Propagate by seeds, by cuttings or by division.

**T. chamaedrys** (kuh-*mee*-dris).
A dense, European subshrub, about 1 ft. high, with toothed, ovate leaves about $^{3}$/$_{4}$ in. long. Small, loose spikes of red-purple to rose flowers, about $^{3}$/$_{4}$ in. long, appear in summer. It makes a neat, low, bordering hedge for herb beds and flower gardens or as an accent in the rock garden or the low flower border. 'Prostratum' is an 8-in. cultivar with rose-pink flowers. Zones 4 to 9.

*Stachys byzantina*
Lamb's-ears

*Stokesia laevis*
Stokes' Aster

## Thalictrum (thal-*lik*-trum).

MEADOW RUE.

Buttercup Family *(Ranunculaceae)*.

Perennials of northern temperate Europe, Asia and North America, with graceful, deeply cut foliage, usually blue-green, and small, delicate, feathery florets in sprays. All are easily grown in well-drained, ordinary garden soil, well turned to a spade's depth. Ample moisture and full sun or partial shade are needed. Propagate by fresh seeds sown in fall or by division in spring (if the latter is done in fall, provide winter protection).

**T. aquilegifolium** (ak-will-ee-jif-*foh*-lee-um).

COLUMBINE MEADOW RUE.

From Europe and Asia, this species grows 2 to 3 ft. high and produces large, decorative panicles of flowers with attractive lilac stamens. It blooms

*Teucrium chamaedrys*
GERMANDER

## Thalictrum

*Thalictrum aquilegifolium*
COLUMBINE MEADOW RUE

*Tiarella cordifolia*
ALLEGHENY FOAMFLOWER

from mid-May to June. The dark green divided leaves are abundant and graceful. It makes a lovely plant in the border, in the wild garden and for cutting. The variety *atropurpureum* has dark purple stems and stamens. 'Alba' has white flowers; 'Dwarf Purple' is 15 in. tall with lilac flowers; 'Roseum' produces pale-pink flowers; 'Thundercloud' has larger flower heads and purple flowers; and 'White Cloud' has whiter flowers than 'Alba'. Zones 5 to 8.

**T. delavayi** (del-ah-*vay*-ee).
YUNNAN MEADOW RUE.
Native to western China. The compound leaves are divided into sections with three leaflets in each section. The effect is fernlike in appearance. Each petalless flower has lilac sepals and pale yellow stamens. Flowers are borne on open, branched panicles held well above the foliage on thin, wiry stems. Bloom begins in midsummer.

The flower stems reach a height of 4 to 6 ft., so some support is needed. Plant in partial shade in rich, moist soil. These are best for northern gardens, as they do not like hot summer temperatures, and they also make good cut flowers. 'Album' has white sepals and is not as vigorous as the species. 'Hewitt's Double' has double lilac flowers that last longer than those of the species; its stamens are petaloid. Two species are similar to T. delavayi: *T. dipterocarpum* (dip-ter-oh-*kar*-pum) and *T. rochebrunianum* (rowsh-brew-nee-*ay*-num). Because of their similarity they are often mislabeled by nurseries. Propagate the species by seeds and the cultivars by division. Zones 4 to 6.

## Thermopsis (ther-*mop*-sis).
FALSE LUPINE.
Pea Family *(Leguminosae).*
Native to North America and Asia, hardy perennials with the characteristic crisp blossoms of the

pea family and abundant, cloverlike leaves. The foliage is handsome most of the summer in northern gardens. They are lovely in masses in the border, with shrubbery or in the wild garden. They require ordinary garden soil, well turned to a spade's depth, and full sun or light shade. This is a member of the pea family and needs little nitrogen; too much will cause leaves to yellow. Propagate by seeds sown in late summer, or, less successfully, by division.

**T. caroliniana** (kar-oh-lin-ee-*ay*-nuh).
SOUTHERN LUPINE.
AARON'S ROD.
A handsome, drought-resistant plant, 5 ft. tall, native to North Carolina. The foliage is divided into three obovate leaflets, each 2 to 3 in. long and having fine hairs. Showy, sulphur-yellow, dense sprays of pea-like florets, 8 in. long, appear in early summer.

**T. montana** (mon-*tay*-nuh).
A species from the Rocky Mountains growing only to 2 ft. It bears yellow flowers in 8-in.-long racemes in June and July. Zones 3 to 7.

# Tiarella (tye-uh-*rell*-uh).
FOAMFLOWER.
Saxifrage Family (*Saxifragaceae*).
Dainty perennials native to moist, rich woodlands of temperate North America. Graceful little plants, they are exquisite in the rock garden and in masses in the wild or fern garden. They require partial shade and humusy soil. Propagate easily by division every three or four years; plants can also be raised from seed.

**T. cordifolia** (kor-di-*foh*-lee-uh).
ALLEGHENY FOAMFLOWER.
This delicate little plant grows 6 to 18 in. high, with three- to five-lobed, slightly crinkled leaves

that form flattish, basal tufts. The leaves have purplish veins that are quite noticeable in winter and spring. Profuse clusters of tiny, starry, creamy-white florets bloom on 3- to 4-in. racemes. Individual flowers are only $1/4$ in. wide and are showy for up to six weeks. The variety *collina* (*kol*-lin-uh) is clump-forming and flowers freely from May to June; it sometimes repeats. It was formerly recognized as *T. wherryi* (*where*-ee-eye) and has the common name Wherry's foamflower. Several cultivars have recently been introduced. Most (but not all) represent *T. cordifolia* var. *collina*: 'Dunvegan' is 12 to 18 in. tall, has light pink flowers and forms a large mat; 'Erika Leigh' is 6 to 10 in. tall, pink-flowered and has fingerlike foliage; 'Montrose Selection' blooms later than the species, has pink flowers and dark foliage, and is clump-forming; 'Oak Leaf' is 12 in. tall with white-blush flowers and leaves resembling a white oak tree; 'Slick Rock' is 8 in. tall, has light pink flowers and is a vigorous spreader; and 'Starburst' is 12 to 18 in. tall and has white flowers and leaves with red starbursts in the center. Zones 3 to 8.

**T. wherryi.** See *T. cordifolia*.

# Tradescantia (trad-es-*kan*-shee-uh).
SPIDERWORT.
Spiderwort Family (*Commelinaceae*).
Perennials of the American continents, of greatly varying form, appearance, growth habit and hardiness. They are extensively grown in baskets, in greenhouses and in the open garden. Propagate by seeds, by cuttings or by division.

**T. × andersoniana** (an-der-sow-nee-*ay*-nuh).
SPIDERWORT.
This hybrid group represents several species. Most resulted from crosses of *T. ohiensis* (oh-ee-*en*-sis), *T. subaspera* (sub-*as*-per-uh) and *T. virginiana*. Plants

## Tradescantia

commonly sold as *T. virginiana* are often *T.* × *andersoniana*. Narrow, straplike leaves, 1 in. wide, reach 1 to 1¹/₂ ft. long. The foliage grows in dense clumps. The flower heads, held just above the foliage, are bunches of buds, which open only one at a time. Each flower lasts one day. The flower parts come in threes: three petals, three sepals and six stamens. These 1- to 2-in. flowers start to open in late spring and continue for eight weeks. By midseason, the leaves get rather ragged looking, so cut the foliage back to the gound. Plants will send up new leaves and rebloom in the fall when cooler weather returns.

If given the right conditions, this plant can become very invasive and hard to eradicate. Plant in full sun in average to poor, well-drained garden soil. Do not over-fertilize. There are many cultivars. Among those with blue and purple flowers, 'Bluestone' bears lavender-blue flowers; 'Isis' has large 3-in. blue flowers; 'James Stratton' has pure blue flowers; 'J.C. Weguelin' is a vigorous cultivar with 2¹/₂-in.-wide China-blue flowers; 'Leonora' has violet-blue flowers on 18-in. stems; 'Pauline' bears lilac flowers 2¹/₂ in. wide; 'Purple Dome' has rich purple flowers on 2-ft. plants; and 'Zwanenburg Blue' has deep blue flowers about 3 in. wide. Among the cultivars with carmine and red flowers, 'Carmine Glow' has deep carmine flowers; 'Purewell Giant' bears flowers between deep rose and purple; and 'Red Cloud' has rosy-red flowers on 2-ft. plants. White-flowered cultivars include 'Innocence', which bears creamy-white flowers; 'Iris Pritchard', which has pure white flowers with violet shading; 'Osprey', which has white flowers with feathery blue stamens; and 'Snowcap', which is a pure white with 3-in. flowers. Zones 4 to 9.

### T. virginiana (vir-jin-ee-*ay*-nuh).
VIRGINIA SPIDERWORT.
Native to eastern North America, a hardy, herba-

ceous perennial, 2 to 3 ft. tall, with slim leaves to 1 ft. long and small clusters of flat, three-petaled flowers 1 in. across. The species has blue flowers, but there are purple, pink, white and rose-colored varieties. All open in the morning but close by mid-afternoon. It is of very easy culture in sun or shade and ordinary garden soil. It can easily become proliferating masses of ropy roots that are all but impossible to eliminate, so it should not be planted where it can crowd out other plants. It is fine in the wild garden, the rock garden and in different locations that are semi-shady, either wet or dry. It blooms from late May through the summer. Zones 4 to 9.

### Tricyrtis (try-*sir*-tis).
TOAD LILY.
Lily Family (*Liliaceae*).
Perennial herbs native to East Asia. These plants have creeping rootstocks; alternate leaves, usually sessile but sometimes clasping; and spotted, bell-shaped flowers. They can be grown in pots or outdoors. The roots should be dried off in the fall and stored indoors over winter for those species grown in pots. Propagate by division.

### T. formosana (for-moh-*say*-nuh).
FORMOSA TOAD LILY.
(Syn. *T. stolonifera.*) The arching stems grow to 2 ft. tall with alternate, 4- to 5-in. long, 1-in.-wide ovate leaves at widely spaced nodes. At the end of the freely branching stems are terminal cymes of many trumpet-shaped flowers. These 1-in. flowers are white with red spots and a yellow eye. Bloom period is unusually extended, because after the terminal cyme is done flowering the last four to six leaf axils produce a flower. Plant this species where it can spread, as a large clump will form in time. It is stoloniferous but not invasive. Also be sure to plant it where it is close at hand, because while it is not a showy

flower, it is quite beautiful when seen up close. Flowering starts in late summer and continues through the fall. Plant in partial shade in moist, deep, humusy, slightly acid soil. The variety *amethystina* (a-me-*this*-ti-nuh) has bluish-purple flowers with a white throat, spotted red. It opens earlier than the species. The variety *stolonifera* (stoh-lon-*if*-er-uh) grows 3$^1$/2 ft. tall and has paler flowers and fewer spots on the petals. Zones 4 to 9.

**T. hirta** (*her*-tuh).
COMMON TOAD LILY.
Native to Japan. It grows to 3 ft. tall, with hairy leaves and stems. Leaves are 6 in. long and 1 to 2 in. wide. Flowers are white, spotted with purple and black, and grow in axils. It blooms in the fall. Zones 4 to 8.

**T. stolonifera.** See *T. formosana.*

# Trillium (*trill*-ee-um).

WAKE-ROBIN.
Lily Family (*Liliaceae*).
Native to North America and Asia. Plants are easily recognized because the leaves and flower petals are always in sets of three. Each plant consists of a single stem growing from a rhizome. Three oval, pointed leaves form a flat whorl, with a single flower in the center. The flower has three pointed sepals and three similarly pointed petals. Trilliums are beautiful spring-blooming plants, growing best in the shade of deciduous trees, in deep, moist soil consisting almost entirely of decayed vegetation. The plants form colonies in established woodlands, making a highly effective, deep-piled ground cover. Flowers are white, pink, yellow, purple or

*Tradescantia* × *andersoniana* 'Isis'
SPIDERWORT

*Tricyrtis formosana*
FORMOSA TOAD LILY

## Trillium

red, long-lasting, and, in some species, sweet-scented. Propagate by bulb offsets or by seeds.

**T. erectum** (ee-*rek*-tum).
PURPLE TRILLIUM.
WAKE-ROBIN.
A native of Canada and the northeastern U.S., about 1 ft. high, with broad leaves. The flower, with 1-in. petals, is erect or slightly drooping, purple or greenish-brown. It has an unpleasant scent. *T. erectum* forma *albiflorum* (al-bi-*floh*-rum) has white flowers. Zones 4 to 9.

**T. grandiflorum** (gran-di-*floh*-rum).
WHITE WAKE-ROBIN.
Native to Canada and the northeastern U.S., perhaps the best known and easily the most dramatic of the trilliums. It grows up to 1½ ft. high, with broad leaves narrowing at each end. The flower petals are up to 3 in. long, broad and wavy, starting out white and turning pink and rose as they age. They are slightly nodding. The plant is especially beautiful when combined with azaleas and ferns in a woodland garden. The variety *roseum* (roh-zee-um), which is sometimes listed as *rubra* (rue-bruh) is a pink-flowered form. 'Flore-plena' is a double selection. Zones 4 to 9.

## Trollius (*troh*-lee-us).
GLOBEFLOWER.
Buttercup Family (*Ranunculaceae*).
Hardy perennials, widely distributed in swampy places in the Northern Temperate Zone. They are moisture-loving plants with showy, bright yellow or orange flowers, usually double and often globular in the cultivated species and the numerous named cultivars of mixed origin. They are of easy culture in sun or shade in ordinary but fairly heavy garden soil. Propagate by division or by seeds; seeds are slow to germinate.

*Trollius europaeus*
GLOBEFLOWER

*Veratrum californicum*
CALIFORNIA FALSE HELLEBORE

**T. × cultorum** (kul-*tor*-um).

HYBRID GLOBEFLOWER.

Plants grown under this name are garden hybrids of *T. europaeus*, *T. asiaticus* (ay-she-at-*i*-kus) and *T. chinensis* (chin-*en*-sis). All have round, buttercup-yellow flowers. The leaves consist of five to six lobes and are ornamental. Some cultivars within this hybrid species are 'Alabaster', a weak grower with ivory-tinged blossoms; 'Canary Bird', with lemon-yellow flowers; 'Earliest of All', with pale orange flowers that open before those of all other hybrids; 'Goldquelle', having pure yellow flowers and one of the most popular; 'Orange Princess', with deep orange flowers on 2-ft. plants; and 'Pritchard's Giant', with medium yellow flowers on 3-ft. stems. Zones 3 to 6.

**T. europaeus** (yew-roh-*pee*-us).

A sturdy plant, growing 1 to 2 ft. high, with bright yellow, globular, double blossoms, 2 in. across, blooming from May and sporadically throughout the summer. It is effective in the rock garden and the spring border, in sun or light shade. It needs a slightly sandier soil and less water than do other species. 'Superbus' flowers more prolifically than the species. Zones 4 to 7.

**T. ledebourii** (led-e-*boor*-ee-eye).

From Siberia. Large, bright golden-yellow, double but open flowers, 3 in. across, are borne on stems 2 ft. high. It blooms all summer and makes a fine border and rock-garden plant. Zones 3 to 6.

## Veratrum (ve-*ray*-trum).

FALSE HELLEBORE.

Lily Family (*Liliaceae*).

Sturdy, coarse perennials native to North America, Europe and Asia. Plants have thick rootstocks, broad leaves and greenish-white or yellow flowers in branching, terminal clusters. All parts of the plant are poisonous. Grow in moist areas and full sun. Occasionally they are grown in the shady border or wild garden. Propagate by division.

**V. album** (*al*-bum).

EUROPEAN WHITE HELLEBORE.

Native to Europe and northern Asia. This grows to 4 ft. tall and has leaves 1 ft. long and 6 in. wide. The flowers are greenish on the outside, white inside, and appear in panicles 2 ft. long. Zones 3 to 6.

**V. californicum** (cal-i-*fore*-ni-cum).

CALIFORNIA FALSE HELLEBORE.

Native to western North America. The large flower heads are composed of drooping spikelets of greenish-white flowers. The 16-in.-long by 8-in.-wide leaves are held cupped and upright on the stem. They are spaced up the stem almost to the flowers. Plants grow to 6 ft. The genus name comes from *vere atrum*, meaning "truly black," a reference to the color of the roots. Propagate by division and seeds. Zone 5.

**V. nigrum** (*nye*-grum).

BLACK FALSE HELLEBORE.

From Europe to Asia. Small ($1/3$-in.), brownish-black flowers are produced on 1- to 3-ft. panicles. Leaves are strikingly handsome and perform best in shade.

## Verbena (ver-*bee*-nuh).

VERVAIN.

Verbena Family (*Verbenaceae*).

A large genus of nearly 200 species of annuals and perennials, most native to the U.S. Attractive, rounded clusters of small, tubular flowers in a large color range—from white through every shade of red and blue—make the hardy species excellent garden plants. Many are fragrant and in bloom all summer. They make fine plants for the border, in the rock garden, as edgings, as ground cover in bulb beds and for cutting. Full sun and

## Verbena

rich garden soil are required. Propagate by seeds started indoors in late March, except in very warm sections, where seeds may be sown outdoors where the plants are wanted. The perennial species can be rooted from cuttings or started by crown divisions in the spring.

### V. bonariensis (bon-ehr-ee-*en*-sis).
BRAZILIAN VERBENA.

An annual or perennial, native to South America. It grows to 4 ft. and has square stems that are branched and long, narrow, toothed leaves. It flowers in lavender clusters that bloom from midsummer until frost. The effect is best if several plants are grown together. Start new plants from tip cuttings. Zones 7 to 9.

### ★ V. canadensis (kan-a-*den*-sis).
CLUMP VERBENA.

A perennial, to 18 in. high, from the Southwest and Mexico, with a creeping rootstock and pink or purple blooms. It is excellent for the front of the border, as stems root and produce many blossoms. Plants may need cutting back to keep them in bounds. Several color forms grow wild. 'Appleblossom' has $^{3}/_{4}$-in. pale pink blossoms splashed with rose-pink in the center. 'Homestead Purple' is a vigorous purple cultivar. Zones 7 to 10.

## Veronica (ve-*ron*-i-kuh).
SPEEDWELL.

Figwort Family (*Scrophulariaceae*).

A large and varied genus of hardy annuals and perennials of Europe, Asia and other parts of the world. The species below are handsome perennials suitable for borders, or rock gardens. They are all characterized by attractive foliage and abundant flowers, usually in showy spikes. They are easily grown in any good garden soil and blend well with other flowers in the garden. They do best in sun but will tolerate partial shade.

Propagate by seeds sown in spring, by cuttings taken in summer or by division in fall.

### V. alpina (al-*pye*-nuh).
ALPINE SPEEDWELL.

Native to Europe and Asia. The foliage is 1 in. long, elliptical, opposite and shiny green. The stems grow to about 6 to 8 in. tall, with a dense raceme of tiny blue flowers at the end of each one. Bloom occurs in spring. Plant in full sun in well-drained garden soil. Plants perform well in both the North and South and are evergreen in the South. 'Alba' is a free-flowering white cultivar. 'Goodness Grows' is a hybrid of *V. alpina* 'Alba' and *V. spicata*. It is 12 in. high with blue flowers. Zones 3 to 8.

### V. incana (in-*kay*-nuh).
WOOLLY SPEEDWELL.

Growing up to $1^{1}/_{2}$ ft. high, this species has downy, gray-green leaves and small blue flowers, borne on numerous slender spikes in June and July. It is a good edging plant for the rock garden or the border but needs good drainage. The variety *glauca* (*glaw*-kuh) has more-silvery foliage than the species. 'Rosea' (*roh*-zee-uh) has pinkish-blue flowers; 'Barcarolle' (*bar*-ka-roll) has pink flowers; 'Minuet' has pink flowers; and 'Sarabande' has violet-blue flowers. Zones 3 to 7.

### V. longifolia (lon-ji-*foh*-lee-uh).
LONG-LEAF VERONICA.

Compact clusters of striking blue flowers appear on 1- to $2^{1}/_{2}$-ft. stems in late summer. Toothed, lance-shaped leaves are up to 4 in. long. This species has naturalized in eastern North America. There are varieties with white, purple or pink flowers. 'Blue Giant' is 3 to $3^{1}/_{2}$ ft. tall with lavender-blue flowers; 'Foester's Blue' is a long-blooming, $1^{1}/_{2}$-ft. blue-flowered form; 'Romilley Purple' has violet-blue flowers on 2-ft. stems;

*Verbena bonariensis*
BRAZILIAN VERBENA

and 'Sunny Border Blue' is a long-blooming 2-ft. plant with dark blue flowers. Zones 4 to 8.

**V. prostrata** (pros-*tray*-tuh).

HAREBELL SPEEDWELL.

From this mat of prostrate stems and leaves rise 8- to 10-in. flower stems, bearing blue flowers. The leaves are 1 to 1½ in. long, opposite, ovate and toothed. The flowers are tiny, ⅓ in. wide, and range from pale to deep blue. While the flowering period is short, only two to three weeks, the show is spectacular in late spring and early summer. When the mats of foliage get out of hand, cut them back to a manageable size. Plant in full sun in well-drained soil. 'Heavenly Blue' has sapphire-blue flowers. 'Loddon Blue' has blue flowers on 4-in. plants. Zones 5 to 8.

**V. spicata** (spy-*kay*-tuh).

SPIKED SPEEDWELL.

One of the most popular species, blooming in summer. Plants are about 1½ ft. high, with dense spikes of clear blue flowers. Cultivars include: 'Blue Peter', 2 ft. tall with dark blue flowers; 'Blue Spires', glossy green foliage and blue flowers on 18-in. plants; 'Heidekind', 12 in. tall and compact rose-pink flowers; 'Icicle', a white hybrid, 18 in. tall; and 'Red Fox', deep rosy-red flowers and glossy leaves. Zones 3 to 8.

## Veronicastrum (ve-ron-i-*kas*-trum).

BOWMAN'S-ROOT.

Figwort Family (*Scrophulariaceae*).

A genus with a close relationship to *Veronica*, native to northeastern American woodlands. Plants are easy to grow but slow to get started.

**V. virginicum** (vir-*jin*-i-kum).

BOWMAN'S-ROOT.

CULVER'S ROOT.

Leaves are lanceolate and arranged in whorls of three to six on unbranched stems. Each leaf is 2 to 4 in. long and sharply toothed. The flowers are pale blue or white. It is slow to establish but very stately when mature. Propagate by seeds, by cuttings or by crown division. The variety *alba* (*al*-buh) has pure-white flowers, while *roseum* (roh-zee-um) has lavender-pink flowers. Zones 3 to 8.

**Viscaria viscosa.** See *Lychnis viscaria*.

## Yucca (*yuk*-uh).

Lily Family (*Liliaceae*).

Evergreen, bold, architectural plants, all native to the American continents. Foliage is sword-shaped, rigid, leathery and sharply pointed. The flowers are fragrant, white or purple, and pendant, in dense pyramidal spires. Full sun and sandy, well-drained soil are required. Propagate

## Yucca

*Veronicastrum virginicum*
BOWMAN'S-ROOT

*Yucca gloriosa*
SPANISH DAGGER

by separating young plants (pups) with pieces of root from the mother plant.

**Y. filamentosa** (fil-a-men-*toh*-suh).
ADAM'S-NEEDLE.
Native to the southeastern U.S. Sprays of creamy-white, cup-shaped, fragrant flowers, 2 in. across, are borne on tall, strong, woody, deciduous stems, 4 to 6 ft. tall. Each year, new stems rise from the center of the sharply pointed leaf clumps. The leaves are evergreen, 15 in. long and 1 in. across, with shaggy threads along the edges. The leaves are not as rigid as in some of the other species. These drought-resistant plants are decorative among shrubs and in large perennial borders. 'Bright Edge' has cream-colored leaf margins; 'Golden Sword' has foliage edged in yellow; and 'Variegata' has leaves striped in cream. Zones 5 to 10.

**Y. glauca** (*glaw*-kuh).
ADAM'S-NEEDLE.
BEAR GRASS.
From the central U.S., a refined yucca growing 2 to 3 ft. wide. The leaves are gray-green, linear and sharply pointed, to $2^{1}/2$ ft. long by $^{1}/2$ in. wide. The flower stems reach 3 ft. The individual flowers are greenish-white flushed with red and $2^{1}/2$ in. wide. Useful in mass plantings or as specimens. Zones 6 to 10.

**Y. gloriosa** (glow-ree-*oh*-suh).
SPANISH DAGGER.
Native from South Carolina to Florida. An evergreen shrub that grows 6 to 8 ft. tall. The leaves are borne on a single fleshy, stiff stem that becomes bare at the bottom. Leaves are 2 ft. long, $2^{1}/2$ in. wide and tipped with a spine. Flowers are pendulous, creamy white and sometimes tinged with red or purple. Propagate by laying the fleshy stems horizontally or by seeds. Zone 7.

# UNDERSTANDING THE ZONE MAP

Gardening is an inexact science, but one unshakable truth is that plants grow, mature, bloom and produce seeds. The key to their success is location—the right plant in the right place will succeed. A plant provided with the right sunlight exposure in a setting where the native climate, moisture and soil conditions meet its needs, will flourish and largely take care of itself.

Climate comes first. The encyclopedic entries in the Hearst Garden Guides are zone-keyed to the United States Department of Agriculture Plant Hardiness Zone Map, which is reproduced on pages 178–179. The lower the number, the lower the winter minimum temperatures are in the zone. The zones identified in the entries describe the recommended range in which the plant will usually thrive. Thus, *Liatris spicata* (spike gay-feather), which is listed as Zones 3 to 9, grows well in Zones 3, 4, 5, 6, 7, 8 and 9. North of Zone 3 (Zones 2 and 1), the winter low temperatures are too cold for it to survive. South of Zone 9 (Zones 10 and 11), the summers are too warm and the winters are not cold enough for it to succeed.

The boundaries of the zone map are oversimplifications, however; they are generalizations that ignore microclimates. For example, an L-shaped wall with a southern exposure or a windbreak to the north, can create pocket climates in which plants prove hardy north of their normal range. Conversely, an exposed or north-facing slope will jeopardize a plant that is marginally hardy in the region.

Plants have individual soil requirements as well as climate preferences. In fact, if the soil is ideal, a plant may stand up to adverse weather conditions. Most evergreens require well-drained, slightly acid soil. Evergreens can be grown in a region where soils are alkaline if the trouble is taken to create and maintain suitable soil conditions. But that plant will not really be in the right place, and it will demand higher maintenance and find the going tougher. Tender cacti and other succulents can be grown in the North—in the heated indoors in winter—and bog plants in the desert—if a bog is created for it. But the low-maintenance way to success is to select plants that thrive naturally in the region.

The most accurate indicator of the type of plants that will flourish in your garden microclimates and soil is the garden next door. What does well there will probably also thrive in your own garden. If you are unsure about the conditions in your area, your local nursery can provide valuable information about the soil, annual rainfall and fluctuations in temperature.

## HARDINESS

Hardiness, commonly accepted as the ability of a plant to withstand low temperatures, should rather be considered a plant's ability to grow well in the presence of a complex variety of physical conditions, of which temperature may be only one factor. Other factors are high temperatures, drought and humidity (rainfall), altitude, soil characteristics, orientation and exposure (sun, shade, available light, prevailing winds), day length (latitude), air quality and ground drainage.

# PLANT HARDINESS

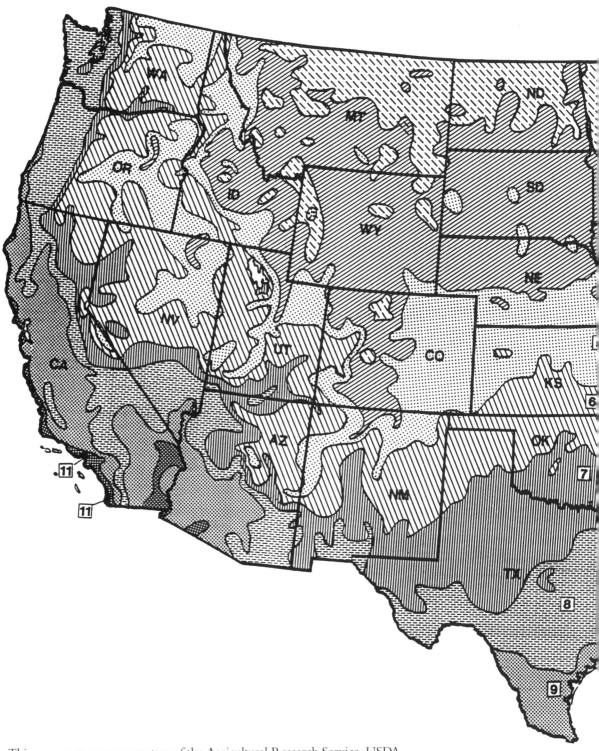

This zone map appears courtesy of the Agricultural Research Service, USDA.

# Z O N E   M A P

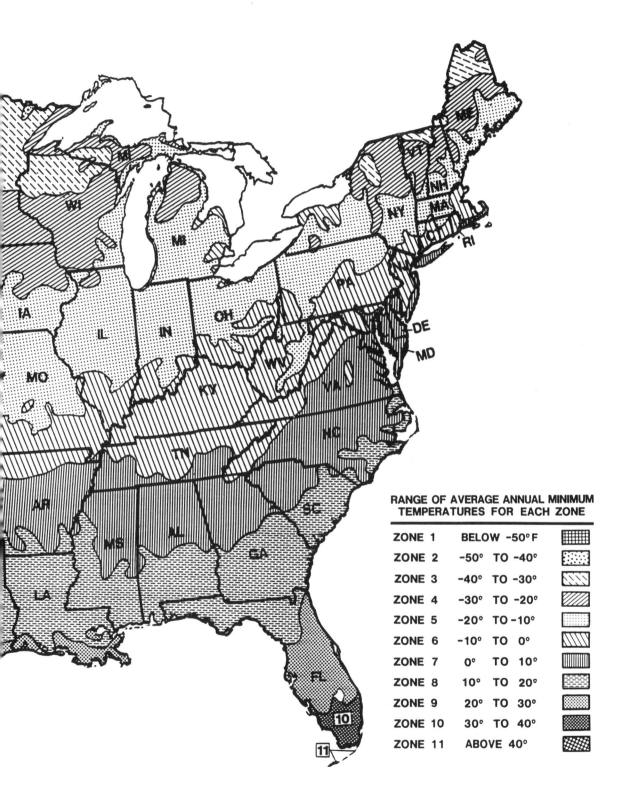

**RANGE OF AVERAGE ANNUAL MINIMUM TEMPERATURES FOR EACH ZONE**

| | | |
|---|---|---|
| ZONE 1 | BELOW −50°F | |
| ZONE 2 | −50° TO −40° | |
| ZONE 3 | −40° TO −30° | |
| ZONE 4 | −30° TO −20° | |
| ZONE 5 | −20° TO −10° | |
| ZONE 6 | −10° TO 0° | |
| ZONE 7 | 0° TO 10° | |
| ZONE 8 | 10° TO 20° | |
| ZONE 9 | 20° TO 30° | |
| ZONE 10 | 30° TO 40° | |
| ZONE 11 | ABOVE 40° | |

# COMMON NAME INDEX

AARON'S ROD. See *Thermopsis caroliniana.*

ACONITE. See *Aconitum.*

ACONITE BUTTERCUP. See *Ranunculus aconitifolius.*

ADAM'S-NEEDLE. See *Yucca filamentosa; Yucca glauca.*

ADONIS, SPRING. See *Adonis vernalis.*

ALKANET. See *Anchusa.*

ALKANET, ITALIAN. See *Anchusa azurea.*

ALLEGHENY FOAMFLOWER. See *Tiarella cordifolia.*

ALLWOOD PINK. See *Dianthus × allwoodii.*

ALPINE PINK. See *Dianthus alpinus.*

ALPINE SEA HOLLY. See *Eryngium alpinum.*

ALPINE SPEEDWELL. See *Veronica alpina.*

ALUMROOT. See *Heuchera.*

ALUMROOT, AMERICAN. See *Heuchera americana.*

ALUMROOT, HAIRY. See *Heuchera villosa.*

ALUMROOT, SMALL-FLOWERED. See *Heuchera micrantha.*

AMERICAN ALUMROOT. See *Heuchera americana.*

AMETHYST SEA HOLLY. See *Eryngium amethystinum.*

AMSONIA, WILLOW. See *Amsonia tabernaemontana.*

AMUR ADONIS. See *Adonis amurensis.*

ANEMONE, GRAPE-LEAVED. See *Anemone tomentosa.*

ANEMONE, JAPANESE. See *Anemone × hybrida.*

ARGENTINE BLUE-EYED GRASS. See *Sisyrinchium striatum.*

ARKWRIGHT'S CAMPION. See *Lychnis × arkwrightii.*

ARMENIAN GERANIUM. See *Geranium psilostemon.*

ARTEMISIA, SILVER-KING. See *Artemisia ludoviciana* var. *albula; Artemisia schmidtiana.*

ASPHODEL. See *Asphodeline lutea.*

ASTER, CALICO. See *Aster lateriflorus.*

ASTER, NEW ENGLAND. See *Aster novae-angliae.*

ASTER, NEW YORK. See *Aster novi-belgii.*

ASTILBE, FALL. See *Astilbe taquetii.*

ASTILBE, STAR. See *Astilbe simplicifolia.*

AUBRETIA. See *Aubrieta.*

AUTUMN JOY SEDUM. See *Sedum* 'Autumn Joy'.

AVENS. See *Geum.*

AVENS, WATER. See *Geum rivale.*

AZURE MONKSHOOD. See *Aconitum carmichaelii.*

AZURE SAGE. See *Salvia azurea.*

BABY'S BREATH. See *Gypsophila paniculata.*

BABY'S BREATH, CREEPING. See *Gypsophila repens.*

BALLOON FLOWER. See *Platycodon.*

BANEBERRY. See *Actaea.*

BANEBERRY, RED. See *Actaea rubra.*

BANEBERRY, WHITE. See *Actaea alba.*

BARRENWORT. See *Epimedium.*

BARRENWORT, BICOLOR. See *Epimedium × versicolor.*

BARRENWORT, RED. See *Epimedium × rubrum.*

BARRENWORT, YOUNG'S. See *Epimedium × youngianum.*

BASKET-OF-GOLD. See *Aurinia saxatilis.*

BEACH WORMWOOD. See *Artemisia stelleriana.*

BEAR GRASS. See *Yucca glauca.*

BEAR'S-BREECH. See *Acanthus.*

BEAR'S-BREECH, COMMON. See *Acanthus mollis.*

BEAR'S-BREECH, SPINY. See
*Acanthus spinosus.*

BEAR'S-FOOT HELLEBORE. See
*Helleborus foetidus.*

BEARD-TONGUE. See
*Penstemon.*

BEARDED PENSTEMON. See
*Penstemon barbatus.*

BEE BALM. See *Monarda
didyma.*

BEE BALM, SCARLET. See
*Monarda didyma.*

BELLADONNA DELPHINIUM. See
*Delphinium × belladonna.*

BELLFLOWER. See *Campanula.*

BELLFLOWER, CARPATHIAN.
See *Campanula carpatica.*

BELLFLOWER, CLUSTERED.
See *Campanula glomerata.*

BELLFLOWER, DALMATIAN. See
*Campanula portenschlagiana.*

BELLFLOWER, MILKY. See
*Campanula lactiflora.*

BELLFLOWER, PEACH-LEAVED.
See *Campanula persicifolia.*

BELLFLOWER, SERBIAN. See
*Campanula poscharskyana.*

BELLFLOWER, SPIRAL. See
*Campanula cochleariifolia.*

BELLS, FOAMY. See
*Heucherella; Heucherella
tiarelloides.*

BERGAMOT. See *Monarda
fistulosa.*

BERGAMOT, WILD. See
*Monarda fistulosa.*

BERGENIA, HEART-LEAVED.
See *Bergenia cordifolia.*

BETHLEHEM SAGE. See
*Pulmonaria saccharata.*

BETONY. See *Stachys.*

BETONY, COMMON. See *Stachys
officinalis.*

BICOLOR BARRENWORT. See
*Epimedium × versicolor.*

BICOLOR MONKSHOOD. See
*Aconitum × bicolor.*

BIGLEAF LIGULARIA. See
*Ligularia dentata.*

BIGROOT GERANIUM. *See
Geranium macrorrhizum.*

BISHOP'S WEED. See
*Aegopodium podagraria.*

BISHOP'S-HAT. See *Epimedium
grandiflorum.*

BLACK COHOSH. See
*Cimicifuga racemosa.*

BLACK FALSE HELLEBORE. See
*Veratrum nigrum.*

BLACK SNAKEROOT. See
*Cimicifuga racemosa.*

BLACKBERRY LILY. See
*Belamcanda chinensis.*

BLADDER CAMPION. See *Silene
vulgaris.*

BLANKET FLOWER. See
*Gaillardia aristata; Gaillardia
× grandiflora.*

BLAZING-STAR. See *Liatris.*

BLEEDING-HEART. See *Dicentra.*

BLEEDING-HEART, COMMON.
See *Dicentra spectabilis.*

BLEEDING-HEART, FRINGED.
See *Dicentra eximia.*

BLOOD-RED GERANIUM. See
*Geranium sanguineum.*

BLOODROOT. See *Sanguinaria
canadensis.*

BLUE HOSTA. See *Hosta
ventricosa.*

BLUE LILYTURF. See *Liriope
muscari.*

BLUE LOBELIA. See *Lobelia
siphilitica.*

BLUE LUNGWORT. See
*Pulmonaria angustifolia.*

BLUE POPPY OF TIBET. See
*Meconopsis betonicifolia.*

BLUE POPPY. See *Meconopsis
betonicifolia.*

BLUE-EYED GRASS. See
*Sisyrinchium.*

BLUEBELLS. See *Mertensia.*

BLUEBELLS, VIRGINIA. See
*Mertensia virginica.*

BLUEBELLS-OF-SCOTLAND.
See *Campanula rotundifolia.*

BLUET, MOUNTAIN. See
*Centaurea montana.*

BONESET. See *Eupatorium.*

BOUNCING BET. See *Saponaria
officinalis.*

BOWMAN'S-ROOT. See
*Porteranthus; Porteranthus
trifoliata; Veronicastrum;
Veronicastrum virginicum.*

BRANCHED BUGBANE. See
*Cimicifuga ramosa.*

BRAZILIAN VERBENA. See
*Verbena bonariensis.*

BRONZELEAF RODGERSIA. See
*Rodgersia podophylla.*

BRUNNERA, HEART-LEAF. See
*Brunnera macrophylla.*

BUGBANE. See *Cimicifuga.*

BUGBANE, BRANCHED. See
*Cimicifuga ramosa.*

BUGBANE, KAMCHATKA. See
*Cimicifuga simplex.*

BUGLEWEED. See *Ajuga; Ajuga reptans.*

BUGLEWEED, CARPET. See *Ajuga reptans.*

BUGLEWEED, UPRIGHT. See *Ajuga pyramidalis.*

BUGLOSS. See *Anchusa.*

BUGLOSS, ITALIAN. See *Anchusa azurea.*

BURNET. See *Sanguisorba officinalis.*

BURNET, CANADIAN. See *Sanguisorba canadensis.*

BURNET, JAPANESE. See *Sanguisorba obtusa.*

BUTTERCUP. See *Ranunculus.*

BUTTERCUP, ACONITE. See *Ranunculus aconitifolius.*

BUTTERCUP, COMMON. See *Ranunculus acris.*

BUTTERCUP, MOUNTAIN. See *Ranunculus montanus.*

BUTTERFLY WEED. See *Asclepias tuberosa.*

CAD-WEED. See *Anaphalis margaritacea.*

CALICO ASTER. See *Aster lateriflorus.*

CAMPION. See *Lychnis; Silene.*

CAMPION, ARKWRIGHT'S. See *Lychnis × arkwrightii.*

CAMPION, BLADDER. See *Silene vulgaris.*

CAMPION, HAAGE. See *Lychnis × haageana.*

CAMPION, ROSE. See *Lychnis coronaria.*

CANADIAN BURNET. See *Sanguisorba canadensis.*

CANADIAN GOLDENROD. See *Solidago canadensis.*

CANDYTUFT. See *Iberis.*

CANDYTUFT, EVERGREEN. See *Iberis sempervirens.*

CARDINAL FLOWER. See *Lobelia cardinalis.*

CARPATHIAN BELLFLOWER. See *Campanula carpatica.*

CARPET BUGLEWEED. See *Ajuga reptans.*

CATCHFLY. See *Lychnis; Silene.*

CATCHFLY, GERMAN. See *Lychnis viscaria.*

CATMINT. See *Nepeta.*

CAUCASIAN LEOPARD'S-BANE. See *Doronicum caucasicum.*

CENTAUREA, GLOBE. See *Centaurea macrocephala.*

CHAMELEON PLANT. See *Houttuynia cordata.*

CHECKERBLOOM. See *Sidalcea malviflora.*

CHEDDAR PINK. See *Dianthus gratianopolitanus.*

CHILEAN AVENS. See *Geum quellyon.*

CHINESE FALSE GOATSBEARD. See *Astilbe chinensis.*

CHINESE-LANTERN. See *Physalis alkekengi.*

CHRISTMAS ROSE. See *Helleborus niger.*

CHRYSANTHEMUM, GOLD-AND-SILVER. See *Chrysanthemum pacificum.*

CHRYSANTHEMUM, HYBRID RED. See *Chrysanthemum × rubellum.*

CITRON DAYLILY. See *Hemerocallis citrina.*

CLARK'S GERANIUM. See *Geranium clarkei.*

CLEMATIS. See *Clematis.*

CLEMATIS, HYBRID. See *Clematis × eriostemon.*

CLEMATIS, TUBE. See *Clematis heracleifolia.*

CLUMP VERBENA. See *Verbena canadensis.*

CLUSTERED BELLFLOWER. See *Campanula glomerata.*

COHOSH. See *Actaea.*

COHOSH, BLACK. See *Cimicifuga racemosa.*

COLEWORT. See *Crambe; Crambe cordifolia.*

COLORADO COLUMBINE. See *Aquilegia caerulea.*

COLUMBINE. See *Aquilegia; Aquilegia × hybrida.*

COLUMBINE, COLORADO. See *Aquilegia caerulea.*

COLUMBINE, FAN. See *Aquilegia flabellata.*

COLUMBINE, GOLDEN-SPURRED. See *Aquilegia chrysantha.*

COLUMBINE, ROCKY MOUNTAIN. See *Aquilegia caerulea.*

COLUMBINE, WILD. See *Aquilegia canadensis.*

COLUMBINE MEADOW RUE. See *Thalictrum aquilegifolium.*

COMMON BEAR'S-BREECH. See
*Acanthus mollis.*

COMMON BETONY. See *Stachys
officinalis.*

COMMON BLEEDING-HEART.
See *Dicentra spectabilis.*

COMMON BUTTERCUP. See
*Ranunculus acris.*

COMMON GARDEN PEONY. See
*Paeonia lactiflora.*

COMMON HAREBELL. See
*Campanula rotundifolia.*

COMMON HOUSELEEK See
*Sempervivum tectorum.*

COMMON LADYBELLS. See
*Adenophora confusa.*

COMMON LAVENDER. See
*Lavandula angustifolia.*

COMMON MONKSHOOD. See
*Aconitum napellus.*

COMMON PEONY. See *Paeonia
officinalis.*

COMMON ROSE MALLOW. See
*Hibiscus moscheutos.*

COMMON SHOOTING-STAR. See
*Dodecatheon meadia.*

COMMON SNEEZEWEED. See
*Helenium autumnale.*

COMMON SUNROSE. See
*Helianthemum nummularium.*

COMMON TOAD LILY. See
*Tricyrtis hirta.*

COMMON TORCH LILY. See
*Kniphofia uvaria.*

COMMON YARROW. See
*Achillea millefolium.*

CONEFLOWER. See *Echinacea.
Rudbeckia.*

CONEFLOWER, CUTLEAF. See
*Rudbeckia laciniata.*

CONEFLOWER, ORANGE. See
*Rudbeckia fulgida.*

CONEFLOWER, PURPLE. See
*Echinacea purpurea.*

CONEFLOWER, SHINING. See
*Rudbeckia nitida.*

CONEFLOWER, THREE-LOBED.
See *Rudbeckia triloba.*

CORALBELLS. See *Heuchera
sanguinea.*

COREOPSIS, LANCE. See
*Coreopsis lanceolata.*

COREOPSIS, MOUSE-EARED.
See *Coreopsis auriculata.*

COREOPSIS, THREAD-LEAVED.
See *Coreopsis verticillata.*

CORONATION GOLD YARROW.
See *Achillea* × 'Coronation
Gold'.

CORSICAN HELLEBORE. See
*Helleborus argutifolius.*

CORYDALIS, WHITE. See
*Corydalis ochroleuca.*

CORYDALIS, YELLOW. See
*Corydalis lutea.*

COTTAGE PINK. See *Dianthus
plumarius.*

CRANESBILL. See *Geranium.*

CRANESBILL, DALMATION. See
*Geranium dalmaticum.*

CRANESBILL, GRAY-LEAVED.
See *Geranium cinereum.*

CRANESBILL, MEADOW. See
*Geranium pratense.*

CREEPING BABY'S BREATH.
See *Gypsophila repens.*

CREEPING JENNY. See
*Lysimachia nummularia.*

CREEPING PHLOX. See *Phlox
stolonifera.*

CREEPING POLEMONIUM. See
*Polemonium reptans.*

CRIMSON PINCUSHION. See
*Knautia macedonica.*

CROWFOOT. See *Ranunculus.*

CULVER'S ROOT. See
*Veronicastrum virginicum.*

CUPID'S DART. See
*Catananche; Catananche
caerulea.*

CUSHION SPURGE. See
*Euphorbia epithymoides.*

CUTLEAF CONEFLOWER. See
*Rudbeckia laciniata.*

DAISY, GIANT. See
*Chrysanthemum uliginosum.*

DAISY, MICHAELMAS. See *Aster.*

DAISY, NIPPON. See
*Chrysanthemum nipponicum.*

DAISY, PAINTED. See
*Chrysanthemum coccineum.*

DAISY, SHASTA. See
*Chrysanthemum* × *superbum.*

DAISY, TATARIAN. See *Aster
tataricus.*

DALMATIAN BELLFLOWER. See
*Campanula portenschlagiana.*

DALMATION CRANESBILL. See
*Geranium dalmaticum.*

DAYLILY. See *Hemerocallis.*

DAYLILY, CITRON. See
*Hemerocallis citrina.*

DAYLILY, DWARF. See
*Hemerocallis minor.*

DAYLILY, EARLY. See
*Hemerocallis dumortieri.*

DAYLILY, KOREAN. See
*Hemerocallis coreana.*

DAYLILY, LEMON. See
*Hemerocallis lilio-asphodelus.*

DAYLILY, MANY-FLOWERED.
See *Hemerocallis multiflora.*

DAYLILY, ORANGE. See
*Hemerocallis × aurantiaca.*

DAYLILY, PURPLE MOUNTAIN.
See *Hemerocallis altissima.*

DAYLILY, THUNBERG'S. See
*Hemerocallis thunbergii.*

DEAD NETTLE, SPOTTED. See
*Lamium maculatum.*

DELPHINIUM, BELLADONNA.
See *Delphinium × belladonna.*

DELPHINIUM, HYBRID BEE. See
*Delphinium × elatum.*

DITTANY. See *Dictamnus.*

DROPWORT. See *Filipendula vulgaris.*

DRUMSTICK PRIMROSE. See
*Primula denticulata.*

DUSTY MILLER. See *Lychnis coronaria.*

DUTCHMAN'S-BREECHES. See
*Dicentra cucullaria.*

DWARF DAYLILY. See
*Hemerocallis minor.*

EARLY DAYLILY. See
*Hemerocallis dumortieri.*

ECHINACEA, PURPLE. See
*Echinacea purpurea.*

ENDRESS' GERANIUM. See
*Geranium endressii.*

ENGLISH LAVENDER. See
*Lavandula angustifolia.*

EPIMEDIUM, LONG-SPUR. See
*Epimedium grandiflorum.*

EPIMEDIUM, PERSIAN. See
*Epimedium pinnatum.*

EUROPEAN STRAWBERRY. See
*Fragaria vesca.*

EUROPEAN WHITE
HELLEBORE. See *Veratrum album.*

EVENING PRIMROSE. See
*Oenothera.*

EVERGREEN CANDYTUFT. See
*Iberis sempervirens.*

EVERLASTING, PEARLY. See
*Anaphalis; Anaphalis margaritacea; Anaphalis triplinervis.*

FAASSEN'S MINT. See *Nepeta × faassenii.*

FAIRY'S-THIMBLE. See
*Campanula cochleariifolia.*

FALL ASTILBE. See *Astilbe taquetii.*

FALSE DRAGONHEAD. See
*Physostegia.*

FALSE GOATSBEARD. See
*Astilbe.*

FALSE GOATSBEARD,
CHINESE. See *Astilbe chinensis.*

FALSE GOLDENROD. See
*Solidago sphacelata.*

FALSE HELLEBORE. See
*Veratrum.*

FALSE HELLEBORE, BLACK.
See *Veratrum nigrum.*

FALSE INDIGO. See *Baptisia.*

FALSE LUPINE. See *Thermopsis.*

FALSE MALLOW. See *Sidalcea.*

FALSE MITTERWORT. See
*Tiarella.*

FALSE SOLOMON'S-SEAL. See
*Smilacina; Smilacina racemosa.*

FALSE STARWORT. See
*Boltonia.*

FAN COLUMBINE. See *Aquilegia flabellata.*

FARRER'S LADYBELLS. See
*Adenophora confusa.*

FEATHERLEAF RODGERSIA.
See *Rodgersia pinnata.*

FERNLEAF PEONY. See *Paeonia tenuifolia.*

FINGERLEAF RODGERSIA. See
*Rodgersia aesculifolia.*

FLAT-LEAVED SEA HOLLY. See
*Eryngium planum.*

FLAX. See *Linum.*

FLAX, GARDEN. See *Linum perenne.*

FLAX, GOLDEN. See *Linum flavum.*

FLEABANE. See *Erigeron.*

FLEABANE, OREGON. See
*Erigeron speciosus.*

FLEECE FLOWER. See
*Polygonum.*

FLEECE FLOWER, HIMALAYAN.
See *Polygonum affine.*

FLORIFEROUS SEDUM. See
*Sedum floriferum.*

FLOWER-OF-JOVE. See *Lychnis flos-jovis.* FLOWERING SEA
KALE. See *Crambe cordifolia.*

FLOWERING SPURGE. See
*Euphorbia corollata.*

FOAMFLOWER, ALLEGHENY.
See *Tiarella cordifolia.*

FOAMY BELLS. See *Heucherella.*
*Heucherella tiarelloides.*

FORGET-ME-NOT. See *Myostis.*

FORMOSA TOAD LILY. See
*Tricyrtis formosana.*

FORTUNE'S HOSTA. See *Hosta fortunei.*

FOXGLOVE. See *Digitalis.*

FOXGLOVE, STRAW. See
*Digitalis lutea.*

FOXGLOVE, STRAWBERRY. See
*Digitalis × mertonensis.*

FOXGLOVE, YELLOW. See
*Digitalis grandiflora.*

FOXGLOVE PENSTEMON. See
*Penstemon digitalis.*

FRAGRANT HOSTA. See *Hosta plantaginea.*

FRAGRANT SOLOMON'S-SEAL.
See *Polygonatum odoratum.*

FRAISES DES BOIS. See
*Fragaria vesca.*

FRAXINELLA. See *Dictamnus.*

FRENCH LAVENDER. See
*Lavandula stoechas.*

FRINGED BLEEDING-HEART.
See *Dicentra eximia.*

FUMARIA. See *Corydalis.*


GARDEN FLAX. See *Linum perenne.*

GARDEN PHLOX. See *Phlox paniculata.*

GARDEN SAGE. See *Salvia officinalis.*

GARLAND LARKSPUR. See
*Delphinium cheilanthum.*

GAS PLANT. See *Dictamnus.*

GAURA, WHITE. See *Gaura lindheimeri.*

GAY-FEATHER. See *Liatris.*

GAY-FEATHER, KANSAS. See
*Liatris pycnostachya.*

GAY-FEATHER, SPIKE. See
*Liatris spicata.*

GAY-FEATHER, TALL. See
*Liatris scariosa.*

GERANIUM, ARMENIAN. See
*Geranium psilostemon.*

GERANIUM, BIGROOT. See
*Geranium macrorrhizum.*

GERANIUM, BLOOD-RED. See
*Geranium sanguineum.*

GERANIUM, CLARK'S. See
*Geranium clarkei.*

GERANIUM, ENDRESS'. See
*Geranium endressii.*

GERANIUM, WILD. See
*Geranium maculatum.*

GERMAN CATCHFLY. See
*Lychnis viscaria.*

GERMANDER. See *Teucrium.*

GIANT DAISY. See
*Chrysanthemum uliginosum.*

GLOBE CENTAUREA. See
*Centaurea macrocephala.*

GLOBE THISTLE. See *Echinops;*
*Echinops ritro.*

GLOBE THISTLE, GREAT. See
*Echinops sphaerocephalus.*

GLOBE THISTLE, RUSSIAN. See
*Echinops exaltatus.*

GLOBE THISTLE, SIBERIAN.
See *Echinops humilis.*

GLOBEFLOWER. See *Trollius.*

GLOBEFLOWER, HYBRID. See
*Trollius × cultorum.*

GLOXINIA PENSTEMON. See
*Penstemon × gloxinioides.*

GOATSBEARD. See *Aruncus.*

GOLD-AND-SILVER
CHRYSANTHEMUM. See
*Chrysanthemum pacificum.*

GOLD-MOSS STONECROP. See
*Sedum acre.*

GOLDEN-CARPET. See *Sedum acre.*

GOLDEN FLAX. See *Linum flavum.*

GOLDEN-ASTER. See
*Chrysopsis.*

GOLDEN-ASTER, HAIRY. See
*Chrysopsis villosa.*

GOLDEN-ASTER, MARYLAND.
See *Chrysopsis mariana.*

GOLDEN-RAY. See *Ligularia.*

GOLDENROD. See *Solidago.*

GOLDENROD, CANADIAN. See
*Solidago canadensis.*

GOLDENROD, SEASIDE. See
*Solidago sempervirens.*

GOLDEN-SPURRED
COLUMBINE. See *Aquilegia chrysantha.*

GOLDEN-STAR. See
*Chrysogonum virginianum.*

GOOSENECK LOOSESTRIFE.
See *Lysimachia clethroides.*

GOUTWEED. See *Aegopodium.*

GRAPE-LEAVED ANEMONE. See
*Anemone tomentosa.*

GRASS PINK. See *Dianthus plumarius.*

GRAY-LEAVED CRANESBILL.
See *Geranium cinereum.*

GREAT GLOBE THISTLE. See
*Echinops sphaerocephalus.*

GREAT LOBELIA. See *Lobelia siphilitica.*

GREAT SOLOMON'S-SEAL. See *Polygonatum commutatum.*

GREEN LAVENDER COTTON. See *Santolina virens.*

GROUND PINK. See *Phlox subulata.*

HAAGE CAMPION. See *Lychnis × haageana.*

HAIRY ALUMROOT. See *Heuchera villosa.*

HAIRY GOLDEN-ASTER. See *Chrysopsis villosa.*

HARDY GARDEN PINK. See *Dianthus knappii.*

HAREBELL, COMMON. See *Campanula rotundifolia.*

HAREBELL PENSTEMON. See *Penstemon campanulatus.*

HAREBELL SPEEDWELL. See *Veronica prostrata.*

HEART-LEAF BRUNNERA. See *Brunnera macrophylla.*

HEART-LEAVED BERGENIA. See *Bergenia cordifolia.*

HELIOPSIS, SUNFLOWER. See *Heliopsis helianthoides.*

HELLEBORE. See *Helleborus.*

HELLEBORE, BEAR'S-FOOT. See *Helleborus foetidus.*

HELLEBORE, CORSICAN. See *Helleborus argutifolius.*

HEN-AND-CHICKENS. See *Sempervivum tectorum.*

HIMALAYAN FLEECE FLOWER. See *Polygonum affine.*

HOLLYHOCK, MINIATURE. See *Sidalcea.*

HOLLYHOCK, WILD. See *Sidalcea malviflora.*

HOLLYHOCK MALLOW. See *Malva alcea.*

HORSE-MINT. See *Monarda.*

HOSTA, BLUE. See *Hosta ventricosa.*

HOSTA, FORTUNE'S. See *Hosta fortunei.*

HOSTA, FRAGRANT. See *Hosta plantaginea.*

HOSTA, LANCE-LEAF. See *Hosta lancifolia.*

HOSTA, LATE-FLOWERING. See *Hosta tardiflora.*

HOSTA, SIEBOLD. See *Hosta sieboldiana.*

HOSTA, TOKUDAMA. See *Hosta tokudama.*

HOSTA, WAVY. See *Hosta undulata.*

HOUSELEEK, COMMON. See *Sempervivum tectorum.*

HYBRID BEE DELPHINIUM. See *Delphinium × elatum.*

HYBRID CLEMATIS. See *Clematis × eriostemon.*

HYBRID GLOBEFLOWER. See *Trollius × cultorum.*

HYBRID RED CHRYSANTHEMUM. See *Chrysanthemum × rubellum.*

INDIAN CHOCOLATE. See *Geum rivale.*

INDIAN PINK. See *Spigelia marilandica.*

INDIAN TURNIP. See *Arisaema triphyllum.*

INDIAN-PHYSIC. See *Porteranthus.*

INULA, SWORDLEAF. See *Inula ensifolia.*

ITALIAN ALKANET. See *Anchusa azurea.*

ITALIAN BUGLOSS. See *Anchusa azurea.*

JACK-IN-THE-PULPIT. See *Arisaema; Arisaema triphyllum.*

JACOB'S ROD. See *Asphodeline.*

JACOB'S-LADDER. See *Polemonium caeruleum.*

JAPANESE ANEMONE. See *Anemone × hybrida.*

JAPANESE BURNET. See *Sanguisorba obtusa.*

JAPANESE LOOSESTRIFE. See *Lysimachia clethroides.*

JAPANESE MEADOWSWEET. See *Filipendula purpurea.*

JAPANESE PRIMROSE. See *Primula japonica.*

JERUSALEM SAGE. See *Phlomis fruticosa.*

JERUSALEM-CROSS. See *Lychnis chalcedonica.*

JOE PYE WEED. See *Eupatorium purpureum.*

JUPITER'S-BEARD. See *Centranthus ruber.*

KAMCHATKA BUGBANE. See *Cimicifuga simplex.*

KAMCHATKA STONECROP. See *Sedum kamtschaticum.*

KANSAS GAY-FEATHER. See
Liatris pycnostachya.
KNAPWEED. See Centaurea
hypoleuca.
KNAPWEED, PERSIAN
CORNFLOWER. See
Centaurea dealbata.
KNOTWEED. See Polygonum.
KOREAN DAYLILY. See
Hemerocallis coreana.

LADY'S MANTLE. See
Alchemilla mollis; Alchemilla
vulgaris.
LADYBELLS, COMMON. See
Adenophora confusa.
LADYBELLS. See Adenophora.
LADYBELLS, FARRER'S. See
Adenophora confusa.
LADYBELLS, LILYLEAF. See
Adenophora liliifolia.
LAMB'S-EARS. See Stachys
byzantina.
LANCE COREOPSIS. Coreopsis
lanceolata.
LANCE-LEAF HOSTA. See Hosta
lancifolia.
LARKSPUR. See Delphinium.
LARKSPUR, GARLAND. See
Delphinium cheilanthum.
LATE-FLOWERING HOSTA. See
Hosta tardiflora.
LAVENDER. See Lavandula.
LAVENDER, COMMON. See
Lavandula angustifolia.
LAVENDER, ENGLISH. See
Lavandula angustifolia.
LAVENDER, FRENCH. See
Lavandula stoechas.

LAVENDER, SEA. See
Limonium.
LAVENDER, SPANISH. See
Lavandula stoechas.
LAVENDER COTTON. See
Santolina chamaecyparissus.
LAVENDER COTTON, GREEN.
See Santolina virens.
LEADWORT. See Ceratostigma
plumbaginoides.
LEBANON STONE CRESS. See
Aethionema coridifolium.
LEMON DAYLILY. See
Hemerocallis lilio-asphodelus.
LENTEN ROSE. See Helleborus
orientalis.
LEOPARD'S-BANE, CAUCASIAN.
See Doronicum caucasicum.
LEOPARD'S-BANE. See
Doronicum.
LIGULARIA, BIGLEAF. See
Ligularia dentata.
LIGULARIA, NARROW-SPIKED.
See Ligularia stenocephala.
LIGULARIA. See Ligularia.
LILY, BLACKBERRY. See
Belamcanda chinensis.
LILY, PLANTAIN. See Hosta.
LILY-OF-THE-VALLEY. See
Convallaria.
LILYLEAF LADYBELLS. See
Adenophora liliifolia.
LILYTURF. See Liriope.
LILYTURF, BLUE. See Liriope
muscari.
LOBELIA, BLUE. See Lobelia
siphilitica.
LOBELIA, GREAT. See Lobelia
siphilitica.

LOBELIA, SCARLET. See Lobelia
cardinalis.
LONG-LEAF VERONICA. See
Veronica longifolia.
LONG-LEAVED LUNGWORT. See
Pulmonaria longifolia.
LONG-SPUR EPIMEDIUM. See
Epimedium grandiflorum.
LOOSESTRIFE. See Lysimachia;
Lythrum.
LOOSESTRIFE, GOOSENECK.
See Lysimachia clethroides.
LOOSESTRIFE, JAPANESE. See
Lysimachia clethroides.
LOOSESTRIFE, PURPLE. See
Lythrum salicaria.
LOOSESTRIFE, WAND. See
Lythrum virgatum.
LUNGWORT. See Pulmonaria.
LUNGWORT, BLUE. See
Pulmonaria angustifolia.
LUNGWORT, LONG-LEAVED.
See Pulmonaria longifolia.
LUNGWORT, RED. See
Pulmonaria rubra.
LUPINE. See Lupinus.
LUPINE, SOUTHERN. See
Thermopsis caroliniana.
LUPINE, TREE. See Lupinus
arboreus.
LUPINE, WASHINGTON. See
Lupinus polyphyllus.
LUPINE, WILD. See Lupinus
perennis.

MAIDEN PINK. See Dianthus
deltoides.
MALLOW, HOLLYHOCK. See
Malva alcea.

MALLOW. See *Malva*.

MALLOW, MUSK. See *Malva moschata*.

MALTESE-CROSS. See *Lychnis chalcedonica*.

MANY-FLOWERED DAYLILY. See *Hemerocallis multiflora*.

MANY-FLOWERED SUNFLOWER. See *Helianthus × multiflorus*.

MARYLAND GOLDEN-ASTER. See *Chrysopsis mariana*.

MASTERWORT. See *Astrantia*.

MEADOW CRANESBILL. See *Geranium pratense*.

MEADOW PHLOX. See *Phlox maculata*.

MEADOW RUE. See *Thalictrum*.

MEADOW RUE, COLUMBINE. See *Thalictrum aquilegifolium*.

MEADOW RUE, YUNNAN. See *Thalictrum delavayi*.

MEADOWSWEET. See *Filipendula*.

MEADOWSWEET, JAPANESE. See *Filipendula purpurea*.

MEADOWSWEET, SIBERIAN. See *Filipendula palmata*.

MICHAELMAS DAISY. See *Aster*.

MILFOIL. See *Achillea millefolium*.

MILKWEED. See *Asclepias*.

MILKWEED, ORANGE. See *Asclepias tuberosa*.

MILKY BELLFLOWER. See *Campanula lactiflora*.

MINIATURE HOLLYHOCK. See *Sidalcea*.

MINT, FAASSEN'S. See *Nepeta × faassenii*.

MIST FLOWER. See *Eupatorium coelestinum*.

MONEYWORT. See *Lysimachia nummularia*.

MONKSHOOD. See *Aconitum*.

MONKSHOOD, AZURE. See *Aconitum carmichaelii*.

MONKSHOOD, BICOLOR. See *Aconitum × bicolor*.

MONKSHOOD, COMMON. See *Aconitum napellus*.

MOSS PINK. See *Phlox subulata*.

MOUNTAIN BLUET. See *Centaurea montana*.

MOUNTAIN BUTTERCUP. See *Ranunculus montanus*.

MOUSE-EARED COREOPSIS. See *Coreopsis auriculata*.

MULLEIN-PINK. See *Lychnis coronaria*.

MUSK MALLOW. See *Malva moschata*.

NARROW-SPIKED LIGULARIA. See *Ligularia stenocephala*.

NEW ENGLAND ASTER. See *Aster novae-angliae*.

NEW YORK ASTER. See *Aster novi-belgii*.

NIPPON DAISY. See *Chrysanthemum nipponicum*.

OBEDIENT PLANT. See *Physostegia; Physostegia virginiana*.

OBOVATE PEONY. See *Paeonia obovata*.

OCONEE-BELLS. See *Shortia galacifolia*.

OLD-MAN-AND-WOMAN. See *Sempervivum tectorum*.

ORANGE CONEFLOWER. See *Rudbeckia fulgida*.

ORANGE DAYLILY. See *Hemerocallis × aurantiaca*.

ORANGE MILKWEED. See *Asclepias tuberosa*.

OREGON FLEABANE. See *Erigeron speciosus*.

ORIENTAL POPPY. See *Papaver orientale*.

ORNAMENTAL RHUBARB. See *Rheum palmatum*.

OSWEGO TEA. See *Monarda didyma*.

OZARK SUNDROPS. See *Oenothera missouriensis*.

PAINTED DAISY. See *Chrysanthemum coccineum*.

PEACH-LEAVED BELLFLOWER. See *Campanula persicifolia*.

PEARLY EVERLASTING. See *Anaphalis; Anaphalis margaritacea; Anaphalis triplinervis*.

PENSTEMON, BEARDED. See *Penstemon barbatus*.

PENSTEMON, FOXGLOVE. See *Penstemon digitalis*.

PENSTEMON, GLOXINIA. See *Penstemon × gloxinoides*.

PENSTEMON, HAREBELL. See *Penstemon campanulatus*.

PEONY. See *Paeonia*.

PEONY, COMMON. See *Paeonia officinalis.*

PEONY, COMMON GARDEN. See *Paeonia lactiflora.*

PEONY, FERNLEAF. See *Paeonia tenuifolia.*

PEONY, OBOVATE. See *Paeonia obovata.*

PEONY, WITTMANN'S. See *Paeonia wittmanniana.*

PERSIAN CORNFLOWER KNAPWEED. See *Centaurea dealbata.*

PERSIAN EPIMEDIUM. See *Epimedium pinnatum.*

PERSIAN STONE CRESS. See *Aethionema grandiflorum.*

PHEASANT'S-EYE. See *Adonis.*

PHLOX, CREEPING. See *Phlox stolonifera.*

PHLOX, GARDEN. See *Phlox paniculata.*

PHLOX, MEADOW. See *Phlox maculata.*

PHLOX, WOODLAND. See *Phlox divaricata.*

PINCUSHION, CRIMSON. See *Knautia macedonica.*

PINCUSHION FLOWER. See *Scabiosa.*

PINK PANDA STRAWBERRY. See *Fragaria frel.*

PINK TURTLEHEAD. See *Chelone lyonii.*

PINK, ALLWOOD. See *Dianthus × allwoodii.*

PINK, ALPINE. See *Dianthus alpinus.*

PINK, CHEDDAR. See *Dianthus gratianopolitanus.*

PINK, COTTAGE. See *Dianthus plumarius.*

PINK, GRASS. See *Dianthus plumarius.*

PINK, GROUND. See *Phlox subulata.*

PINK, HARDY GARDEN. See *Dianthus knappii.*

PINK, INDIAN. See *Spigelia marilandica.*

PINK, MAIDEN. See *Dianthus deltoides.*

PINK, MOSS. See *Phlox subulata.*

PINK, SEA. See *Armeria maritima; Limonium.*

PLANTAIN LILY. See *Hosta.*

PLUME POPPY. See *Macleaya cordata.*

POLEMONIUM, CREEPING. See *Polemonium reptans.*

POPPY. See *Papaver.*

POPPY, ORIENTAL. See *Papaver orientale.*

POPPY, PLUME. See *Macleaya cordata.*

POPPY MALLOW. See *Callirhoe.*

PRIMROSE. See *Primula.*

PRIMROSE, DRUMSTICK. See *Primula denticulata.*

PRIMROSE, EVENING. See *Oenothera.*

PRIMROSE, JAPANESE. See *Primula japonica.*

PRIMROSE, SHOWY. See *Oenothera speciosa.*

PRIMULA, SIEBOLD. See *Primula sieboldiana.*

PURPLE CONEFLOWER. See *Echinacea purpurea.*

PURPLE ECHINACEA. See *Echinacea purpurea.*

PURPLE LOOSESTRIFE. See *Lythrum salicaria.*

PURPLE MOUNTAIN DAYLILY. See *Hemerocallis altissima.*

PURPLE ROCK CRESS. See *Aubrieta deltoidea.*

PURPLE TOADFLAX. See *Linaria purpurea.*

PURPLE TRILLIUM. See *Trillium erectum.*

PYRETHRUM. See *Chrysanthemum coccineum.*

QUEEN-OF-THE-MEADOW. See *Filipendula ulmaria.*

QUEEN-OF-THE-PRAIRIE. See *Filipendula rubra.*

RABBIT-TOBACCO. See *Anaphalis margaritacea.*

RATTLESNAKE-MASTER. See *Eryngium yuccifolium.*

RED BANEBERRY. See *Actaea rubra.*

RED BARRENWORT. See *Epimedium × rubrum.*

RED LUNGWORT. See *Pulmonaria rubra.*

RED VALERIAN. See *Centranthus ruber.*

RED-HOT-POKER. See *Kniphofia.*

RHUBARB. See *Rheum.*

RHUBARB, ORNAMENTAL. See *Rheum palmatum.*

ROCK CRESS. See *Arabis.*

ROCK CRESS, PURPLE. See
*Aubrieta deltoidea.*

ROCK CRESS, WALL. See
*Arabis albida.*

ROCK SOAPWORT. See
*Saponaria ocymoides.*

ROCKY MOUNTAIN
COLUMBINE. See *Aquilegia
caerulea.*

RODGERSIA, BRONZELEAF. See
*Rodgersia podophylla.*

RODGERSIA, FEATHERLEAF.
See *Rodgersia pinnata.*

RODGERSIA, FINGERLEAF. See
*Rodgersia aesculifolia.*

RODGERSIA, SHIELDLEAF. See
*Rodgersia tabularis.*

ROSE, LENTEN. See *Helleborus
orientalis.*

ROSE CAMPION. See *Lychnis
coronaria.*

ROSE MALLOW, COMMON. See
*Hibiscus moscheutos.*

ROSE TICKSEED. See *Coreopsis
rosea.*

ROSE TURTLEHEAD. See
*Chelone obliqua.*

RUSSIAN GLOBE THISTLE. See
*Echinops exaltatus.*

RUSSIAN SAGE. See *Perovskia;
Perovskia × superba.*

SAGE. See *Salvia*

SAGE, AZURE. See *Salvia
azurea.*

SAGE, BETHLEHEM. See
*Pulmonaria saccharata.*

SAGE, GARDEN. See *Salvia
officinalis.*

SAGE, JERUSALEM. See
*Phlomis fruticosa.*

SAGE, RUSSIAN. See *Perovskia
× superba.*

SAGE, RUSSIAN. See *Perovskia.*

SAGE, WOOD. See *Salvia
nemorosa.*

SCABIOUS. See *Scabiosa.*

SCARLET BEE BALM. See
*Monarda didyma.*

SCARLET LOBELIA. See *Lobelia
cardinalis.*

SEA HOLLY. See *Eryngium.*

SEA HOLLY, ALPINE. See
*Eryngium alpinum.*

SEA HOLLY, AMETHYST. See
*Eryngium amethystinum.*

SEA HOLLY, FLAT-LEAVED. See
*Eryngium planum.*

SEA KALE, FLOWERING. See
*Crambe cordifolia.*

SEA LAVENDER. See *Limonium.*

SEA PINK. See *Armeria
maritima; Limonium.*

SEASIDE GOLDENROD. See
*Solidago sempervirens.*

SEDUM, AUTUMN JOY. See
*Sedum* 'Autumn Joy'.

SEDUM, FLORIFEROUS. See
*Sedum floriferum.*

SELF-HEAL. See *Prunella ×
webbiana.*

SERBIAN BELLFLOWER. *See
Campanula poscharskyana.*

SHASTA DAISY. See
*Chrysanthemum × superbum.*

SHIELDLEAF RODGERSIA. See
*Rodgersia tabularis.*

SHINING CONEFLOWER. See
*Rudbeckia nitida.*

SHOOTING-STAR. See
*Dodecatheon.*

SHOOTING-STAR, COMMON.
See *Dodecatheon meadia.*

SHOWY PRIMROSE. See
*Oenothera speciosa.*

SHOWY STONECROP. See
*Sedum spectabile.*

SIBERIAN GLOBE THISTLE. See
*Echinops humilis.*

SIBERIAN MEADOWSWEET. See
*Filipendula palmata.*

SIEBOLD HOSTA. See *Hosta
sieboldiana.*

SIEBOLD PRIMULA. See *Primula
sieboldiana.*

SIEBOLD STONECROP. See
*Sedum sieboldii.*

SILVER-KING ARTEMISIA. See
*Artemisia ludoviciana* var.
*albula.*

SILVER-MOUND ARTEMISIA.
See *Artemisia schmidtiana.*

SMALL SOLOMON'S-SEAL. See
*Polygonatum biflorum.*

SMALL-FLOWERED ALUMROOT.
See *Heuchera micrantha.*

SNAKEROOT, BLACK. See
*Cimicifuga racemosa.*

SNAKEROOT, WHITE. See
*Eupatorium rugosum.*

SNAKEWEED. See *Polygonum
bistorta.*

SNEEZEWEED, COMMON. See
*Helenium autumnale.*

SNEEZEWEED. See *Helenium.*

SNEEZEWORT. See *Achillea
ptarmica.*

SNOW-IN-SUMMER. See
*Cerastium; Cerastium
tomentosum.*

SNOW RICE-CAKE PLANT. See
*Arisaema sikokianum.*

SOAPWORT. See *Saponaria.*

SOAPWORT, ROCK. See
*Saponaria ocymoides.*

SOLOMON'S-SEAL. See
*Polygonatum.*

SOLOMON'S-SEAL, FRAGRANT.
See *Polygonatum odoratum.*

SOLOMON'S-SEAL, GREAT. See
*Polygonatum commutatum.*

SOLOMON'S-SEAL, SMALL. See
*Polygonatum biflorum.*

SOUTHERN LUPINE. See
*Thermopsis caroliniana.*

SOUTHERNWOOD. See
*Artemisia abrotanum.*

SPANISH LAVENDER. See
*Lavandula stoechas.*

SPEEDWELL. See *Veronica.*

SPEEDWELL, ALPINE. See
*Veronica alpina.*

SPEEDWELL, HAREBELL. See
*Veronica prostrata.*

SPEEDWELL, SPIKED. See
*Veronica spicata.*

SPEEDWELL, WOOLLY. See
*Veronica incana.*

SPIDERWORT. See *Tradescantia;
Tradescantia × andersoniana.*

SPIDERWORT, VIRGINIA. See
*Tradescantia virginiana.*

SPIGELIA. See *Spigelia.*

SPIKE GAY-FEATHER. See
*Liatris spicata.*

SPIKED SPEEDWELL. See
*Veronica spicata.*

SPINY BEAR'S-BREECH. See
*Acanthus spinosus.*

SPIRAL BELLFLOWER. See
*Campanula cochleariifolia.*

SPOTTED DEAD NETTLE. See
*Lamium maculatum.*

SPRING ADONIS. See *Adonis
vernalis.*

SPRING VETCHLING. See
*Lathyrus vernus.*

SPURGE. See *Euphorbia.*

SPURGE, CUSHION. See
*Euphorbia epithymoides.*

SPURGE, FLOWERING. See
*Euphorbia corollata.*

STAR ASTILBE. See *Astilbe
simplicifolia.*

STATICE. See *Limonium.*

STOKE'S ASTER. See *Stokesia;
Stokesia laevis.*

STONE CRESS. See
*Aethionema.*

STONE CRESS, LEBANON. See
*Aethionema coridifolium.*

STONE CRESS, PERSIAN. See
*Aethionema grandiflorum.*

STONECROP. See *Sedum.*

STONECROP, GOLD-MOSS. See
*Sedum acre.*

STONECROP, KAMCHATKA. See
*Sedum kamtschaticum.*

STONECROP, SHOWY. See
*Sedum spectabile.*

STONECROP, SIEBOLD. See
*Sedum sieboldii.*

STONECROP, TWO ROW. See
*Sedum spurium.*

STONECROP, VERA JAMESON.
See *Sedum 'Vera Jameson'.*

STRAW FOXGLOVE. See
*Digitalis lutea.*

STRAWBERRY. See *Fragaria.*

STRAWBERRY, EUROPEAN. See
*Fragaria vesca.*

STRAWBERRY, PINK PANDA.
See *Fragaria frel.*

STRAWBERRY FOXGLOVE. See
*Digitalis × mertonensis.*

SUNDROPS. See *Oenothera
tetragona.*

SUNDROPS, OZARK. See
*Oenothera missouriensis.*

SUNFLOWER. See *Helianthus*

SUNFLOWER, MANY-
FLOWERED. See *Helianthus ×
multiflorus.*

SUNFLOWER, SWAMP. See
*Helianthus angustifolius.*

SUNFLOWER, WILLOW-LEAVED.
See *Helianthus salicifolius.*

SUNFLOWER HELIOPSIS. See
*Heliopsis helianthoides.*

SUNROSE. See *Helianthemum.*

SUNROSE, COMMON. See
*Helianthemum nummularium.*

SWAMP SUNFLOWER. See
*Helianthus angustifolius.*

SWEET WILLIAM. See *Dianthus
barbatus.*

SWEET WILLIAM, WILD. See
*Phlox maculata.*

SWORDLEAF INULA. See *Inula
ensifolia.*


TALL GAY-FEATHER. See *Liatris
scariosa.*

TATARIAN DAISY. See *Aster
tataricus.*

THREAD-LEAVED COREOPSIS.
See *Coreopsis verticillata.*

THREE-LOBED CONEFLOWER.
See *Rudbeckia triloba.*

THRIFT. See *Armeria.*

THUNBERG'S DAYLILY. See
*Hemerocallis thunbergii.*

TICKSEED. See *Coreopsis;
Coreopsis grandiflora.*

TICKSEED, ROSE. See
*Coreopsis rosea.*

TOAD LILY. See *Tricyrtis.*

TOAD LILY, COMMON. See
*Tricyrtis hirta.*

TOAD LILY, FORMOSA. See
*Tricyrtis formosana.*

TOADFLAX. See *Linaria.*

TOADFLAX, PURPLE. See
*Linaria purpurea.*

TOKUDAMA HOSTA. See *Hosta
tokudama.*

TORCH LILY. See *Kniphofia.*

TORCH LILY, COMMON. See
*Kniphofia uvaria.*

TREE LUPINE. See *Lupinus
arboreus.*

TRILLIUM, PURPLE. See
*Trillium erectum.*

TRITOMA. See *Kniphofia.*

TUBE CLEMATIS. See *Clematis
heracleifolia.*

TURNIP, INDIAN. See *Arisaema
triphyllum.*

TURTLEHEAD. See *Chelone.*

TURTLEHEAD, PINK. See
*Chelone lyonii.*

TURTLEHEAD, ROSE. See
*Chelone obliqua.*

TURTLEHEAD, WHITE. See
*Chelone glabra.*

TWO ROW STONECROP. See
*Sedum spurium.*

UPRIGHT BUGLEWEED. See
*Ajuga pyramidalis.*

VALERIAN. See *Centranthus;
Centranthus ruber.*

VALERIAN, RED. See
*Centranthus ruber.*

VERA JAMESON STONECROP.
See *Sedum 'Vera Jameson'.*

VERBENA, BRAZILIAN. See
*Verbena bonariensis.*

VERBENA, CLUMP. See *Verbena
canadensis.*

VERBENA, RIGID. See *Verbena
rigida.*

VERONICA, LONG-LEAF. See
*Veronica longifolia.*

VERVAIN. See *Verbena.*

VETCHLING, SPRING. See
*Lathyrus vernus.*

VIRGINIA BLUEBELLS. See
*Mertensia virginica.*

VIRGINIA SPIDERWORT. See
*Tradescantia virginiana.*

WAKE-ROBIN. See *Trillium;
Trillium erectum.*

WAKE-ROBIN, WHITE. See
*Trillium grandiflorum.*

WALL ROCK CRESS. See
*Arabis albida.*

WAND LOOSESTRIFE. See
*Lythrum virgatum.*

WASHINGTON LUPINE. See
*Lupinus polyphyllus.*

WATER AVENS. See *Geum
rivale.*

WAVY HOSTA. See *Hosta
undulata.*

WAXBELLS, YELLOW. See
*Kirengeshoma; Kirengeshoma
palmata.*

WELSH POPPY. See *Meconopsis
cambrica.*

WHITE BANEBERRY. See *Actaea
alba.*

WHITE CORYDALIS. See
*Corydalis ochroleuca.*

WHITE GAURA. See *Gaura
lindheimeri.*

WHITE HELLEBORE,
EUROPEAN. See *Veratrum
album.*

WHITE SNAKEROOT. See
*Eupatorium rugosum.*

WHITE TURTLEHEAD. See
*Chelone glabra.*

WHITE WAKE-ROBIN. See
*Trillium grandiflorum.*

WILD BERGAMOT. See *Monarda
fistulosa.*

WILD COLUMBINE. See
*Aquilegia canadensis.*

WILD GERANIUM. See
*Geranium maculatum.*

WILD HOLLYHOCK. See *Sidalcea
malviflora.*

WILD LUPINE. See *Lupinus
perennis.*

WILD SWEET WILLIAM. See
*Phlox maculata.*

WILLOW AMSONIA. See
*Amsonia tabernaemontana.*

WILLOW HERB. See *Lythrum salicaria.*

WILLOW-LEAVED SUNFLOWER. See *Helianthus salicifolius.*

WINDFLOWER. See *Anemone.*

WITTMANN'S PEONY. See *Paeonia wittmanniana.*

WOOD SAGE. See *Salvia nemorosa.*

WOODLAND PHLOX. See *Phlox divaricata.*

WOOLLY SPEEDWELL. See *Veronica incana.*

WORMWOOD, BEACH. See *Artemisia stelleriana.*

WORMWOOD. See *Artemisia; Artemisia absinthium.*

YARROW. See *Achillea.*

YARROW, COMMON. See *Achillea millefolium.*

YARROW, CORONATION GOLD. See *Achillea* × 'Coronation Gold'.

YELLOW CORYDALIS. See *Corydalis lutea.*

YELLOW FOXGLOVE. See *Digitalis grandiflora.*

YELLOW WAXBELLS. See *Kirengeshoma; Kirengeshoma palmata.*

YOUNG'S BARRENWORT. See *Epimedium* × *youngianum.*

YUNNAN MEADOW RUE. See *Thalictrum delavayi.*

# GLOSSARY

**achene.** A single-seeded, dry fruit that does not split open when ripe. The seeds of *Fragaria* (strawberry) are achenes, as are *Helianthus* (sunflower) seeds.

**alternate.** Referring to the way twigs, branches or, especially, leaves have their point of attachment or emergence at different levels, not opposite one another, on stem or trunk. Technically, one leaf at each node (joint) of a stem. Compare OPPPOSITE and WHORL.

**annual.** A plant that completes its lifecycle, from germination to seed formation, in one year. Contrast BIENNIAL, PERENNIAL.

**anther.** The part of a stamen in which pollen is produced by a seed plant. The anther opens when the pollen is ripe.

**apomixis.** Nonsexual reproduction, in which contact between male and female gametes is not necessary, as in *Hosta ventricosa* (blue hosta). Often, the development of unfertilized egg cells or non-egg cells. The new plants are called apomicts, and have the same genetic make-up as the parent plant.

**aril.** An outer covering or appendage on some seeds. It is often colored, as in *Celastrus* (bittersweet).

**awn.** A bristly appendage on some anthers and on the fruits of some plants, notably on grains such as wheat and oats.

**axil.** The angle formed where a leaf, stalk or branch diverges from the main stem.

**axillary.** Forming part of an axil. For example, the flowers of *Clematis heracleifolia* (tube clematis) grow in axillary clusters; the clusters grow out of the axil—the angle between the main stem and leaf stalks.

**biennial.** A plant that requires two years to complete its life cycle. In the first year, it makes only vegetative growth (although some biennials will flower if started early in the year). In the second year, it flowers and produces seed, then dies. Contrast ANNUAL, PERENNIAL.

**bigeneric.** Involving two genera. Commonly referring to a hybrid produced by crossing plants of different genera.

**bipinnate.** Twice pinnate; with leaves arranged in double-feather fashion.

**bisexual.** Term commonly applied to a flower having both stamens and pistils.

**blade.** Strictly, the more or less flat, expanded part of any leaf (not to be confused with the leaf-stalk or petiole). Loosely, blade is a common term for any long, narrow, pointed leaf, as in grass.

**botrytis.** Also known as gray mold, this common fungal problem thrives on fruits and flowers, such as *Paeonia* (peony), in moist conditions, usually infecting dead tissue first.

**bract.** One of the small, scalelike leaves that emerge from a flower stalk and enclose a flower bud. Although usually green, bracts may be beautifully colored. The "flowers" of *Cornus* (dogwood) and *Euphorbia* (poinsettia), for example, are really bracts.

**bulb.** Loosely, any globular or markedly swollen underground stem that produces top growth and basal roots. Strictly, a true bulb is a modified plant bud enclosed in thick, fleshy scales held together by a fibrous base that sends forth roots.

**calyx.** The small, petal-like parts, called sepals that surround the true petals of a flower. The calyx is commonly green, but in some flowers, such as the lily and *Anemone*, it assumes the flower's color.

**carpel.** A pistil or one of the units of a pistil; a simple pistil is made up of one carpel, and a compound pistil is made up of a number of carpels.

**clone.** A group of identical plants, all descended by vegetative or asexual reproduction by cuttings, division, layering, from a single plant produced from seed. Examples: 'Baldwin' apple, 'Concord' grape and named varieties of many common garden plants.

**cold frame.** An outdoor, boxlike construction, without a bottom and usually covered in glass or clear plastic on top, used to control weather conditions; often used to germinate seeds.

**compound.** Composite; composed of two or more similar parts in one organ, usually in a flower or leaf. A compound leaf, for example, has two or more leaflets.

**cordate.** Describing a leaf that is ovate in form, and that has lobes at its base on either side of the point where the leaf and the leaf stalk meet, resulting in a heart-like shape.

**corm.** A swollen but flattish underground stem that resembles a bulb but is more solid and lacks the typical thick scale leaves of a bulb. Gladiolus and crocus are cormous plants.

**cormel.** A small corm produced at the base of a corm.

**corolla.** Usually, the showy parts of a flower, consisting of petals.

**corona.** The circular crown—which may be cup-shaped or tube-shaped—immediately surrounding the stamen of a flower. For example, the cup of a daffodil.

**corymb.** A flower cluster that is flat on top because of the elongation of the side stems to match the height of the central stem. The flowers bloom from the edges inward. Contrast CYME.

**cotyledon.** The first seed leaf (or one of the first pairs or whorl) to develop within a seed.

**crested.** Having an elevated, sometimes toothed, ridge. The fasciated inflorescence of cockscomb is described as crested.

**crown.** The upper part of the rootstock from which shoots grow, as in *Lupinus*, *Paeonia*, *Delphinium* and *Chrysanthemum × superba* (Shasta daisy). Also, the entire foliage of a tree and the corona or corolla of a flower, which is usually the part between petals and stamens.

**cultivar.** Abbreviation: cv. A new plant developed in cultivation through a breeding program. By contrast, a VARIETY occurs spontaneously, either in the wild or in cultivation, and is simply selected, propagated and named by the grower.

**cutting.** A rootless piece of plant used to produce a new plant.

**cyme.** A large, broad, sometimes flat flower cluster that blooms from the center outward—always with a flower at the end of the main or central stalk. Example: *Phlox*. Contrast CORYMB.

**deciduous.** A plant that drops its leaves every year and always before new leaves come. Contrast EVERGREEN.

**decumbent.** Growing close to the ground, but with ascending tips; *Campanula poscharskyana* (Serbian bellflower), for example.

**dicotyledon.** Sometimes shortened to dicot. A plant with two seed leaves (two leaflike structures on the embryo plant within a seed). Contrast MONOCOTYLEDON.

**dioecious.** With staminate and pistillate flowers on separate plants. Contrast MONOECIOUS.

**disbud.** To remove certain buds in order to produce better flowers from remaining buds or to induce stronger growth or a more symmetrical shape.

**disk.** The central portion of the flower head of plants of the *Compostiae* (Daisy) Family. Also, the part of the inflorescence producing the tubular central flowers.

**diurnal.** Flowers that open only during daylight hours, as in *Hemerocallis*.

**divide.** To cut, pull apart or otherwise separate the roots or crowns of a plant or clump in order to produce additional plants. See DIVISION, PROPAGATION.

**division.** A method of propagating multi-crowned plants (usually herbaceous ones) by separating the roots into smaller portions capable of independent growth.

**double.** Flower form that has a greater than normal number of petals.

**down.** Soft hairs that cover a plant surface, usually the leaves.

**encurved.** Curved upward or inward. Contrast REFLEXED.

**endemic.** Referring to a plant native to, and found wild only in, a particular region.

**entire.** Referring to a leaf with smooth, continuous edges. For example, a rhododendron leaf. An elm or beech leaf is not entire, because its edges are toothed.

**epidermis.** The "skin" of a leaf.

**escape.** Colloquially, a cultivated plant that has gone wild and perpetuates itself without further care. Also, the naturalization of such a plant. *Convallaria* (lily-of-the-valley) and *Hemerocallis* (daylily) frequently escape from the strictly cultivated state.

**evergreen.** A plant that does not lose all its foliage in the autumn, hence appears to retain its leaves the year round. Contrast DECIDUOUS.

**everlasting.** A plant that retains its form and color when dried.

**exotic.** A plant being grown in a region to which it is not indigenous. Contrast NATIVE.

**exserted.** By derivation, extended or protruding. In application, relating especially to staminate or pistillate flower parts that project beyond the corolla. Contrast INCLUDED.

**eye.** The growth bud on a tuber or on the stem of a plant. Also, the distinctive center of a flower, as in some members of the *Compositae* (Daisy) Family.

**female.** Referring to pistillate flowers or flower parts. Also, colloquially, a plant having pistillate flowers.

**fertile.** Referring to a plant able to produce fruit (seeds); to a flower possessing the organs of reproduction; to a soil abundantly supplied with the ingredients necessary to plant growth and in a condition appropriate to the support of that growth.

**filament.** The slender stalk that supports the anther and, with it, constitutes the stamen of a flower.

**floret.** One of the flowers in a composite cluster; loosely, any single flower, usually small, in any multiple inflorescence.

**flower.** The popular term for the combination of sexual structures having to do with complex, plants. The concept usually includes color and a definite organization. If plants did not have flowers, they could not produce seed with which to reproduce their kind.

**fruit.** Botanically, a fruit is the mature seed-bearing ovary of any plant. It may or may not be edible or ornamental, large or small, borne singly or in clusters—on trees, bushes or herbaceous plants.

**funnelform.** The shape of certain flowers, in which the tube gradually widens upward and outward like a trumpet.

**gamopetalous.** A flower whose petals are completely or almost completely fused. For example, *Campanula* (bellflower). Contrast APETALOUS.

**genus.** Plural, genera. A quite closely related and definable group of plants that includes one or more species. The genus name is the first half of the horticultural name of a species.

**glabrous.** Smooth; lacking hairs. Contrast PUBESCENT.

**glaucous.** Covered with a waxy or powdery, bluish-white to bluish-gray bloom which can easily be rubbed off. Generally a reference to foliage.

**glomerate.** Clustered, often referring to dense, globular flower heads.

**hair.** Fine filaments growing from a plant surface.

**hardiness zone.** The region in which a plant can overwinter outdoors, and in which summers are not too hot for the plant.

**hardy.** A plant which can overwinter outdoors. Compare HALF-HARDY.

**head.** A dense flower or leaf cluster that more or less resembles a head. Commonly, anything from a composite flowerhead (daisies) to a head of lettuce.

**heart-shaped.** Usually applied to leaves that are ovate (egg-shaped) and bear two rounded basal lobes; see CORDATE.

**heaving.** Swelling or bulging (as in a plant bed). Changing temperatures cause freezing, defrosting and refreezing of soil water, causing it to expand and contract, damaging plants.

**herb.** By definition, a seed plant having soft, fleshy tissue rather than the persistently woody tissue associated with trees and shrubs. Such plants are generally termed herbaceous. Commonly, "herb" refers to plants used for medicinal or culinary purposes.

**herbaceous.** Plants that have soft, fleshy tissues; not WOODY.

**hip.** The enlarged, fleshy, berrylike, often quite handsome fruit of the rose.

**humus.** Decomposed plant and animal matter used as a soil ingredient. Humus provides nutrients, natural drainage and the ideal pH.

**hybrid.** The progeny resulting from the cross-fertilization of one genus, species or variety of plant with another, different plant. Hybrids occur naturally in nature; they are also the preoccupation of many plant breeders.

**hypocotyl.** In a newly germinated seedling, the stem below the cotyledons and above the root. (The stem above the cotyledons is part of the EPICOTYL.)

**imperfect.** A flower that produces male or female reproductive organs (stamens or pistils) but not both. Contrast PERFECT.

**incurved.** Referring to flowers having parts curved toward the center; also to the parts themselves, such as an incurved ray petal. Contrast RECURVED.

**inferior.** A plant ovary that develops beneath a flower calyx. The rose has an inferior ovary, familiarly known as the rose hip. Compare SEMNIFEROUS, SUPERIOR.

**inflorescence.** The general and total flowering arrangement of a plant; also, the way individual florets are arranged in a cluster.

**inserted.** Attached by natural growth (as with certain flower parts).

**internode.** The part of a plant stem between nodes.

**involucre.** A whorl of bracts or small, often scalelike leaves around the base of a flower or fruit (conspicuously on *Centaurea*, zinnia and many other members of the *Compositae* Family).

**irregular.** An unsymmetrical flower, in which various parts differ in size or shape from the other parts in the same flower group. For example, all orchid flowers are irregular.

**keel.** A ridge on the back of a leaf or petal, somewhat resembling a boat keel and V-shaped in section.

**lanceolate.** Of a much greater length than width, tapering at the ends (lance-shaped), and having convex sides; generally refering to leaf shape. Compare OBLANCEOLATE.

**lateral.** A branch, shoot or bud borne at the side of a plant. Contrast TERMINAL.

**leaf.** Basically, a leaf consists of a more or less flat, wide part, known as the BLADE, and a stalk, known as the PETIOLE. Some leaves also have two small bracts, called STIPULES, at the base of the petiole, where it joins the stem. Though variously shaped, most leaves have a one-piece blade and are therefore called SIMPLE leaves. But in some leaves, such as in the rose, the blade is divided into several leaflets. Such leaves are called COMPOUND.

**leaflet.** One part of a compound leaf's whole blade.

**leafmold.** A layer of soil made up mainly of decayed vegetable matter.

**linear.** Long and uniformly narrow, as are many leaves.

**male.** Referring loosely to a plant bearing only STAMINATE (pollen-producing) flowers.

**marginal.** Partial. For instance, a marginal water plant, such as *Asclepias* (milkweed), is one that grows either partially submerged in shallow water or in the moist soil alongside a body of water.

**mildew.** A fungus-caused plant disease characterized by a usually-white, cottony coating on surfaces of affected parts of the plant.

**monocarp.** A plant that flowers and sets seeds once, then dies. All annuals and biennials are monocarps.

**monocotyledon.** Sometimes called monocot. A flowering plant with only one seedleaf (a single leaflike structure on the embryo). Its flowers have three (or a multiple of three) petals, sepals and stamens; its leaves are parallel-veined. Among the monocotyledons are amaryllis, irises, lilies, orchids and the grasses. Contrast DICOTYLEDON.

**monoecious.** A plant with separate male and female flowers, but with both kinds on the same plant. For example, cucumber, oak and walnut. Contrast DIOECIOUS.

**monotypic.** Referring to a genus having only one species.

**mulch.** An insulating layer, made of peat, compost, dried leaves, straw or other material, used to cover a planting. Spread around plant bases, it serves to protect against frost, conserve water and fight weed growth.

**multifid.** Divided into many parts, referring especially to leaves; compare PINNATIFID.

**mutant.** A SPORT resulting from a mutation, due to genetic changes in a particular plant or part of a plant.

**mutation.** A natural, spontaneous change in a plant gene that results in the development of a new variety. Also, the result of such a change.

**native.** A plant indigenous to a particular region. Contrast EXOTIC.

**nectar.** A dilute sugar solution formed by many flowers. By attracting insects and birds, it aids in pollination.

**nectary.** A flower part, usually a gland near the base of petal or stamen, that exudes nectar.

**nematode.** Microscopic, threadlike worm, also known as an eelworm. Although there are many types, both beneficial to the soil and parasitic, gardeners are generally only concerned with the parasitic nematodes, which can be very destructive.

**node.** The joint at which a leaf, bud or branch meets the stem; hence, often, a joint, sometimes quite conspicuous. The space between two nodes is an INTERNODE.

**nodule.** A tubercle or small outgrowth on the root of a legume; *Lupinus* (lupines), for instance, have nodules. These nodules take nitrogen from the air and put it in the soil.

**oblanceolate.** Refers to leaf shape; widest toward the leaf edge and tapering to the base; inversely LANCEOLATE.

**obovate.** Egg-shaped, with the wide part upward; commonly referring to the shape of a leaf. Contrast OVATE.

**offset.** A short shoot that runs laterally from the base of a plant, producing leaves and usually roots at the end, thus forming a new plant. For example, a strawberry runner. Also, a small bulb that forms at the base of a mature bulb.

**opposite.** Referring to two leaves or branches attached to a stem directly across from each other, so they seem like pairs. Whether a plant has opposite or alternate leaves is one of the chief and obvious determinants of plant identification. Contrast ALTERNATE and WHORL.

**orbicular.** Round or almost round.

**ovary.** In the flowers of angiosperms, the enlarged organ at the base of the pistil that holds one or more ovules. After pollination, the ovules develop into seeds. The ovary, containing the seeds, develops into a fruit.

**ovate.** Egg-shaped, with the wide end downward; commonly referring to the shape of a leaf. Contrast OBOVATE.

**ovule.** One of the globular bodies within an ovary that develop into seeds after fertilization.

**panicle.** A loose flower cluster with the earliest-blooming florets at the bottom. The flower stem does not have a terminal floret bloom. *Yucca* produces a typical panicle, as do *Phlox paniculata* (garden phlox) and many grasses.

**parasite.** A plant (often a fungus) that lives on, and at the expense of, another living plant, called the host plant. Examples: mistletoe, corn smut.

**parted.** Leaves, or sometimes petals, divided almost to the base.

**pedicel.** The stalk of any floret in a flower cluster; a division of a PEDUNCLE.

**peduncle.** The stalk of a single or solitary flower when branched. The branches are PEDICELS

**peltate.** A leaf with its stem attached at or near the center, not at the margin. Examples: nasturtium, lotus.

**perennial.** A plant that lives from year to year. All trees, shrubs and many flowering bulbs are perennial; but the word is applied most commonly to herbaceous plants, especially the better-known border flowers. Contrast ANNUAL, BIENNIAL.

**perfect.** A bloom that contains both male and female reproductive organs (STAMENS and PISTILS). Contrast IMPERFECT.

**perianth.** Technically, all the floral leaves of a blossom. The word is used especially where the calyx is almost indistinguishable from the corolla. Among gardeners, perianth most commonly designates the petals from which the cup or crown of a narcissus rises.

**persistent.** Leaves, fruits or seed pods that remain or hang on, even if withered.

**petal.** Strictly, the leaf of a corolla. Colloquially, the leaf or segment blossom, which is usually showy.

**petiole.** The stalk of a leaf.

**petiolule.** Strictly, the petiole of the leaflet in a compound leaf.

**pinnate.** A compound leaf of which the leaflets or leaf parts are similarly arranged on either side of a principal stem, feather-fashion. Also, a single leaf of which the principal veins branch off at a number of points along a midrib.

**pinnatifid.** Divided or parted in a pinnate manner. Contrast MULTIFID.

**pinnule.** The smallest and ultimate division of a compound leaf.

**pip.** Commonly, the individual root-stock (a single stem bud with roots) of *Convallaria* (lily-of-the-valley); occasionally also *Anemone* and some others. Colloquially, a seed of an apple, orange or pear.

**pistil.** The female reproductive organ of a flower. It consists of three parts: The swollen, bulbous base—the OVARY—contains the ovules that develop into seeds. Leading from it is a fleshy, tubelike stalk called the STYLE (not always definable). The enlarged tip of the style is the STIGMA, with a sticky surface on which pollen adheres and is conveyed through the style to the ovary.

**pistillate.** Having only a pistil (no stamens); female.

**pod.** Strictly, a dry, dehiscent fruit, such as a peapod. Loosely, any dry fruit or podlike organ that contains seeds.

**pollen.** The microscopic grains, usually resembling yellow dust, produced on the anther of a stamen. When ripe, dry pollen becomes windborne; sticky pollen is picked up by insects and birds. After pollen is deposited on the stigma of a pistil, it will produce the sperm cells that may fertilize ovules.

**polycotyledon.** A plant with more than two cotyledons or seed leaves, as the pine and other conifers.

**polygamous.** A plant with both perfect and imperfect flowers.

**propagation.** Plant reproduction, which can occur by a variety of means, including seeds, division of the CROWN, bulblets produced by mature bulbs, and shoots emerging from roots or stolons.

**pubescent.** Covered with soft, fine hairs. Contrast GLABROUS.

**raceme.** A long flower cluster with only one main stem, from which the stems of individual florets branch. The cluster blooms from the bottom upward. There is no flower at the end of the main stem. (A compound raceme is produced when the main stem is branched.) Examples: honey locust, *Convallaria* (lily-of-the-valley).

**rachis.** The main stalk of a flower cluster; the main leaf stem or PETIOLE of a compound leaf.

**radical.** Pertaining to or proceeding from the root.

**radicle.** The root portion of an embryo. Also, the first root developed by a germinating seed.

**ray.** Strictly, a flattened corolla radiating from the central disk of a composite flower head, as in *Aster* and *Helianthus* (sunflower). Loosely, any flat, straplike petal in the outer part of a flower.

**receptacle.** The part of the stem on which the flowers are borne. A rose hip is an enlarged receptacle. So is *Fragaria* (strawberry).

**recurved.** Backward- or downward-curving, usually in reference to petals. Contrast INCURVED.

**reflexed.** Curved sharply backward or downward, usually in reference to petals. Contrast ENCURVED.

**regular.** A flower that is basically symmetrical in the arrrangement of its parts, such as petals, sepals, and so forth; *Chrysanthemum* (daisy) is an example. Most flowers are regular.

**remontant.** A plant that blooms twice in the same season; some roses, for example.

**revolute.** Leaves or petals with margins or tips rolled backward or downward.

**rhizomatous.** Having or producing rhizomes, such as *Anemone*.

**rhizome.** The fleshy, somewhat elongated rootstock (underground stem) of some herbaceous perennials. It has stem buds on the upper side and small roots on the lower side.

**root cutting.** A piece of root or rootstock used for propagation.

**root-hardy.** Referring to perennial plants whose roots survive even though above ground parts may die because of climatic extremes.

**rootstock.** A fleshy, underground stem with eyes and roots, as herbaceous *Paeonia* (peony) or *Rheum* (rhubarb). It differs from the actual root in that it stores food but does not gather it. Also, colloquially, the root or rooted understock upon which a scion or bud is grafted.

**rust.** Any of a number of specific plant diseases, usually requiring two different hosts during their lifecycle and manifesting in reddening or browning of twigs and needles and the release of rust-colored spores.

**salver-form.** A flower with a slender tube topped by an expanded, flat circle of petals; a *Phlox* blossom, for example.

**scale.** One of the scalelike leaves protecting a bud before it opens. Also, a small, thin, often dry bract. Also, short for scale insect.

**scalloped.** Having a pattern of bulging extensions at the edges.

**scape.** A single leafless, branchless stem rising from the ground and topped by a flower or an inflorescence, as in *Amaryllis* spp., *Sanguinaria canadensis* (bloodroot), *Hemerocallis* (daylilies), *Narcissus* (daffoldils).

**seed.** The fertilized and ripened ovule capable of germination and growth.

**self-sow.** Referring to plants that seed themselves and produce new plants without human assistance.

**self-sterile.** A plant that cannot be fertilized by itself or by another plant of the same variety is self-sterile. This is true of many species of *Dianthus* (carnations) and *Papaver* (poppies).

**semidouble.** Flower form that has an incomplete extra floral envelope, for example *Anemone × hybrida*.

**semniferous.** Usually a plant ovary surrounded by a cup formed by the perianth and stamens, which are fused together. Compare INFERIOR, SUPERIOR.

**sepal.** One of the outermost, usually green, scales of a flower bud. First leaflike, later often petal-like, the sepals make up the CALYX.

**serrate.** Having a pattern of pointed extensions at the edges; saw-toothed.

**sessile.** Lacking a stalk.

**shoot.** A young branch that may produce flowers or leaves or both.

**simple.** A single flower or a leaf with a single whole blade. Also, but rarely, a medicinal herb.

**single.** Flower head made up of only one floral envelope.

**spadix.** The thick flower spike (with fleshy, cylindrical center) characteristic of plants in the *Aracae* (Arum) Family and some others. The spadix is usually enclosed in a SPATHE.

**spathe.** The leaflike bract or pair of bracts sheathing an inflorescence (often a SPADIX), as in calla lily and *Arisaema triphyllum* (Jack-in-the-pulpit).

**spatulate.** Oblong, with a narrow base and a pointed tip; spatula-shaped.

**species.** A group of plants within a genus. Species of the same genus are all different but contain one or more common characteristics. Species may reproduce themselves from seeds and may often be interbred, sometimes in nature.

**spike.** An elongated flower cluster in which each individual blossom is connected without a stalk to the main stem. Example, mignonette.

**spore.** The microscopic, unicellular reproductive body of fungi, algae, ferns, mosses and lichens.

**sport.** A mutant plant, with different characteristics than the parent plant. Sports occur naturally or can be induced by gardeners.

**spray.** A single, fragile shoot, stem or branch, along with its leaves and flowers.

**sprig.** A young shoot. Also, the act of planting stolons of some turf species to make a lawn.

**stalk.** The stem or main axis of a plant. The word also has such specialized meanings as leafstalk (PETIOLE), flower stalk (PEDUNCLE), a slender stalk (PEDICEL), the stalk of an anther (FILAMENT).

**stamen.** The male reproductive organ of a flower. It comprises a slender stalk (the FILAMENT) and a swollen tip (the ANTHER). The latter produces pollen.

**staminate.** Having stamens; MALE.

**stem.** A confusing term with several meanings: Most commonly, it refers to the main axis of a plant, as the trunk of a tree or the stalk of a zinnia. A rootstock or rhizome is an underground stem. Broadly, any leaf- or flower-bearing stalk is also a stem.

**sterility.** A plant's inability to reproduce. Some plants are absolutely sterile; others are sterile only under certain circumstances.

**stigma.** In pistillate flowers, that part of the style, usually the expanded tip, that receives the pollen from the anthers of staminate flowers. A stigma is said to be receptive when its surface becomes sticky, so that it holds the pollen for the initiation of the fertilization process.

**stock.** The rooted plant to which a scion is grafted.

**stolon.** A shoot that runs along the ground and takes root, and from which new plants sprout.

**strain.** A group of plants of the same variety that have a distinct common characteristic, such as greater vigor, longer stems, better flowers than the type.

**style.** The stalklike or tubelike growth that connects the ovary to the terminal stigma of a pistil.

**subspecies.** A subdivision of a species, ranking between species and variety.

**subshrub.** A small, generally herbaceous plant that has woody and shrubby stems, as *Chrysanthemum* and *Pachysandra*.

**succulent.** A fleshy plant, such as a cactus, that stores water in stems or leaves in order to survive in hot, dry, desert regions.

**superior.** Usually a plant ovary borne above rather than below the calyx, as in lilies. Compare INFERIOR, SEMNIFEROUS.

**systemic.** A pesticide applied to the roots of a plant and absorbed through the plant's system.

**taproot.** The large, central root of many plants. It usually goes straight down to considerable depth.

**temperate.** Neither excessively cold nor excessively hot. In the Northern Hemisphere, the Temperate Zone lies between the Tropic of Cancer and the Arctic Circle.

**tender.** Plants that cannot survive winter in the regions where frost is common.

**tendril.** A slender, springy, coiling part of climbing plants. Usually an extension of a stalk or leaf, it wraps around any available means of support.

**terminal.** Buds or flowers at the tip of a stem. Contrast LATERAL.

**ternate.** In threes, as in compound leaves, or divided into three parts or lobes.

**tomentose.** Having a covering layer of short, dense, matted woolly hairs.

**tuber.** A fleshy, swollen stem, having lateral as well as terminal growth buds or "eyes" and producing roots along its length or at the end.

**umbel.** A flat-topped or dome-shaped flower cluster. All the flower stems rise from a common point on the main stalk.

**unisexual.** Flowers having stamens or pistils but not both. Also, loosely, plants having such flowers on separate plants.

**variegation.** Variation in appearance or color; patches of different colors, as in leaves.

**variety.** The final natural classification of plants. Not all species have natural varieties, but most species have several.

**vegetative.** Reproducing asexually.

**vein.** Strand or bundle of vascular tissue forming the frame or skeleton of a leaf.

**whorl.** A circle of three or more petals, leaves, twigs or flowers, all from the same point on a stalk.

**woody.** Describes plants whose stems are made of hard, tough fibers that do not die back (i.e. are PERSISTENT). Contrast HERBACEOUS.

**xerophyte.** A plant adapted by nature to withstand drought, by storing water or by resisting waterless conditions for long periods.

# ACKNOWLEDGMENTS

The text for *The Hearst Garden Guides* is based on *The Good Housekeeping Illustrated Encyclopedia of Gardening*, a sixteen-volume set originally compiled under the auspices of the Editors of *Good Housekeeping* and published in 1972. The project began as the work of Ralph Sargent Bailey, garden editor for more than a quarter of a century at *House Beautiful* and *House and Garden* (now *HG*); unfinished at the time of Mr. Bailey's death, the work was completed by then Garden Editor at *House Beautiful*, Elvin McDonald.

Mr. McDonald assembled some of the finest garden writers of the day to work on different sections of the encyclopedia. In addition to Messrs. Bailey and McDonald, we would like in particular to acknowledge Marjorie J. Dietz, former editor of *Plants and Garden* for the Brooklyn Botanic Garden and author of *The Concise Encyclopedia of Favorite Wild Flowers*, for her fine essay on perennials, which was the basis for the essay herein.

For this edition, Sue Baldwin-Way and her husband Robert G. Way did a great deal of work on organizing the manuscript. We would like also to thank Ruth Lively for her impressive horticultural knowledge, Tom Starace for his computer expertise and Durrae Johanek for thoroughly copyediting the text.

Andrew Lawson shot the glorious specimen and general garden photographs. Lisa Zador's and Wendy Frost's beautiful illustrations lend beauty as well as crisp visual reference to the book.

# PHOTOGRAPHY CREDITS

Andrew Lawson provided the photography for this book, except for the following:.

p. 73 (top left), Joanne Pavia;

p. 77 (top), Joanne Pavia;

p. 77 (bottom), Jerry Pavia

p. 102 (top), Darrel Apps;

p. 102 (bottom left), Darrel Apps;

p. 106 (top right), Elvin McDonald;

p. 130 (top), Elvin McDonald;

p. 134 (top), Darrel Apps;

p. 134 (bottom), Darrel Apps;

p. 148 (right), Darrel Apps;

p. 155 (top left), Clive Nichols;

p. 164 (right), Darrel Apps.

The following photographs are copyright © by Andrew Lawson:

p. 36 (top),

p. 79 (left),

p. 86 (top),

p. 92 (top right),

p. 145 (top),

p. 146 (top left),

p. 148 (left),

p. 160 (bottom left),

p. 160 (top right),

p. 171 (right).